NEW PRODUCT PLANNING

To Mary Kay and our two products,
Alexander and Michael

NEW PRODUCT PLANNING

KENNETH B. KAHN

Los Angeles | London | New Delhi
Singapore | Washington DC | Melbourne

Originally Published in 2001 by SAGE Publications, Inc.,
2455 Teller Road, Thousand Oaks, California 91320 under the title
Product Planning Essentials

First published in 2001 by

SAGE Publications India Pvt Ltd
B1/I-1 Mohan Cooperative Industrial Area
Mathura Road, New Delhi 110 044, India
www.sagepub.in

SAGE Publications Inc
2455 Teller Road
Thousand Oaks, California 91320, USA

SAGE Publications Ltd
1 Oliver's Yard, 55 City Road
London EC1Y 1SP, United Kingdom

SAGE Publications Asia-Pacific Pte Ltd
18 Cross Street #10-10/11/12
China Square Central
Singapore 048423

Published by Vivek Mehra for SAGE Publications India Pvt Ltd.

ISBN: 978-81-782-9026-3 (PB)

Contents

PREFACE

Over the past 6 years, I have been teaching a course entitled product planning at the undergraduate, graduate, and executive education levels. All the while, I have failed to find a book that provides a broad, interdisciplinary view of product planning. Instead, most books focus predominantly on either product development or product management topics. Typical books on product development and product management also are either too qualitative or too quantitative in nature. I, therefore, imagined a book that would unify product development and product management topics under a product planning framework. I also envisioned a book that would balance qualitative and quantitative topics, providing key managerial insights and perspectives along with a set of useful analytical tools that could be readily applied during product planning.

With these objectives in mind, I have worked diligently to compose the following book. As the title states, this book is a product planning primer. It is not intended to be a comprehensive review of the product planning field. I decided to write a primer because of the dynamic nature of the product planning field and the vast scope of industrial contexts to which product planning applies, characteristics that inhibit a truly comprehensive view. However, even with such dynamics and scope, certain general principles underlying product planning can be and are documented in this book. Accordingly, this book outlines the product planning endeavor by describing the various initiatives that are necessary for successful product planning and by illustrating various tools that can be used in managing the product planning effort. Following an introduction to product planning and key definitions, the books covers strategic issues that emerge during the product life cycle, from product strategy to idea generation, to technical development, commercialization, and life cycle management, and then eventual product dismissal. Such issues include defining customer needs; translating customer needs into technical specifications; generating concepts; evaluating results; conducting market analyses, marketing plan development, market testing, product launch, and brand management; and attending to public policy issues. My hope is that the book will help readers understand good managerial practices for successful product planning. Hence, executives and students alike who want to gain an understanding of the complex, interdisciplinary nature of product planning should find this book a useful desk reference. Those who have reviewed this book have agreed that it indeed meets this objective. I hope this book will be a welcome addition to your management book collection.

Before beginning, it is necessary to mention several key individuals and companies who have contributed to this book and thereby helped to bring it to fruition. Ms. Julie Wood of the Georgia Tech Library and Information Center is duly recognized for her assistance in compiling the list of situation analysis data sources found in Appendix A of this book. Note that I have used this list in all my product planning classes and have received a great deal of positive feedback from executives and students on its usefulness. I am grateful to Great Lakes Chemical Corporation and S. C. Johnson Wax Company for granting permission to show their product development processes in Chapter 2, proving that companies actually apply the material discussed in this book. Special appreciation goes to the many individuals who took the time to review draft manuscripts of this book and to my product planning classes, whose feedback helped me to refine the content. Last, I wish to thank my family, Mary Kay, Alexander, and Michael who afforded me the time to complete this endeavor.

Kenneth Kahn

Chapter One

Introduction

Companies represent themselves in the marketplace by way of their offerings. These offerings can be in the form of products, services, or ideas and, in many cases, a combination of all three.

The objective in providing such offerings can derive from many reasons. Profitability is often a key objective, directly corresponding to a company's bottom line. Other objectives, such as company image, company awareness, customer satisfaction, and market share, are common as well, and these are important for long-term viability and competitiveness. In light of these objectives, it should be evident that the success of a company offering has strategic implications. However, as will be discussed later in this chapter, success is not guaranteed. Special efforts are necessary to increase the likelihood of success.

Such efforts are part of a company process called *product planning*. Product planning is formally defined as the process of envisioning, conceptualizing, developing, producing, testing, commercializing, sustaining, and disposing of organizational offerings to satisfy consumer needs/wants and achieve organizational objectives. By this definition, product planning is certainly a broad and complex endeavor, comprising numerous issues and activities, many of which are cross-disciplinary in nature.

To simplify one's understanding of the topic, product planning can be characterized as comprising the two processes of product development and product management. Product development represents the "up-front" process, where the product/service is conceived, developed, produced, and tested. All these activities occur prior to the formal offering of the product/service to the marketplace, which is termed the "launch."

Product management represents the "back-end" process, where the product/service is commercialized, sustained, and eventually withdrawn. Product management includes the launch endeavor along with all activities that occur after the launch.

Although distinguishing product planning into two phases of product development and product management is useful in understanding the endeavor, separating the two processes can lead to certain unfortunate results. For one thing, the separation of product development and product management implicitly assumes a break between the two processes, which overlooks the necessary transition. Various new product offerings have failed to reach their potential because product development was not properly linked to product management, and thus, misunderstanding about the new product offering abounded. Separating the two processes also implies that product development has a stopping point, which is not really true. Even after launch, product developers should work with product managers to improve and possibly broaden the brand or product line. Conversely, product management should not be seen as just a launch and post launch activity. In fact, product managers can work with product developers on delineating market trends and customer needs that future offerings should serve. Overall, a philosophy of product planning should acknowledge the important processes of product development and product management, as well as the necessary link between them, to secure a full "inception-to-termination" view of company offerings.

■ PRODUCT PLANNING ROLES

Product planning serves various key roles in the company. One of these roles is resource allocation. Product planning analyzes each product/service, whether current or new, to determine the resources that it will need to be successful and to prioritize the impact that it has for the company. The company's finite resources are then apportioned to those products deserving of investment and support. Assuming most, if not all, products are deserving of resources, product planning forces the company to optimize the division of its resources across products.

Related to the role of resource allocation is that of product mix coordination. Here, the objective is to balance the various products that the company offers to ensure that a particular type of product is not overwhelming the company's offerings or diluting customer interest. The role of product mix coordination is to provide a product mix that comprises distinguished products where some or all are complementary products and that provides the strongest market presence possible.

Another role is marketing program support. Product planning can provide market information based on the current performance of existing products. Product planning also can inform the marketing function about customer comments regarding current products and customer needs. As a result, new marketing programs can be better focused to meet the intended target market(s), and current marketing programs can be refined.

A fourth role is the appraisal of company offerings. Product planning evaluates the performance of current products (and services) to reveal their impact on the business. In many instances, this impact is measured in terms of cash flow. Products are found to be either generating a profit or losing money for the company. In the former case, product planners consider how to increase the profit being generated; in the latter, product planners consider actions needed to turn the product around.

Of course, one action that could be taken is the termination of the product. This is another role of product planning, that is, product deletion. Product planners identify products that should be deleted and chart a course of action for proper termination of the product. This course might include programs to transition customers to alternative products, and possibly, a plan to maintain a spare parts inventory for the product being deleted so as to not alienate customers of the product.

■ PRODUCT, SERVICE, OR BOTH

In the above paragraphs, I have described a company offering as a product, service, or even an idea. Although historically products and services have been considered distinct, they have become innately intertwined in today's market scenarios. For example, the product components of a car include chassis, engine, tires, and windows—among other things. But the buyer also receives warranties on various components of the car, gets a customer service telephone number for complaints, and may participate in a special program for car financing or servicing (e.g., free oil changes, tire rotation). Together, these items serve as the total package of what the customer gets when "buying a car." Truly distinguishing products and services can be purposeless or even misleading.

Aside from slight nuances associated with their inherent characteristics, products and services should be considered equivalent in terms of the issues related to their development and management. Henceforth, the term *product* is used in this book, but the term *service* could be easily substituted, if preferred.

WHAT IS A PRODUCT?

Having clarified the issue of product versus service, the term product needs to be defined. Basically, a product is a particular offering that a company provides to customers. This does not mean that the product is in a form that would be recognized by the final consumer market; the product may be a raw material for the buyer's product planning process. For example, integrated circuit chip manufacturers such as Intel and AMD sell their products to computer manufacturers such as Dell, Gateway, and IBM, who in turn produce desktop computer Systems to be sold to businesses and final consumers. Just because the product in a business-to-business market differs from the product in a final consumer market does not mean that it is not a product. Following the definition used here, it is just as much a product and requires equal attention to systematic product planning.

With this said, it is necessary to clarify what *product* means across different contexts. This is because product can mean different things to different people based on the given context. Three particular contexts are considered: the nature of innovation, the nature of market demand, and the nature of the company's internal perspective.

Defining Product by the Nature of Innovation

One way to define product is by the nature of innovation underlying the respective product. Specifically, the terms of invention, innovation, and imitation can be associated with product.

Inventions are not products. They are technical devices that contain features, are packaged into some form, and provide a function. The distinction of inventions is that these features, forms, or functions may or may not match a need, want, or desire in the marketplace. Crawford (1987) defines inventions as taking pre-existing knowledge and combining it in such a way as to develop something that never before existed.

Innovations are basically inventions around which a marketing program has been built to clearly offer a benefit to customers, a benefit that satisfies a market need, want, or desire. Innovations are considered products because customers clearly understand how they satisfy a need, want, or desire. In other words, innovations represent a total package of features, forms, and functions concentrated on delivering the benefit to customers.

Innovations can be classified as continuous and discontinuous innovations. Continuous innovations involve slight product changes that customers can readily understand and use. Such innovations can be the result of the normal upgrading, of products, and in most cases, they do not require a change in customer behavior. New flavors or brands of potato chips would be continuous innovations. Discontinuous innovations revolutionize the market infrastructure, making other technologies obsolete and, in many cases, changing the lifestyles of consumers. A technology like fusion-powered vehicles would be a discontinuous innovation.

At this point, it should be recognized that many new products do *not* succeed because they were not actual products but rather inventions. Even famous products may have inauspicious beginnings. One example is the photocopier.

Plagued by the need for copies of patent drawings and specifications, Chester Carlson investigated ways of automatic text and illustration reproduction, working out of his apartment. Whereas others sought chemical or photographic solutions to "instant copying" problems, Carlson turned to electrostatics. In 1938, he succeeded in obtaining his first "dry copy," and 2 years later, he was awarded the first of many patents. However, he was initially unsuccessful in convincing companies that the technology would be preferable to the use of carbon paper. In fact, Carlson had called on 20 companies when the Batelle Development Corporation agreed to invest in his concept in 1944. Batelle's investment provided the necessary resources to "commercialize" the technology. In 1947, the Haloid Corporation acquired a license for Carlson's basic xerographic patents from Batelle. In 1948, Haloid and Batelle announced the development of "xerography," and a year later, the first xerographic printer, the Model A, was introduced. Of course, today, the photocopy machine is an invaluable business tool.

So why did 20 companies pass on the idea over a period of 4 years? In short, Carlson's patent was an invention. As previously stated, inventions lack clear benefits and are not in a recognizable form. Batelle's vision and resources took the invention and transformed it into an innovation, which Haloid Corporation then realized it could use. As defined, an innovation is a product because the marketing component clarifies the benefits and helps prospective customers understand the offering. Customers do not buy inventions, they buy innovations. This corresponds to the general marketing tenet that customers buy benefits, not features.

Various versions of the photocopy machine have emerged since the 1950s. Some of these were branded by different companies and, more or less, were imitations of photocopiers on the market. Yet, imitations are products, too. Imitations are copies of innovations, which may or may not have enhanced features, enhanced form, and/or enhanced function. Successful products can and, in many cases, have been imitations or "me-too" products. Their success might derive from a lower price or an enhanced feature, even though the product is essentially the same as the original innovation.

Defining Product by the Nature of Market Demand

Product also can be defined from a market perspective. This perspective is based on the premise that all products extend from a core benefit and that products can be represented as building on the core benefit. Product, therefore, can be portrayed as a group of concentric circles building on the issues of the inner circles, as shown in Exhibit 1.1.

The essential component of any product is the core benefit. The core benefit represents the fundamental service or benefit that the consumer is really buying and is derived from the consumer's need or want. However, consumers cannot buy just a benefit. The benefit must be put into some form or given some features through which the benefit can be delivered. Based on this framework, decisions regarding products (or services) must begin with what the core benefit is (or should be).

The second level of a product is the generic product. The generic product is the basic version of the product and is typically a "less developed" product. Less developed means that the product does not have features or forms that distinguish the given product or service.

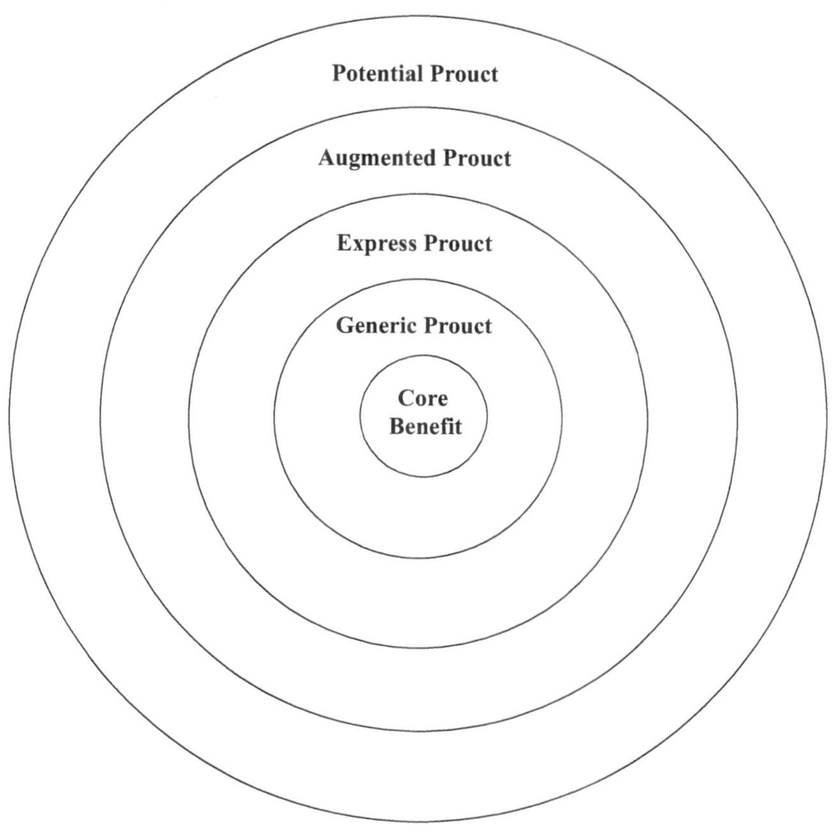

EXHIBIT 1.1. Product Model

However, the features and/or forms given to the product or service allow consumers to receive the benefit that they want.

The third level is the expected product. The expected product includes a set of attributes and conditions that buyers normally expect and agree to when they purchase this product.

The fourth level is the augmented product. The augmented product is one that includes additional services and benefits that distinguish the company's offering from competitors' offerings. At this level, the product is complemented by services and vice versa.

At the fifth and top level is the potential product. The potential product is all the augmentations and transformations that the product might undergo in the future. The potential product represents a product that attempts to satisfy all consumers' needs and wants, related to the product and thereby to create "customer delight."

For example, the core benefit of a hotel is shelter. But one cannot buy the concept of shelter by itself. All the associated features and services associated with consumer assumptions of what a hotel is boil down to the need for shelter. The generic level might comprise hostels and YMCAs, which provide a bed and a roof over the consumer's head. At this point, an argument could be made to include tents or similar options. But if the product/service being considered is a hotel, tents should not be considered a solution in the hotel set because the concept of a hotel characteristically suggests that someone else is providing consumers' shelter—they are not providing their own shelter. Of course, a service that would provide consumers with a tent for shelter would be considered a valid generic option.

Simpler hotels such as those in the Motel 6 or Super 8 chains could be characteristic of the expected level. These products provide expected features associated with a hotel room, for example, a private room, a television, a telephone, and a private bathroom (a characteristically U.S. hotel expectation).

The augmented level would represent hotels such as those in the Hilton, Hyatt, Marriott, Omni, and Westin chains. These provide multiple services in association with shelter, including room service, a newspaper at the door every morning, a concierge, a business support center, a fitness center, and in-room computerized check-out.

Arguably, the potential level would be hotels that attempt to cater to hotel guests: resort hotels such as Marriott Resorts, Westin Resorts. One particular hotel chain that prides itself on exceptional service and may be characteristic of the potential level is Ritz-Carlton.

A simple product example can be macaroni and cheese. The core benefit associated with macaroni and cheese is satisfaction of hunger and/or provision of nutrition. The generic level would be a plain, generic version of the product—a simple box with little use of color. The expected level would be a branded product with more use of color. The augmented level would be a nationally branded product with a consumer complaint line and a kids club. The potential product might be a delivery service that would provide macaroni and cheese whenever the customer wanted.

Realize that as we move toward the outer circles, the product becomes a premium product, be it a Ritz-Carlton hotel or a macaroni and cheese delivery service. Here, customers would pay (and be willing to pay) a higher price for a better product and service. As we move inward, the product becomes less expensive and more basic. The model can, therefore, be used to devise a strategic product portfolio comprising products based on a margin strategy (at the outer levels) and simplified products based on a volume strategy (at the inner levels).

Related to the point of a product portfolio is the fact that many companies offer different versions of the same product category. Each of these versions vary on price, features, and associated services. For example, Marriott Corporation has multiple hotel offerings that fall across the different levels: Fairfield Inn could be considered a generic product; Courtyard by Marriott and Residence Inn could be considered expected products; Marriott Hotels and Marriott Suites could be considered augmented products; and Marriott Resorts could be considered a potential product (see Exhibit 1.2).

Another issue inherent in the product model of Exhibit 1.1 is the affirmation that all products must have a core benefit. As shown in this exhibit, the core benefit serves as the focal point of the product, not its features or form (styling). However, customers cannot buy a benefit directly. It is encapsulated with features and form to make the respective product understandable and compatible within the customer's environment.

One final point needs to be made about the effect of customer learning. That is, the services that enhance a product at the augmented product level can, over time, become expected services. Thus, the given product model can be viewed as an onion, with multiple levels cascading down to the center. The important point is that a company cannot be satisfied with existing offerings because customers can be trained to expect certain features/add-on services as a result of continued augmentation of the product by the company and/or augmentation activities by competitors. One approach to managing this situation is to provide multiple offerings, as described in the case of Marriott. Another option is to not provide a potential product immediately but, instead, to offer various versions of the product over time, each time enhancing the product, so customers do not expect everything at once.

Defining Product by the Company's Internal Perspective

A third way to define product is from an internal company perspective. Specifically, product can be defined in terms of a product item,

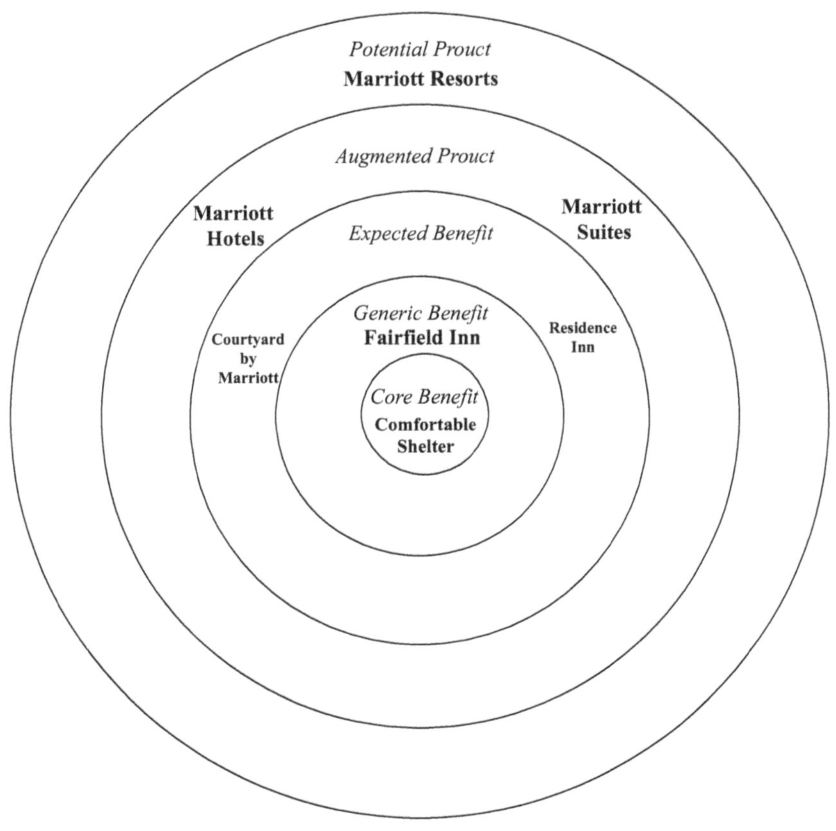

EXHIBIT **1.2.** Marriott Corporation's Product Mix

Marriott International is a leading worldwide hospitality company, with more than 1,800 units. The company operates and franchises the broadest portfolio of lodging brands in the world, offering travelers more than 325,000 rooms and time-share villas worldwide. Marriott also operates 113 senior living communities, as Well as a nationwide network of food distribution centers.

Description of above offerings (Marriott Corporation, 2000):

- Marriott Hotels, Resorts and Suites is the company's line of upscale, full-service hotels and suites. Marriott Hotels, Resorts and Suites offers a full array of quality services, including multiple restaurants and lounges, fully equipped health clubs, swimming pool, gift shop, concierge level, business center, and meeting facilities. It is the original and parent brand of all of Marriott's lodging portfolio, dating back to 1957. The system encompasses 346 hotels: 250 properties in the United States and 96 in 42 other countries and territories.

EXHIBIT 1.2. Continued

- Courtyard by Marriott, the leading U.S. moderate price chain, features superior guest accommodations for both the business and pleasure traveler. Courtyard hotels resemble contemporary residences in their landscaping and architecture. Most of the rooms overlook a central landscaped courtyard with an outdoor swimming pool (indoor at some locations) and socializing area with a gazebo. Encompassing 406 hotels in the United States and 34 international properties, Courtyard by Marriott hotels have from 80 to 150 spacious guest rooms designed for business travelers.
- Residence Inn by Marriott is the top extended-stay chain in the world. Designed as a "home away from home," Residence Inn hotels feature complimentary breakfast and newspaper every morning, swimming pool, and heated whirlpool. Guest suites provide in-room modem jacks, separate living and sleeping areas, and a fully equipped kitchen with appliances and cooking utensils. Generally built as a neighborhood of two-story, residential-style buildings, Residence Inn has 303 properties in the United States and 7 in Canada and Mexico.
- Fairfield Inn by Marriott is an economy lodging chain appealing to business and leisure travelers. Fairfield Inn provides clean, convenient, quality accommodations and friendly hospitality at an economical price. The system consists of over 392 inns nationwide. Fairfield Inn features complimentary continental breakfast served daily, free local calls, large and well-lit work desks, and an outdoor pool (indoor at some locations).

product line, product family, or product mix. A product item is the individual product that a particular customer may buy. The product item, therefore, is a specific model, brand, or size of a product that a company offers.

A product line is a group of closely related product items. Distinguishing product items by product lines is important for a variety of reasons. Organizing products by product lines may indicate a new opportunity. Product lines can help to spread resources across products, using company resources in a more optimal fashion. Product lines also can serve as a signal to the consumer about quality and/or desirable characteristics, and thus, product lines can serve as a mechanism for gaining market acceptance as well as promoting product items.

A product family is a collection of product lines in a related group. Sometimes, a product family is referred to as a product category or even a product platform. Determining product families can allow for better use of manufacturing capabilities or other company resources. Companies also sometimes organize their organizational structures in accordance with product families.

At the highest level of aggregation is the product mix. Product mix consists of all the different product lines a firm offers. Three characteristics are used to describe the product mix: width, depth, and consistency. Width represents the number of different product lines. A wide product mix suggests many product lines, whereas a narrow product mix suggests fewer product lines. Depth represents the number of product items within each line. A deep product mix suggests many product items per product line; a shallow product line suggests fewer product items per line. And consistency is the degree of commonality among lines with respect to end use, distribution outlets, consumer groups, and/or price range. A consistent product mix would suggest similar product lines; an inconsistent product mix would suggest a diverse mix of product lines.

The characteristics of width, depth, and consistency can be illustrated with the product mixes of Pillsbury and MCI WorldCom. As shown in Exhibit 1.3, Pillsbury has a wide and deep product mix that comprises seven product families: Pillsbury, Haagen-Dazs, Green Giant, Old El Paso, Progresso Products, Pizza and Snacks, and Martha White. Within each of these families are multiple product lines. As shown, the Pillsbury brand comprises three broad product lines: desserts and baking mixes, refrigerated baked goods, and breakfast products. Within each of these lines are multiple product items, such as flour, cake mix, frosting, brownies, dessert bars, muffins, quick breads, and specialty desserts. In fact, each of these items could conceivably be characterized as a line within which a particular package size, such as a 16-ounce chocolate cake mix, would represent a specific product item. In comparison, MCI WorldCom, as shown in Exhibit 1.4, has a narrower but relatively deep product mix. Conceivably, MCI WorldCom has three product families: home services, small business services, and business services. Within each of these families of services are different types of services, representing product lines. A particular service plan within each type of service would represent a product item.

An issue faced by product planners is product proliferation. *Product proliferation* is a term used to describe the current trend of companies to expand the width and depth of their mixes. Product planners, therefore, face an explosion of product items that need to be managed. Even with the use of product platforms (which are discussed later in this book), product proliferation makes product planning more difficult. In the final consumer market, especially, manufacturers typically must provide multiple mass merchants (e.g., Kmart, Target, Wal-Mart) with their own universal product code or UPC—the bar

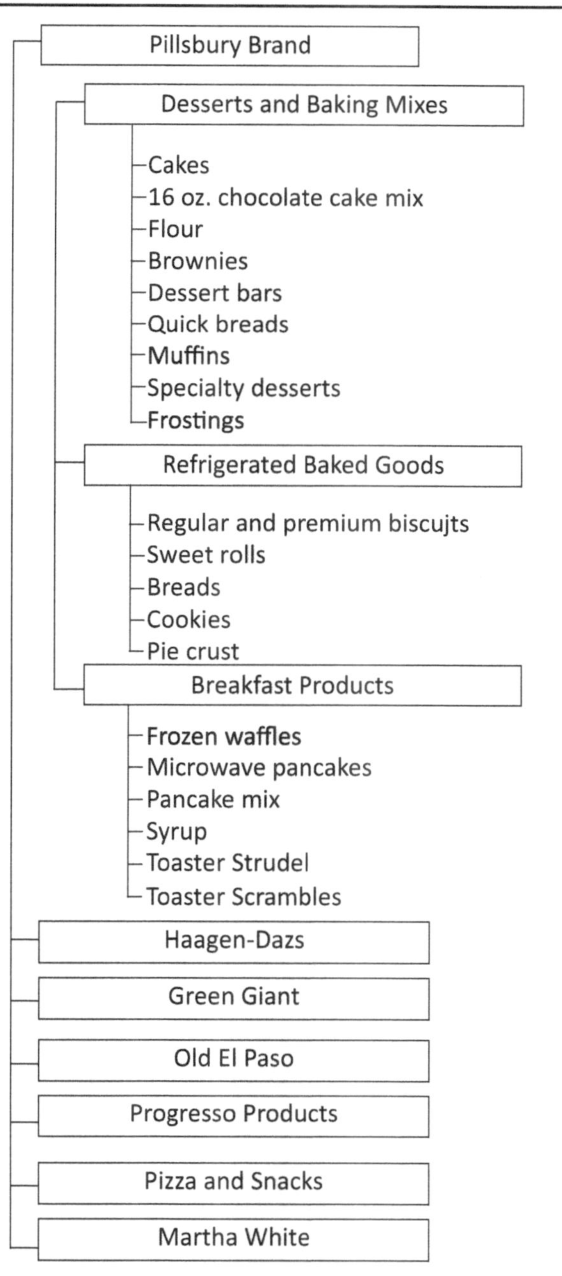

EXHIBIT **1.3.** Illustrating the Product Mix: Pillsbury

Home	Small Business	Business
Long distance plans	Long distance plans	MCI WorldCom on-net services
Local toll calling	Local toll calling	Voice services
International calling	Toll-free service	Data services
Calling card	International calling	Internet services
Personal 800 number	Calling cards	Messaging services
Local service	Wireless	Call center services
Prepaid cards	Internet	Business solutions
Internet		Partnerships and buying programs

EXHIBIT 1.4. Illustrating the Product Mix: MCI WorldCom

code on packages. Because of this, the individual product item now represents a set of products. For example, one television model being shipped to three mass merchandisers would be three products (one product item × three unique customer UPCs equals three separate product items to be managed). Obviously, this get more complicated if there are three different television models going to three different mass merchandisers; a total of nine products would need to be managed (three television models × three unique customer UPCs equals nine separate product items to be managed).

Related to product proliferation is the issue of cannibalization. Cannibalization occurs when one product takes sales from another product offering. Typically, companies want to avoid new product introductions that cannibalize their own product offerings. However, there is a saying that "if you are going to have to deal with cannibals, you may as well keep the cannibals in the family." In other words, companies would rather cannibalize their own sales than have a competitor cannibalize sales. Sometimes, however, companies introduce new products without considering the potential for cannibalization of existing product sales. Cannibalization should be a necessary consideration to ensure that products are positioned correctly to minimize cannibalization. Reducing cannibalization also minimizes the duplication of resources and the lack of efficiency in the product planning effort.

Overall, companies can use three general questions to evaluate their product mix and thus highlight company competencies, identify lagging products, and pinpoint new product opportunities:

- What product lines does the company offer?
- How deep are the offerings within each product line?
- What gaps exist within the product line that could be filled by new products or modified current products?

DEFINING A NEW PRODUCT

Having defined what *product* means, it is time to distinguish what is meant by *new product*. Like the term product, new product can mean different things. Conceivably, there are six types of new products: cost improvements, product improvements, line extensions, market extensions, new category entries, and new-to-the-world products.

Cost improvements are not dramatic changes to the product and may not be noticeable by the consumer. However, cost improvements may provide a competitive advantage. Toyota's redesign of the 1996 Camry, which emerged as the 1997 Camry, was predominantly based on the objective of cost reduction.

Product improvements are product enhancements that improve the product's form or function. An example of a product improvement would be products that are labeled as "new and improved" or "better flavor." A product improvement serves as a replacement for the original product. A new and improved Tide laundry detergent—now "even better than before"—is an example of a product improvement.

Line extensions are copies of an existing product that contain unique features the original product (or set of products) does not have. An example of a line extension is the lengthening of the Colgate toothpaste product line. Starting with the original Colgate toothpaste, the line extensions include Colgate Toothpaste Gel, Colgate Tartar Control Toothpaste, Colgate Whitening Toothpaste, and so on. The key distinction between a product improvement and a line extension is that when the line extension is introduced, the original product can still be acquired by the consumer. A product improvement always serves as the replacement for the original product.

Market extensions are original products positioned in new markets without any (or with minimal) changes to the product. A classic example of a market extension is Arm and Hammer Baking Soda. Originally, positioned as a baking product, the yellow box of Arm & Hammer Baking Soda was positioned as a deodorizer for refrigerators and sinks and as a mouthwash when used with hydrogen peroxide. Later, Arm and Hammer introduced new lines of products such as toothpaste and laundry detergents—products that were in a new form and new packaging, providing different functions. Most energy companies are pursuing market extensions by marketing their power generation expertise to utilities in developing countries. The reason for this is that the U.S. market is saturated compared to foreign markets such as Latin America, and power generation expertise is applied in the same fashion across domestic and foreign markets.

New category entries are products that are new to the company, but as a category, the product is not new to the consumer. For example, the entry of Kodak into the battery market represents a new category market. Batteries represented a new market and a new set of customers for Kodak, although a portion of this market would include Kodak customers needing batteries for their camera equipment. However, the batteries sold were not exclusively for camera equipment.

New-to-the-world products are technological innovations that create a completely new market that previously did not exist. These innovations would be characterized as discontinuous innovations. The introduction of the first commercial cellular telephone, or recently, the first DVD system, represent new-to-the-world products.

It is important to recognize that companies do not just deal with one type of new product. Rather, multiple types of new products permeate the product planning process. For example, Coca-Cola may redesign a fountain dispenser to reduce material costs, which would be characteristic of cost improvement; the redesign of an existing soda can to be more colorful would represent a product improvement; a new package size would represent a line extension; Coca-Cola's entry into an untapped market such as China would represent a market extension; and Coca-Cola clothing represents a new category entry.

■ THE GROWING EMPHASIS ON PRODUCT PLANNING

Product planning is gaining more and more attention due to its impact on the business. Recently, the chief executive officer (CEO) of Gillette indicated a plan to have sales of products less than 5 years old make up 50% of total sales. Benchmarking work by the Product Development and Management Association (Griffin et al., 1997) indicates that, on average, about 33% of company sales come from new products introduced within the last 5 years. This percentage is expected to increase, placing greater pressure on new products being developed, launched, and managed.

Such pressure exists because research has found that more than 90% of product concepts fail during the product development process. An even smaller percentage of products are considered successful after launch. Booz, Allen, and Hamilton (1982) found that the failure rate of new products that made it to the marketplace ranged from 33% to 35% between 1963 and 1981. Research by Cooper (1982) found that, on average, 31% of industrial products fail, and 46% of consumer products fail. And a report by the Association of National Advertisers (1984) estimated that 27% of product line extensions fail; 31% of new brands introduced in categories where the company already had a product fail; and 46% of the new products that were introduced to new categories fail.

These statistics are noteworthy, but what exactly is meant by *new product success* and *new product failure*. Indeed, what may be considered a failure from one perspective may be a success from another. For

Customer-Based	*Competitive-Based*	*Financial*	*Technical Performance*
• Customer satisfaction	• Market share	• Revenue	• Performance specifications
• Customer acceptance	• Competitive benchmarks	• Profit	• Speed-to-market
• Number of original customers	• Competitive advantage	• Rate of return	• Development cost
• Unit volume		• Payback period	• Quality
• Number of repeat customers			• On-time launch
			• Innovativeness

EXHIBIT **1.5.** *A* Sample of Product Success Measures

example, a new technological innovation may be a commercial failure, but the fact that the technology functions properly makes it a technological success.

Griffin and Page (1996) classify new product success measures into four general categories: customer-based measures, competitive-based measures, financial measures, and technical performance measures. Customer-based success can be based on customer satisfaction, customer acceptance, number of original customers, unit volume, and number of repeat customers. Competitive-based measures can include achieving market share, competitive benchmarking, and establishing a competitive advantage. Financial measures can be revenue, profit, margin, rate of return, and payback. Technical performance measures can include performance specifications, speed to market, development cost, quality specifications, on-time launch, and innovativeness. The use of particular success measures will obviously be dependent on the departments involved and the point in the development process (see Exhibit 1.5).

■ SO WHY IS PRODUCT PLANNING DIFFICULT?

Product planning is difficult because of the uncertainty that new technology will function properly and that the market will accept the new product. Product planning also is a multifunctional process, and because of the involvement of multiple functions, the process becomes complicated. Factors related to organizational culture, organizational politics, and individual personalities come into the process, creating further complications.

Although there is no silver bullet ensuring success, some steps improve the odds when developing, launching, and managing products. These include (a) learning about previous experiences to understand what does or does not work, (b) understanding a systematic approach to product planning to organize the process, and (c) assembling a toolbox of ideas/heuristics/tools to aid in planning and managing the product planning process.

The overriding intent of this book is to present a product planning perspective in this manner and to impress on readers the broad, integrated product planning perspective. To do this, the book is organized along the lines of the eight elements of the definition for product planning. To reiterate, product planning is defined as the process of envisioning, conceptualizing, developing, producing, testing, commercializing, sustaining, and disposing of organizational offerings to satisfy consumer needs/wants and achieve organizational objectives.

Chapter 1 has introduced the product planning topic, provided key definitions, and identified issues inherent to product planning. Chapters 2, 3, and 4 address the *envisioning* step: Chapter 2 discusses strategic planning, product strategy, the product planning process, and product development charters; Chapter 3 discusses product planning teams; and Chapter 4 discusses opportunity identification. Chapters 5 and 6 address the *conceptualizing* step, with Chapter 5 presenting concept generation techniques and Chapter 6 presenting concept evaluation techniques. Chapter 7 covers the *developing* and *producing* steps, as well as some aspects of the *testing* step. Topics include design for excellence and product use testing. Chapters 8 and 9 cover other aspects of *developing* and *testing* and address the *commercializing* step of product planning. Chapter 8 provides an overview of market planning and market testing, whereas Chapter 9 does the same for launch management. Chapter 10 covers the steps of *sustaining* and *disposing* of products/ services by way of the topics of life cycle management, product families, and brand management. Chapter 11 discusses special topics related to product planning endeavors. Chapter 12, then, closes the book with key learning about product planning, prescriptions, and best-practice benchmarks.

Obviously, covering the breadth of these topics is a daunting task. Yet, it is an imperative task so that readers can be attuned to and have an understanding of the complex product planning process. Moreover, being attuned to and having an understanding of these topics will ensure a greater likelihood of success as a product planner. It is hoped that after going through this book, readers will agree and realize the need for a broader view of product planning.

Prior to learning about these topics, some degree of preparation by readers is necessary. First, shake off any particular functional viewpoint. Product planning is characteristically cross-functional. Second, be prepared to be inquisitively analytical. Product planners cannot afford to base all decisions on gut feelings alone; product data must be examined to determine what is truly going on before an informed decision can be made. Third, be creative and not critical of creative ideas. Creative product planning often leads to success. Fourth, be tolerant of failure and examine why failure occurred. Not all products succeed, and product planners make it a point to learn from mistakes to avoid repeating them in the future. Failure is very much a part of the process for ensuring success in the product planning process.

Having said all this, let's begin.

Key Concepts

- Product
- Product planning
- Product development
- Product management
- New product

Chapter Questions

1. What is product planning?
2. What is a product?
3. What is the difference between product and service?
4. What is a new product?
5. Why is product planning important?

Chapter Two

Strategy and Process

Successful product planning companies commonly share the following characteristics:

- They have clearly defined goals.
- They seek future customer needs.
- They build organizations dedicated to accomplishing focused goals.
- They partner with customers in the development process.

Such characteristics are ingrained into the company's strategic planning process, permeating all activities in the company. Among the various ways to envision the strategic planning process, strategic planning can be illustrated as a pyramid, with mission at the top, objectives at the next level, and goals, strategies, and programs at the lower level (see Exhibit 2.1).

By definition, mission defines the company's central purpose, direction, and scope. Objectives derive from the mission and represent specific elements to be achieved by the company (objectives are often prefaced by the phrase *to be).* Goals are time-specific metrics by which to measure successful attainment of a particular objective. Strategies characterize the way in which the objectives are to be realized. And

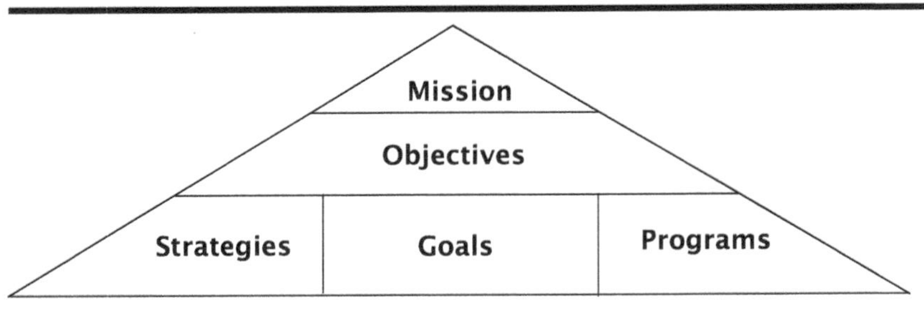

EXHIBIT **2.1.** Corporate Strategy Framework

programs are a way to execute individual strategies. For example, a corporate mission may reflect a desire for innovation. In turn, a company objective "to be the recognized leader in technological innovation in our industry" may lead to a next-generation new product strategy, implemented through the company's product development program. The goal, "50% of company revenues will come from new product introduced in the past 3 years," would be one way to measure whether the given objective is being met.

■ NEW PRODUCT STRATEGY

A common misconception of product development is that new products correspond to major changes. In fact, new product strategy can mean different types of new product products, depending on how the company delineates the type of market to be served (current or new customers) and type of technology (current or new technology). *Current* customers here does not necessarily mean direct customers. Rather, current customers are those within or associated with the target market or market segment, who may be immediate customers, a competitor's customers, or noncustomers (potential customers who have not made a purchase yet). Similarly, *current technology* means the company has the technology, whereas *new technology* indicates a technology that needs to be created or Required from somewhere else.

Based on this schematic, which marketers call the Product-Market Matrix, four general strategies for product planning are identified: market penetration, product development, market development, and diversification (see Exhibit 2.2).

Current	New
Market Penetration (Product improvements, cost reductions)	**Product Development** (line extensions)
Market Extensions (new uses, new markets)	**Diversification** (new-to-the-compnay, new-to-the-world)

EXHIBIT **2.2.** Product-Market Matrix

A market penetration strategy is based on an objective to increase market share and/or increase product usage. The current customer base is pursued with no major changes to the existing product technology. Cost improvements and product improvements are characteristic of a market penetration strategy. Naturally, these two types of new products attempt to attract customers through a lower price, more features, and/or improved features.

A product development strategy derives from an objective to capitalize on new product technology and offer more options to the customer base. In this way, the company with a more diverse product line can fend off competitors. Line extensions are characteristically associated with a product development strategy.

A market development strategy stems from a desire to expand sales volume of existing products through new markets. This would include expanding geographically, for example, to international markets, and targeting new market segments. The company is not interested in pursuing any product technology changes; the predominant interest is to take the product "as is" and find new viable markets. Market extensions are characteristic of a market development strategy.

Diversification is pursued when the company wishes to expand its business into related businesses and unrelated businesses. Thus, new customer markets and new product technologies will face the company. New category entries and new-to-the-world products are pursued in the course of a diversification strategy.

Although it is a simple representation of product planning, the Product-Market Matrix suggests that product planning itself becomes more complex and risky along the diagonal of the matrix from the upper left corner to the lower right corner. Plotting the different types of new products, the riskier projects of new category entries and new-to-the-world products are in the riskiest cell, the cell representing the diversification strategy. Diversification would be the riskiest, as such products as new category entries and new-to-the-world products would be the most unfamiliar and untested for the company. The least risky are cost improvements and product improvements because of company knowledge of the market and technology. These efforts would offer a more comfortable business situation for a company than diversification. However, greater risk can translate into a greater return for the company. Thus, diversification offers the potential for a greater "bottom line" impact than the other strategies.

■ THE PRODUCT DEVELOPMENT PROCESS

As indicated, strategy is implemented through programs. In the case of new product development, a strategy of new products is typically coordinated through the product development process. In the past, such a process was haphazard and unstructured, but companies have found that a systematic process creates a great propensity for new product success. Consequently, companies employ a structured product development process.

There is a debate over how the product development process should begin, however. Some contend that the product development process begins with a company objective or strategy that, in turn, orients the product development endeavor. Others argue that an idea (inspiration) is first needed to stimulate the process and that such an idea should not be constrained by strategic planning. Both are valid ways to initiate the product development process.

Pursuing product development via a strategy is a systematic approach to product development. The company first determines the objectives and goals that it wants to achieve and then charts a course of product development that would indeed achieve these objectives and goals.

Idea-directed product development may be systematic or haphazard. It is systematic if a promising idea is proposed, investigated, and, if found to have potential, pursued. It is haphazard if the idea is quickly pursued without an investigation phase and rushed to market. Both approaches can be successful, but more often than not, a systematic approach has a better chance of success.

Another view of product development is market-pull versus technology-push. Market-pull product development is focused on satisfying customer needs and closely parallels the strategy-directed approach to product development. The process begins with an analysis of the marketplace to determine customer needs and their views of the competition. These needs and views are then used to develop a set of possible company objectives and goals. Continued analysis of the customer base occurs throughout the process.

Technology-push product development closely parallels the idea-directed approach to product development. A new technology (either incremental or discontinuous in nature) is developed, with or without an investigation into its potential. In many cases, a technology-push process ends with a feasible product looking for a suitable market. Consequently, there is a lot of postdevelopment work focused on selling the product.

This does not mean that a technology-push approach is inappropriate. Many radical innovations have come through a technology-push product development process. In fact, in certain cases, customers can have trouble articulating innovative or next-generation products. The company, therefore, can aid customers in envisioning what is possible. However, technology-push product development is a risky endeavor when the customer is overlooked. In comparison, market-pull product development is generally more successful than technology-push product development, especially when it comes to launching the product.

Conceivably, a merging of the philosophies underlying market-pull and technology-push product development processes would seem reasonable. However, the typical product development organization/function is biased toward one of these two processes; there is never a true merging of both. Furthermore, companies typically favor a particular department during product development—be it the marketing department for a market-pull approach or the engineering department for a technology-push approach.

Overall, the purpose of any systematic product development process is to

- Transfer technology to a commercial application
- Mate technical characteristics and market needs
- Integrate multiple functional efforts to create the product

- Implement company strategy via the development of a new product
- Provide managerial control but not be overwhelmingly intrusive

Also common to any type of systematic product development process is the organization of product development activities into multiple phases or stages. In addition, a review point or gate is placed between phases/stages such that a particular new product concept cannot enter a subsequent development phase/stage without satisfying a given set of company criteria. This product process is called a "stage-gate™" or "phase-review" product development process. Another parallel form of the product development process is called the PACE process, which was designed by the PRTM consulting group. This process parallels the typical stage-gate™ process but focuses on product development speed to expedite time to market.

Interestingly, product development processes are similar across companies and industries: Commonalities can be found regardless of the underlying philosophical principles that created the process. Indeed, most product development processes will reflect similar stages: opportunity identification, concept generation, pretechnical evaluation, technical development, and launch. One common shortcoming is the omission of a sixth product development stage, life cycle management, which should be considered and which some companies include as part of their continuous product development process. Those companies that do not include a life cycle management stage hold the philosophy that the product development process ends at launch.

Opportunity identification represents the first stage of the product development process. The purpose of this stage is to delineate a direction for the product development initiative. At the conclusion of the opportunity identification stage comes the first gate. In many cases, an outline of the opportunities is generated and approved. A more formal approach is to develop a product development charter, also referred to as a product innovation charter, which would then be approved before moving on to the next stage.

Concept generation represents the second stage of the product development process. The purpose of this stage is to put together a set of potential new product ideas. Typically, the more ideas/concepts generated, the better. A variety of concept generation techniques can facilitate the effort. The gate after the concept generation stage is the affirmation of a pool of interesting concepts that meet a preliminary set of criteria.

As previously mentioned, some companies prefer to conduct the concept generation stage prior to the opportunity identification stage. The rationale is that concept generation should not be biased by any preconceived notions of what should be developed. Instead, these companies prefer to begin the process with a clean slate, providing an environment for greater innovation.

Other companies, however, prefer to conduct an opportunity identification stage first to provide boundaries for their product development process. The rationale is that concept generation can get off track and present ideas that go beyond what the company would want to offer. The opportunity identification stage has management delineate what is acceptable as a new product opportunity, thereby providing a greater focus in the concept generation stage.

Pretechnical evaluation is the third stage in the product development process. Here, product concepts are evaluated and prioritized. An important element in the pretechnical evaluation stage is a business analysis of the product concept. Those concepts showing the greatest potential to meet company objectives and goals are further defined via product protocols (i.e., product definition statements). The gate at the end of the pretechnical evaluation stage is selection of a final set of concepts to continue in the product development process and approval of their respective product protocols.

The fourth stage in the product development process is technical development. In this stage, the technology behind the product concept is realized and tested to ensure that it meets the specifications in the product protocol. Construction of a viable business/marketing plan also occurs. The gate at the conclusion of this stage assesses whether a tangible product has been developed and functions as desired. The financial viability and marketability (profit potential) of the product also is gauged to make a determination of whether to commit resources and continue work on the product.

The fifth stage of the product development process is launch. This stage comprises activities related to solidifying market acceptance of the new product, including market testing, prelaunch preparation, launch, and postlaunch control. The gate at the conclusion of the launch stage is the successful launch of the product and favorable sales levels.

The sixth stage of the product development process is life cycle management. This stage represents continuous monitoring, the possible refinement of the launched product, and the possible augmentation of the product to create a product line, should one not already exist. Such refinements would be necessary to keep up with changing consumer needs and wants, competitor actions, government regulations, and/or new technologies. The latter part of this stage focuses on the eventual market withdrawal and disposal of the product and substitution by the next-generation product.

Several points are to be made about the product development process. Although the process is illustrated as sequential, it is actually concurrent. At times, steps will overlap. The process also is inherently multifunctional. That is, multiple company departments are involved in the process to cover the variety of activities necessary to develop, launch, and manage the product successfully.

There also is the "fuzzy front end." Depending on the company, the fuzzy front end precedes the opportunity identification stage. The fuzzy front end is the amassing of new technologies and is characteristic of research and development (R&D). The big issue in the fuzzy front end is determining which technologies should be pursued.

The following are criteria that any good product development process should have:

- Some structure of checkpoints along the way for making decisions and committing resources
- Substantial degrees of freedom for the product development team and its support group
- Flexibility to changing conditions
- Success in passing especially critical points in development
- Integration of the team with the rest of the firm and the world
- Facilitation of a smooth launch
- Provision for organization learning

This generic product development process somewhat simplifies what truly happens in practice. The process does not necessarily follow a path as described. For example, sometimes the process needs to be expedited so "fuzzy gates" are used. By fuzzy gates, we mean that a new product concept will go through a gate without resistance to allow the project to continue. The goal is to ensure that the process continues, with the expectation that a more stringent gate will be used later in the product development process. Fuzzy gates are commonly used when being "first to market" is critical to success and when a gate review meeting cannot be scheduled because key members of the review team are unavailable.

All the steps in a product development process are not necessarily delineated in this schematic of the product development process. Many times, bottlenecks occur when, for example, technology problems or market changes force a change in the expected course of action.

Nonetheless, many companies provide a schematic of their product development process to frame expectations for their product development initiatives. In this way, company personnel understand the general steps and criteria necessary to get products to the marketplace. Exhibit 2.3 presents some sample product development processes for Great Lakes Chemical Corporation and S. C. Johnson Wax.

Note that even if a product development process exists, companies can abuse how the way the product development process is used. Several of these abuses include

- Too much faith in the product being developed
- Lack of concern for the customer
- Faulty research (skewed findings)
- Incorrect signals from good research
- Meeting of technical needs and certain customer needs, but not all customer needs

Special attention must be taken to ensure that these abuses do not emerge, or else the respective product development process will not reach its potential for success.

■ IMPLEMENTING A PRODUCT DEVELOPMENT PROCESS

Although many companies have a structured product development process, other companies do not. In some situations, the current product development process should be revised to be more effective.

To do this, O'Connor (1994) lays out a five-step process:

1. Lay the foundation: gather information, establish the need for a product development process, analyze current practices and benchmark with best practices, identify and attempt to understand hurdles for implementation
2. Gain initial commitment: sell senior management on the need for a product development process, note and address management concerns, detail the activities per stage and criteria per gate, compose an implementation plan, obtain a budget to implement the process

	GATE 1 SCREENING		GATE 2 ASSESSMENT		GATE 3 DEVELOPMENT		GATE 4 VALIDATION		GATE 5 COMMERCIALIZATION		
	♦ Completed and signed Idea Form		♦ If sufficient opportunity authorize modest resources to further quantify opportunity and develop criteria for next gate.		♦ Authorize development funds and develop criteria for next gate.		♦ Authorize continued funding and commitments to customers and develop criteria for next gate.		♦ Last assessment before launching product. ♦ Approve commercialization plan. ♦ Authorize funding		
IDEA GENERATION	1	STAGE 1 PRELIMINAY INVESTIGATION	2	STAGE 2 DETAILED ASSESSMENT	3	STAGE 3 DEVELOPMENT	4	STAGE 4 VALIDATION	5	STAGE 5 COMMERCIALIZATION	REVIEW
♦ Generate and document ideas. ♦ Complete an Idea Form and submit it to Facilitator. ♦ Champion the idea through the initial gate reviews. ♦ Prepare information required for Screening gate review.		♦ Preliminary literature search and consultations with internal and industry resources to assess value of an idea		♦ Determine if opportunity warrants development funds.		♦ Complete product, process and market development activities and reassess value of project.		♦ Develop confidence that product specifications, volume, cost, and price targets can be met. ♦ Develop commercialization plan.		♦ Launch product. ♦ Commence full-scale production. ♦ Complete transfer to ongoing business operations.	♦ Assess effectiveness of process to deliver objectives. ♦ Make appropriate changes to the process for future projects.

EXHIBIT **2.3a.** Examples of Company Product Development Processes: Great Lakes Chemical

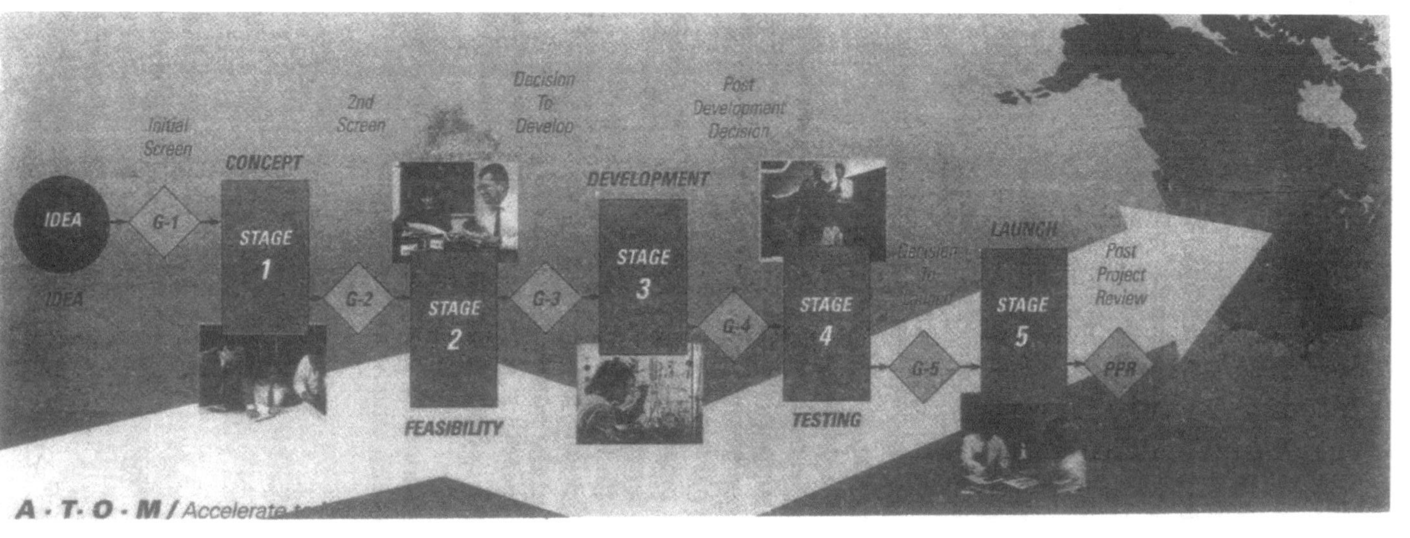

EXHIBIT 2.3B. S. C. Johnson Wax

3. Effect change: train management and participating players, sustain active participation in the process, develop tools to support the process, put new projects into the process
4. Work the transition: seek continual feedback, analyze feedback and take appropriate action, continue training, improve tools
5. Monitor and improve: benchmark process with best practices, seek improvements in tools and product development activities, refresh product development process if needed

O'Connor also indicates a variety of challenges to implementation of a product development process. These also apply to the ongoing use of existing product development processes:

Optimizing and validating the process: Achieving an optimal process may be unfeasible; a workable process may be just as, if not more, efficient and effective.

Gaining top management commitment and involvement: Without top management support, the process will not be sustained.

Structuring decision making: Who makes which decisions must be clarified to avoid confusion and/or conflict.

Developing new product development leaders and high-performance teams: Cross-functional communication and collaboration are necessary to effect product development activities.

Training for critical skills and knowledge: Such skills and knowledge help to support the process.

Optimizing the portfolio: A portfolio management process must be developed that decides which projects to pursue and which projects to shelve.

Linking and positioning the process: The product development process must fit with other company processes.

EVALUATING THE PRODUCT DEVELOPMENT PROCESS

There are various ways to evaluate the effectiveness and efficiency of the product development process. One technique is statistical in nature and can be readily applied to assess the risk, cost, and time characteristics inherent in the product development process. Results can indicate the riskiest, costliest, and most time-consuming product development stages.

To apply this technique, the risk, cost, and time associated with each product development stage must be determined. Risk should be given in terms of the percentage of product concepts that successfully make it through the stage (i.e., successfully pass the respective stage's gate review). Cost should be given as the standard cost for one product concept to progress through the given stage. Time should be given as the standard time for one product concept to progress through the given stage.

For example, assume a new product development comprises the five stages of opportunity identification, concept generation, pretechnical review, technical development, and launch. Note that the life cycle management stage is not considered in this analysis because it is an ongoing stage after launch. Assume that 90% of the proposed product concepts (ideas) successfully go through the opportunity identification stage; 60%, through the concept generation stage; 40%, through the pretechnical evaluation stage; 50%, through the technical development stage, and 80% successfully launch (see Exhibit 2.4).

Using these percentages, the overall probability of success for one product concept at the beginning of the product development process is 8.64%. In other words, fewer than 9 concepts out of a 100 will ever be officially launched. To ensure that the company can successfully launch one product, 12 likely product concepts will be needed at the beginning of the product development process. This is calculated by taking the reciprocal of 8.64% or 11.57 product concepts (note that 11.57 is rounded up to 12 because .57 product concepts cannot be achieved). If the company wants to launch two new products in a given year, then 24 (two launched products × 11.57 concepts necessary for each launch = 23.15, rounded up to 24) product concepts will be needed at the beginning of the product development process.

This approach can be used to show how many product concepts will enter each stage. For example, assume that one launched product is the goal. If 11.57 enter the process, 10.41 (11.57 × .9) concepts would enter the concept generation stage; 6.25 (10.4 × .6) concepts, the pretechnical evaluation stage; 2.50 (6.25 × .4) concepts, the technical development stage; 1.25 (2.50 × .5) concepts, the launch stage; and 1 (1.25 × .8) concept would be launched as a product. These values are also shown in Exhibit 2.4.

Using these values, one can construct a "decay curve." A decay curve is a representation of the funneling effect the respective product development process has. In other words, the decay curve shows how stringent the product development process is in reducing the total sample of product concepts to eventually launch one product.

Stage	*Risk*	*Cost*	*Time (in Person - Weeks)*	*Number of Concepts Needed*	*Cost to Complete Stage*	*Time to Complete Stage (in Person-Weeks)*
Opportunity identification	90%	$2,000	2	11.57	$ 23,140	23.14
Concept generation	60%	$10,000	6	10.41	$104,100	62.46
Pretechnical evaluation	40%	$30,000	6	6.25	$187,500	37.50
Technical development	50%	$200,000	12	2.50	$500,000	30.00
Launch	80%	$125,000	4	1.25	$156,250	5.00
TOTAL					$970,990	158.10 person-weeks

Probability of success for a given product concept	.9 × .6 × .4 × .5 × .8 = .0864 or 8.64%
Number of product concepts needed for one success	1 / .0864 = 11.57 product concepts

EXHIBIT **2.4.** Evaluating the Product Development Process

The decay curve can be used as a benchmark for comparison with industry decay curves. Every 5 years, the Product Development Management Association (PDMA) surveys its members and determines a standard decay curve. Companies can then compare their process to an industry standard to see if it is too stringent or too lax. The data of the previous example are compared to PDMA's standard decay curve (Griffin et al., 1997) in Exhibit 2.5.

The decay curve can be used as an evaluative tool with individual product development project teams, too. In particular, the decay curve suggests two regions. Being above the curve indicates a "slow decay," or a situation where product concepts are not necessarily be-

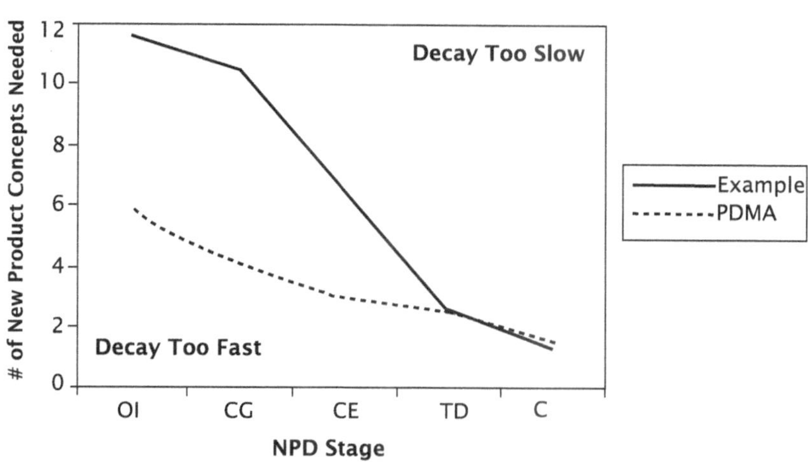

EXHIBIT 2.5. The Decay Curve

ing eliminated as they should be. A product development project team staying above the curve might be allowing too many product concepts through the process and might have too many product concepts at the end of the process. Being below the curve indicates a "fast decay," or a situation where many product concepts are being eliminated. A product development project team staying below the curve might not have enough product concepts to sustain the product development process and will not have a product to launch. A product development project team staying near the company's decay curve would closely approximate the expected product development process for that company.

The number of product concepts needed per stage also can be used to calculate cost and time estimates for each of the product development stages. Assume the cost and time necessary to have one product concept complete each of the product development stages are as follows (please note that these data are for illustrative purposes only and should not be viewed as real industry benchmarks): opportunity identification, $2,000 in 2 person-weeks; concept generation, $10,000 in 6 person-weeks; pretechnical evaluation, $30,000 in 6 person-weeks; technical development, $200,000 in 12 person-weeks; and launch, $125,000 in 4 person-weeks. The cost and time necessary across each product development stage to ensure one launched product are determined by multiplying the number of product concepts in each stage by the cost and time figures. Hence, in the example, to ensure one launched product, opportunity identification will cost \$23,140 (11.57 × \$2,000) and consume 23.14 (11.57 × 2) person-weeks; concept generation will cost \$104,100 (10.41 × \$10,000) and consume 62.46 (10.41 × 6) person-weeks; pretechnical evaluation will cost \$187,500 (6.25 × \$30,000) and consume 37.50 (6.25 × 6) person-weeks; technical development will cost \$500,000 (2.50 × \$200,000) and consume 30.00 (2.50 × 12) person-weeks; and launch will cost \$156,250 (1.25 × \$125,000) and consume 5.00 (1.25 × 4) person-weeks (see Exhibit 2.4).

These calculations provide insightful information into the product development process. Added information can be gained by calculating the relative and cumulative percentages for cost and time across each product development stage, as shown in Exhibit 2.6. In the example, the costliest product development stage is technical development, which accounts for over half of the total project cost of developing one product. The most time-consuming stage is concept generation, which accounts for more than half of total project time to develop one product. The cumulative percentages indicate that only a third of costs are expended before technical development. However, almost 80% of the time required to complete the product development project occurs before technical development. A company could reflect on whether this seems appropriate.

Additional information can be gained by constructing an "expenditures curve." This curve portrays the cumulative percentage of cost versus the cumulative percentage of time (see Exhibit 2.7). This curve can then be used to benchmark company product development projects to determine if costs are running too high versus time. If a project falls above the curve, the budget is perhaps being spent too quickly. Being below the curve could suggest that not enough money is being expended on the project to achieve completion.

■ INITIATIVES TO REDUCE COST OR TIME

Performing an assessment of a company's product development process can identify particular product development stages that would appear to be too costly or time-consuming, based on company expec-

Stage	*Cost to Complete Stage*	*Percentage of Total Cost*	*Cumulative Percentage of Total Cost*	*Time to Complete Stage (in person-weeks)*	*Percentage of Total Cost*	*Cumulative Percentage of Total Cost*
Opportunity identification	$ 23,140	2	2	23.14	15	15
Concept generation	$104,100	11	13	62.46	39	54
Pretechnical evaluation	$187,500	19	32	37.50	24	78
Technical development	$500,000	52	84	30.00	19	97
Launch	$156,250	16	100%	5.00	3	100%
TOTAL	$970,990	100%		158.10 person-weeks	100%	

EXHIBIT **2.6.** Evaluating Cost and Time Per Product Development Stage

tations or relative to the other product development stages. Various initiatives can be undertaken to reduce costs and time consumed in the product development process. A sample of such initiatives are described below:

Get slack out of the system: Avoid unnecessary steps or work on reducing the number of activities pursued in a particular product development stage.

Use technology to shorten steps: Computer-aided design, computer-aided manufacturing, and rapid prototyping may be useful in shortening product development cycle time.

Invite early customer input to prevent redesign: Early customer involvement can help to focus the product development effort on key issues/attributes.

Conduct inventory up-front marketing and engineering projects: Consider using off-the-shelf ideas so that projects do not necessarily have to go through a full product development process.

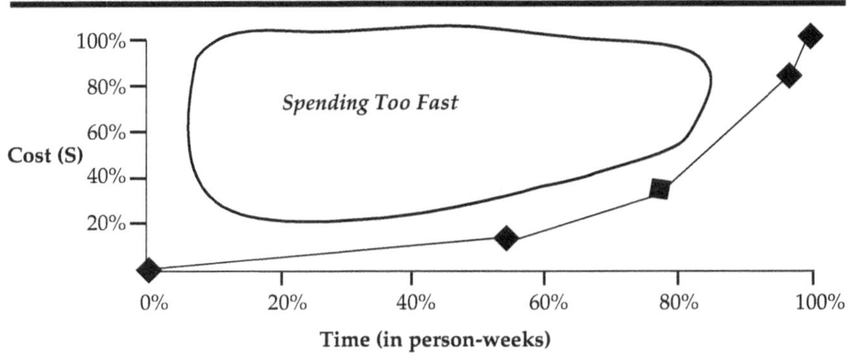

EXHIBIT 2.7. The Cost-Expenditure Curve

Try flexible manufacturing: A flexible manufacturing process offers a wider variety of options for product development.

Form alliances: Alliances can sometimes reduce the time and resources necessary to achieve a product development objective because of shared resources.

Skip a step in the process : Although this is not preferred, sometimes, it is necessary to skip a product development activity to get to the market quickly; this should only be employed when being first to market is critical (even when skipping a step, it is necessary to make sure that everything is ready to go before launching the new product).

KEY CONCEPTS

- New product strategy
- Product-market matrix
- Product development process
- Technology-push versus market-pull
- Decay curve
- Cost-expenditure curve

CHAPTER QUESTIONS

1. Delineate the differences between market penetration, product development, market extension, and diversification strategies.
2. Describe the different stages of the product development process.
3. How can the effectiveness and efficiency of the product development process be evaluated?
4. How is a product development process implemented?
5. How are the cost and time parameters associated with the product development process managed?

Chapter Three

Organizing People

A major element impinging on product planning activities is how people are organized to carry out these activities. Among the inherent issues, several are important to understand: traditional department responsibilities, general organization structure, team structure, and team roles.

■ DEPARTMENT RESPONSIBILITIES

Within the company organization, product planning activities can be the responsibility of various departments. Preference for which department oversees product development and product management activities depends on company history, tradition, and culture, as well as the objectives of the company's product planning activities. Note that terminology of departments is used due to the fact that departments can serve multiple functions.

Product development may be under the auspices of the technical or marketing side of the organization. This would include research and development (R&D), engineering, and marketing departments. In certain companies, product development is a stand-alone department. Product management can fall under the auspices of the marketing or operations side of the organization. This would include marketing, distribution, logistics, manufacturing, or operations departments. In certain companies, product management is a standalone department. For the most part, product development and product management represent traditional department responsibilities and not stand-alone departments.

Generally, the technical side of the organization serves a product techoscientific role for the company. That is, the role is focused on discovery of new product technology and the refinement of the discovery into feasible product technology. The research department would be responsible for finding promising new technology inventions, whereas the development department would be responsible for building on the benefits offered by such technology to provide innovations. In some companies, separate research and development departments are combined into R&D. Some companies use the terminology of engineering departments; their purpose is akin to development and not fundamental research. The decision to have product development under the auspices of the technical organization would be based on objectives to be technically driven and to be a technology leader.

The marketing side of the organization serves a demand management role for the company. Such a role includes identifying, understanding, stimulating, and servicing market demand, which would encompass demand among current, potential, and competitor customers. Various departments can compose the marketing side of the organization, including marketing, advertising, promotion, sales, market research, and distribution, to name a few. Most commonly, marketing and sales are separated, with marketing serving a general market interface role and sales a specific customer interface role. The decision to have product development and/or product management under the auspices of the marketing organization would be based on objectives to be market driven.

The operations side of the organization serves a production technoeconomic role for the organization. That is, the role is focused on development of new production processes, techniques, and capabilities to improve company effectiveness and efficiencies in offering products. Manufacturing, operations, and production departments are responsible for composing the actual product so that it can be offered to the market (service companies typically have an operations department). Logistics is responsible for the proper delivery of the product to the marketplace. The decision to have product management under the auspices of the operations organization would be based on objectives to be price-competitive or a low-price provider.

■ INTERDEPARTMENTAL INTEGRATION

One of the emerging themes for successful product planning is the integration of departments. However, a common definition for interdepartmental integration is not apparent. Various literature has stressed the need for communication or interaction, where meetings and "documented information exchange" describe the relationships between departments (e.g., Fisher, Maltz, & Jaworski, 1997; Griffin & Hauser, 1993; Lim & Reid, 1992; Moenaert, Souder, DeMeyer, & Deschoolmeester, 1994; Ruekert & Walker, 1987). This characterization would favor the use of more meetings, greater written documentation, and increased information flows to promote interdepartmental unity.

Other literature has used the terminology of collaboration, where teamwork and resource sharing typify interfunctional relationships (e.g., Clark & Fujimoto, 1991; Lawrence & Lorsch, 1986; Schrage, 1990; Souder, 1987). In this vein, efforts that instill collective goals, mutual respect, and teamwork between departments would be favored.

And other literature suggests that integration via information sharing and involvement describes marketing's relationship with other functions (Gupta, Raj, & Wilemon, 1986; Kahn, 1996; Kahn & Mentzer, 1998; Song & Parry, 1993). This composite view implies that interaction and collaboration are both important elements of marketing's relationship with other functions and that interdepartmental integration depends on the balancing of interaction and collaboration.

Empirical work by various researchers (e.g., Fisher et al., 1997; Kahn, 1996; Kahn & Mentzer, 1998; Maltz & Kohli, 1996) finds that collaboration appears to be most important for product development and product management performance. This does not necessarily mean that communication/interaction is not important. Rather, it is generally concluded that communication should be viewed as a necessary but not sufficient factor for improved performance; collaboration appears to be the distinguishing factor for improved performance.

Given the various characterizations of interdepartmental integration, how might a company successfully integrate departments? The work of Griffin and Hauser (1996) suggests six general approaches for integrating departments: co-location; personnel movement; formal product planning processes; informal social systems; incentives, rewards, and recognitions; and organizational structure.

Co-location represents the relocation of departmental personnel to the same location to reduce the distance between these personnel. The underlying premise of co-location is that close proximity of personnel will provide a higher level of information transfer and opportunities to collaborate.

Personnel movement is the rotation of personnel between departments so that individuals are cross-trained and appreciate the contributions of each department to the product planning process. The underlying premise is that job rotation increases department familiarity and sensitivity. This, in turn, would facilitate interchanges between departments. Because of the difficulty in truly comprehending multiple skill sets characteristic of different departments, it is recommended that such personnel movements be temporary.

Formal processes are akin to the previously discussed stage-gate™ process and other processes that specify activities in the product planning endeavor. The underlying premise for formal processes is to structure the decision-making process across departments, organize the process, indicate information requirements and information flows, and establish process responsibilities.

Informal social systems are needed in addition to traditional formal mechanisms such as scheduled meetings. Informal meetings—impromptu hall meetings, lunches, and outings—will build familiarity and a willingness to communicate and collaborate.

Incentives and *rewards* involve performance evaluations and compensation to motivate department personnel to accomplish their department objectives, interdepartmental objectives, and corporate objectives. The use of such incentives, rewards, and recognitions helps to encourage interdepartmental participation and task completion.

Organizational structure represents the design of the company's hierarchy to facilitate interdepartmental integration. Various types of organization structures are possible, including a change in the entire organizational structure or the use of project teams. Because of the prevalence of organizational structure solutions for interdepartmental integration, especially with respect to the use of teams, organization and team structure are further discussed.

Note that each of these approaches is valid in the product planning process. However, each approach consumes resources and requires a carefully thought-out plan of implementation. Furthermore, each approach alone may not provide an immediate level of commitment on the part of personnel to attempt to integrate themselves. Multiple approaches may be necessary over a longer time horizon.

■ ORGANIZATION STRUCTURE

Of the above approaches, organization structure represents a prevalent approach. Decisions on how to structure the organization, and thereby capitalize on department strengths and company core competencies, are driven by industry forces, company tradition, and management preferences. In simplest forms, there are three general ways to structure the organization for conducting product development and product management activities.

The most popular structure is the functional approach (Exhibit 3.1), which represents the use of departments specializing in a core set of activities. A vice president heads each department, with the responsibility of coordinating the department's activities. The advantage of this approach is simpler administration of activities. The disadvantage is that specialization divides the organization and often leads to conflict over resource needs and organizational status.

A second type of organizational structure is the matrix management approach (Exhibit 3.2). In this approach, the functional organization is retained, but a project management department is created. The project management department assigns project managers or team leaders to product planning projects and coordinates these projects. The individual project managers (team leaders) form project teams by selecting key representatives from the other departments. The premise of the matrix management approach is that responsibility for functional performance is vertical and responsibility for getting projects done is horizontal. The advantage of this approach is merging of department capabilities to create a cross-functional perspective and, thus, capitalize on department abilities. The disadvantage is that this approach can become complicated, especially with regards to authority, responsibility, and reward issues.

A third general approach is the project program approach (Exhibit 3.3). This approach is only valid when a given project is large, and personnel work full-time on the project over the long term, as in the case of designing and building the space shuttle or an aircraft carrier. The project manager heads the project and serves essentially as the vice president for the project, coordinating traditional department responsibilities within the project. The advantages of this approach are

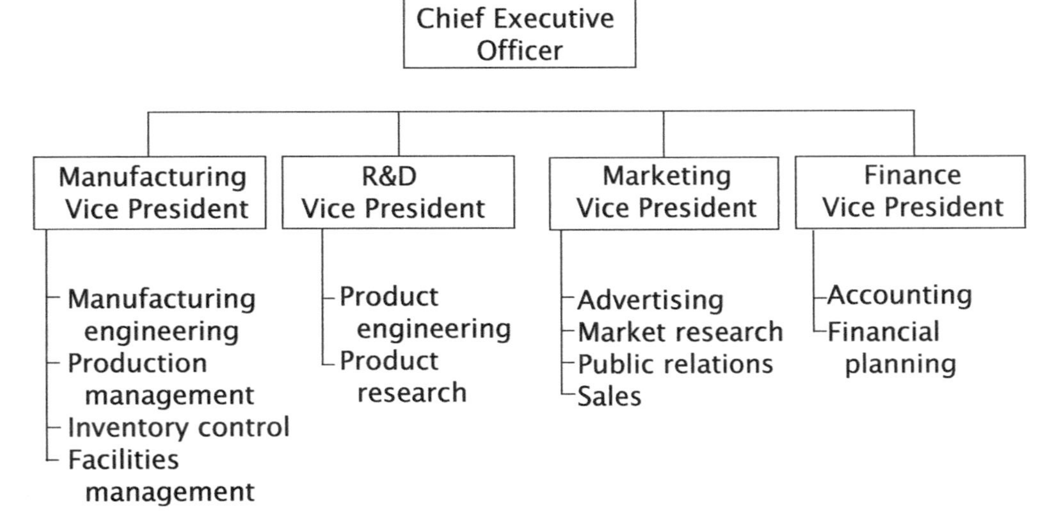

EXHIBIT 3.1. Functional Organization

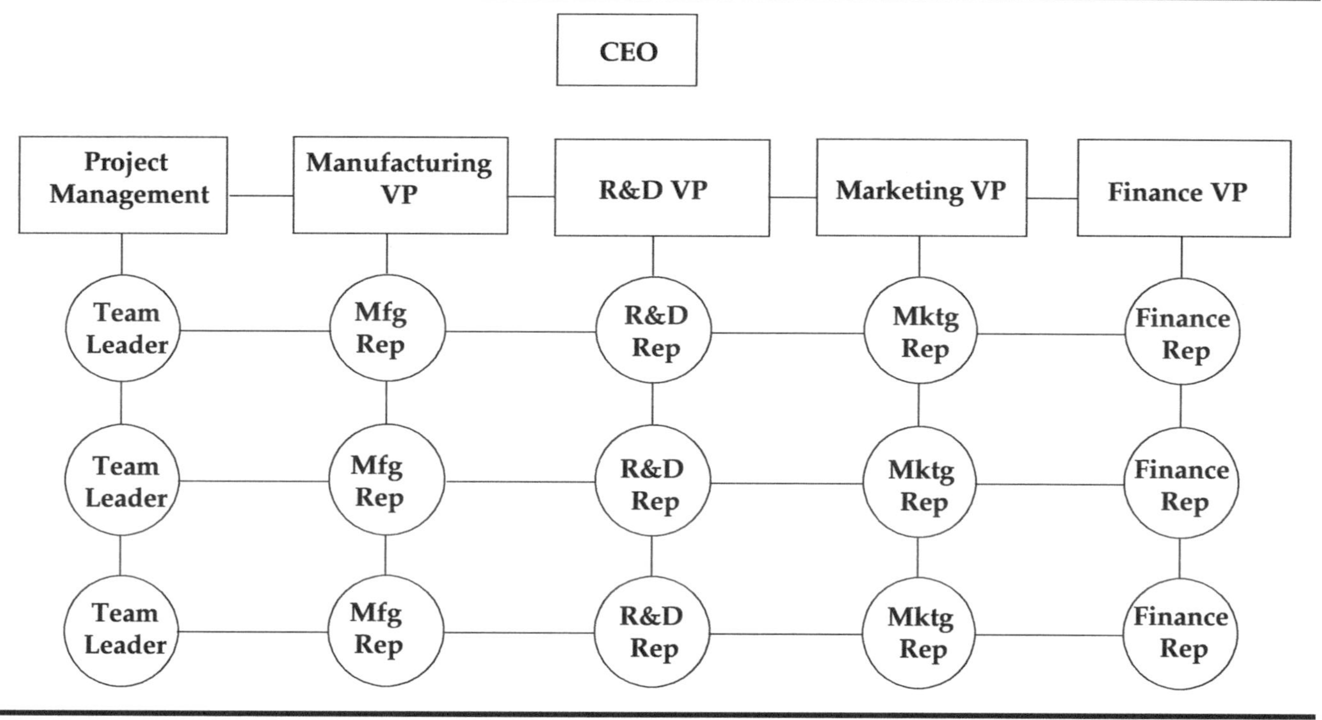

Exhibit 3.2. Matrix Organization

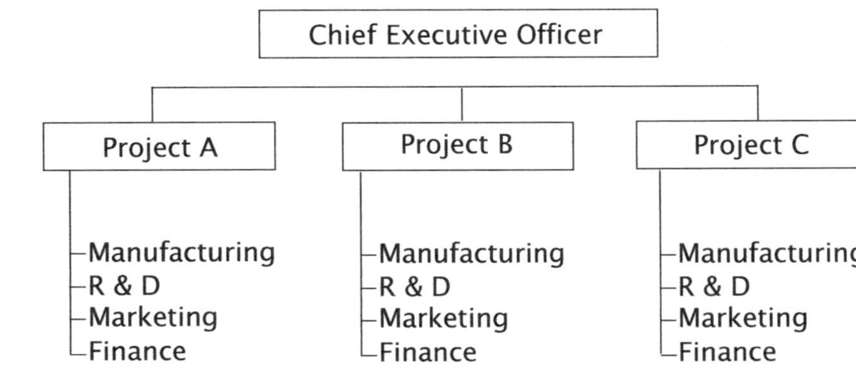

EXHIBIT 3.3. Project Management Organization

greater focus and control of the respective project, but the disadvantages are higher resource requirements due to the need to duplicate activities.

■ TEAM TYPES

Regardless of the type of organization structure, most if not all companies employ teams to manage product planning activities. Teams represent a temporary organization structure focusing on the achievement of a specific objective. Although the organization structure influences the types of teams that a particular company might use, there are generally five types of teams: functional, multifunctional, balanced matrix, project matrix, and venture teams. The characteristics of each of these types of teams are shown in Exhibit 3.4.

A functional team works within an individual department and has minimal to no contact with other department personnel. Activities best served by a functional team would be department-specific activities that are narrow in scope and have a specific, distinct goal: for example, electrical engineering personnel working on a solution to a power "glitch" in a new amplifier system. The addition of other department personnel would not necessarily benefit the project, and in fact, could inhibit engineering's ability to resolve the matter in a cost-effective and timely fashion. Functional teams have a team leader from the given department and are under the auspices of the respective department and that department's manager. Rewards and recognition are 100% the responsibility of the department manager.

Multifunctional teams are a predominant form of team employed for both product development and product management purposes. Multifunctional teams comprise personnel from those departments having skills necessary to achieve the team's objectives. In some respects, multifunctional team members are liaisons to the team, representing each of their respective department's views. The team leader may be one of these team representatives or a preselected team leader outside of the departments, for example, from product development, product management, or product planning. This team leader directs the project effort but has no control of rewards and recognitions because 100% of such compensation still comes from each representative's department. This is a disadvantage because loyalty to the team may be low, leading to lower motivation to work on the project. Multifunctional teams also contend with interdepartmental conflict

	Functional Team	*Multifunctional Team*	*Balanced Matrix*	*Cross-functional Team*	*Venture Team*
Department representation	Single department	Multiple departments	Multiple departments	Multiple departments	Multiple departments
Accountability	100% department	Mostly department	50% department, 50% team	Mostly team	100% team
Appropriate product development projects	Cost improvements, simple product improvements	All types of product development projects	All types of product development projects	All types of product development projects	New category entries, new-to-the-world products
Issues	Focused on single, specific product issue	Addresses issues affecting multiple departments, but conflict can arise due to team members' loyalties to their own department	Team member confusion can arise due to uncertainty over equally splitting time between department and team	Team members work on team issues predominantly, although there are departmental responsibilities as well	Personnel removed from organization to address key corporate objective(s); department managers may resist

EXHIBIT 3.4. Team Characteristics

because each team member represents a different department's views. Nonetheless, multifunctional teams offer an ability to be flexible for many situations.

Balanced matrix teams also are composed of representatives from different departments, with a preselected team leader from a department responsible for team management, for example, product development, product management, or project planning. The distinction of balanced matrix teams is that team member rewards and recognitions for a particular employee come equally from the respective team member's department and the team. That is, 50% of an employee's rewards and recognition are decided by the department, and 50% are decided by the team leader. The advantage of balanced matrix teams is an attempt to equalize the team effort with department efforts. Unfortunately, it becomes difficult to equalize team and department efforts, leading to team member confusion over compensation and conflicts between department managers and team leaders over team member responsibilities. Balanced matrix teams are not common due to the complexity surrounding rewards and recognition to team members.

Cross-functional teams, also called project matrix teams, are composed of representatives from different departments with a preselected team leader from a department responsible for team management. The distinction of cross-functional teams is that team member rewards and recognitions are mostly the responsibility of the team leader. This means that team members are mostly dedicated to the project. Although there still can be conflict between department and team priorities and responsibilities, cross-functional teams provide a greater focus on the part of team members.

In venture teams, members are pulled out of departments to serve on a self-contained team, and members' time is 100% dedicated to the project. Department managers may resist venture teams because the best people in their department may be pulled out to serve on the venture team. There also is the need to provide adequate resources to support a stand-alone team. However, venture teams offer the advantage of being completely focused on the given task. Because of these issues, venture teams are typically reserved for new-to-the-world product development projects. Another more subtle reason for the use of venture teams is the possibility of creating a new division around the venture team, should the product being developed achieve success. Even more subtly, separating the venture team allows the company to sell off the new division (venture team) more easily, should company management decide that the developed product is outside of corporate objectives.

Two types of venture teams are possible. An in-house venture team is one that meets within the company infrastructure and facilities. A spin-out venture team meets at a different location and creates its own quasi-organization, if not an entirely new organization. The latter type of venture team obviously is more expensive to support, given the duplication of resources.

■ DISTINGUISHING THE CORE TEAM, AD HOC TEAM, AND EXTENDED TEAM

For each of the above types of teams, there is an implicit team structure. This structure encompasses a core team, an ad hoc team, and an extended team. The core team is the original, permanent team members, who represent the key skill sets necessary for achieving the team's given objective. The ad hoc team represents team members who are added if specialized skills or knowledge outside of the team skill/knowledge set is needed. For example, a purchasing staffer may be added to a product development team if discussions of how to acquire a new material persist. Ad hoc team members only remain on the team for as long as they are needed. The extended team represents support personnel that help the core team to accomplish its given objective. Administrative staffers are characteristically members of the extended team.

■ TEAM ROLES

Another consideration for team structure is team member roles. There are multiple roles prevalent in teams. The following are a sample of the major roles played:

Team Leader (also known as the project manager): The team leader has responsibility for organizing, directing, monitoring, and motivating team members to achieve the given team objective.

Inventor: The inventor is the original source of the product concept/idea on which the team is working; the inventor educates team members on basic knowledge underlying the concept/idea.

Champion: The champion promotes the team project, substantiates its importance to the company, and works to surpass roadblocks. In some cases, the team leader is the product champion. In other cases, a champion is not an official member of the team but rather an upper-level company manager who is intimately knowledgeable about the team project.

Sponsor: A sponsor is an upper-level company manager who is supportive of the team project and assists in providing necessary resources. The sponsor is not a team member and is typically a higher level manager than the champion.

Rationalist: The rationalist attempts to ground the team with a sense of reality by questioning team decisions. The rationalist's role is to ensure that team decisions are sound ones.

The importance of recognizing these multiple roles is that teams require multiple skill sets to function properly. Thus, team leaders need to find team members and upper managers that can play critical roles to help the team achieve its objective.

■ FACTORS FOR TEAM EFFECTIVENESS

Holahan and Markham (1996) present three sets of factors that underlie effective teams. These factors include the structure of the product development process, organizational support for teams, and general team management issues.

Two issues inherent in the structure of the product development process are an ability to link departmental activities and provide opportunities for interdepartmental activities to exist. Failure of the existing product development process to account for either of these two considerations precludes the use of teams (aside from functional teams).

Organizational support for teams concerns issues related to performance appraisal, career development, pay and promotion, and organizational culture. Each of these issues correlates to the motivation of individual team members and their willingness to work toward the given team objective.

General team management issues include issues related to team size, team leader selection, team member selection, team training, and team decision making and conflict resolution. Some specific recommendations are that teams remain small (8 to 12 members generally);

employ team leaders that have interpersonal, technical, and political skills; and obtain team members that have team player and technical skills. Overall, general team management issues recognize the need for team functioning and the ability to perform as a cohesive unit.

KEY CONCEPTS

- Traditional department responsibilities during product planning
- Types of organization structures for product planning
- Types of teams for use in product planning
- Team roles

CHAPTER QUESTIONS

1. Which department(s) may oversee product development activities?
2. Which department(s) may oversee product management activities?
3. How can departments be integrated?
4. Describe the three general ways to structure the organization for conducting product development and product management activities.
5. Describe the different types of teams that can be employed during product planning and when each type of team would be most appropriate.
6. What is the difference between core team, ad hoc team, and extended team members?
7. What are the various roles that may exist in any given team?

Chapter Four

Opportunity Identification

Not all companies begin the product development process with strategic planning. Most companies, however, engage in some sort of opportunity identification stage at the start of the product development process. That is, there is an assessment of what potential opportunities currently present themselves to the company, and of these, which opportunities are the best ones for the company to pursue.

In general, there are four sources for opportunities. Opportunities can come about because of underused resources, new resources, external mandate, and internal mandate. Underused resources such as excess production capacity can offer a new product opportunity. Companies typically are able to pursue most line and market extensions because of an ability of the production system to handle a greater variety of product types and volume.

New resources can emerge from the development of new skills or technologies, as in the case of high-technology companies, or from corporate acquisition. With respect to the latter, IBM's acquisition of Lotus in 1995 helped IBM to enter the groupware market and allowed IBM to become the largest software company at the time.

External mandates can come from multiple sources, stimulating the product development endeavor. New government regulations, self-imposed industry standards, changes in customer attitudes, and competitor actions all can lead to new product opportunities. For example, the U.S. government's mandate for the elimination of chlorofluorocarbons (CFCs) in air conditioning and refrigeration equipment forced manufacturers to develop new types of refrigerants, equipment, and systems. Another example is the emergence of minivans and sport utility vehicles, now being offered by almost all major car manufacturers, because of strong emerging consumer preference for these vehicles.

Internal mandates, like upper management mandates from a company president, also can stimulate the company and lead to new product opportunities. Steve Jobs, on his return to Apple Computer Company as chief executive officer (CEO) in 1996, proclaimed that Apple needed to develop a web-friendly machine. His vision and emphasis led to the development and launch of the IMAC in 1998.

Of course, an opportunity is not necessarily a firm product concept. An opportunity can be an insight, a raw technology, a new customer, or something else. Basically, the purpose of opportunity identification is to delineate a valid arena for product development considerations.

■ USE OF BREAKDOWN STRUCTURES

One way to conceive opportunities is to employ breakdown structures of the given market or technology. Breakdown analysis is essentially a segmenting of the total market or the respective technology in an attempt to provide an underlying structure and thereby identify possible unforeseen opportunities.

Constructing a market breakdown structure requires an understanding of what is meant by market, market segment, and target market. By definition, the market represents all current and potential buyers sharing a particular need or want who might be willing and able to engage in exchange to satisfy that need or want. A market segment is a subset of customers who behave in the same way, reflect similar characteristics, and/or have similar needs. And a target market is the particular group(s) of customers the company proposes to serve or whose needs the company proposes to satisfy with a particular marketing program.

By applying a market breakdown structure, a market is divided into distinct customer subsets until valid market segments or target markets are identified. Validity of these segments or target markets is based on the following criteria:

Size: The market segment or target market should be of sufficient size in terms of potential sales to make it worth pursuing.

Identification: It must be possible to recognize and describe the market segment or target market.

Access: It should be feasible to contact the market segment or target market in an efficient manner.

Different response: Each of the market segments should respond uniquely to different product attributes and promotion programs. Otherwise, market segments can be combined.

Coherence: Members of the same market segment or target market should be basically homogeneous in that they behave in the same way and/or have the same preferences.

Stability: Customer patterns and preferences in the market segment or target market will not drastically change in the near future.

The theoretical rationale behind segmentation is that market demand can come in three basic forms: homogeneous demand, diffused demand, and clustered demand. Homogenous demand characterizes a situation where market demand is relatively similar across customers. Consequently, a common approach to the marketplace can be undertaken because customers will conceivably respond alike. Diffused demand characterizes a situation where market demand is distinct among customers in the marketplace; that is, customers have different reasons for purchasing the same product. In this case, an undifferentiated approach to the marketplace may be warranted because customers are distinct in the reasoning behind their purchase behavior. Clustered demand characterizes most market situations where demand is distinct among subsets of customers within a given marketplace. Here, a differentiated approach to the market would be used to address the individual demand characteristics per each subset. Because clustered demand is typical of market situations, the identification of clusters via a process of segmentation is a natural course to follow.

In particular, there are five options for segmenting the market. One option is demographic segmentation, which divides the market by objective, quantifiable characteristics that describe customers. Consumer demographics include gender, marital status, location, age, and education. Business-to-business demographics include company age, type of product manufactured as indicated by the company's standard industry classification code, and employment size. Another option is psychographic segmentation, which divides the market by subjective characteristics such as lifestyle, personality, and culture, in the case of consumer psychographics, and organizational culture and customer orientation in the case of business-to-business psychographics. A third option is geographic segmentation, which distinguishes segments by geography, for example, Northeast, Southeast, Midwest, West Coast, and international markets. A fourth option is benefit segmentation, which distinguishes segments according to the benefit desired by the respective customer base. A fifth option is usage segmentation, which distinguishes segments according to the way the product is used by the respective customer base. Although there are five options to segmentation, a combined use of options is the more effective approach.

An example of a market breakdown structure is shown in Exhibit 4.1. This simple business-to-business example attempts to identify possible opportunities within the corrugated box market via a process of market segmentation. As shown, the corrugated box market can be broken down by demographics in terms of perishable versus nonperishable products offered by customers. Geographic segmentation is used to break down the perishable products side, whereas psychographics are employed to break down the nonperishable side. Benefit segmentation is used to divide the West Coast perishable products into two possible opportunities identified as (a) corrugated boxes for perishable products on the West Coast that keep water out, and (b) corrugated boxes for perishable products on the West Coast that are easy to handle. Usage segmentation is used to break innovative firms providing nonperishable products and identify these two possible opportunities: (a) corrugated boxes for nonperishable products of innovative firms for use in work-in-process storage and (b) corrugated boxes for nonperishable products of innovative firms for use in finished goods storage. In short, this simple market breakdown structure identifies four possible opportunities. Further analysis on such issues as market potential, technical feasibility, and financial attractiveness would be necessary to determine which opportunities should be pursued.

A technology breakdown structure would follow a similar course. Subtechnologies, subcomponents, product attributes, or product functions would break down a particular technology or product structure. Exhibit 4.2 presents a breakdown structure applied to a stapler. As shown, a breakdown by functions, attributes, and subcomponents

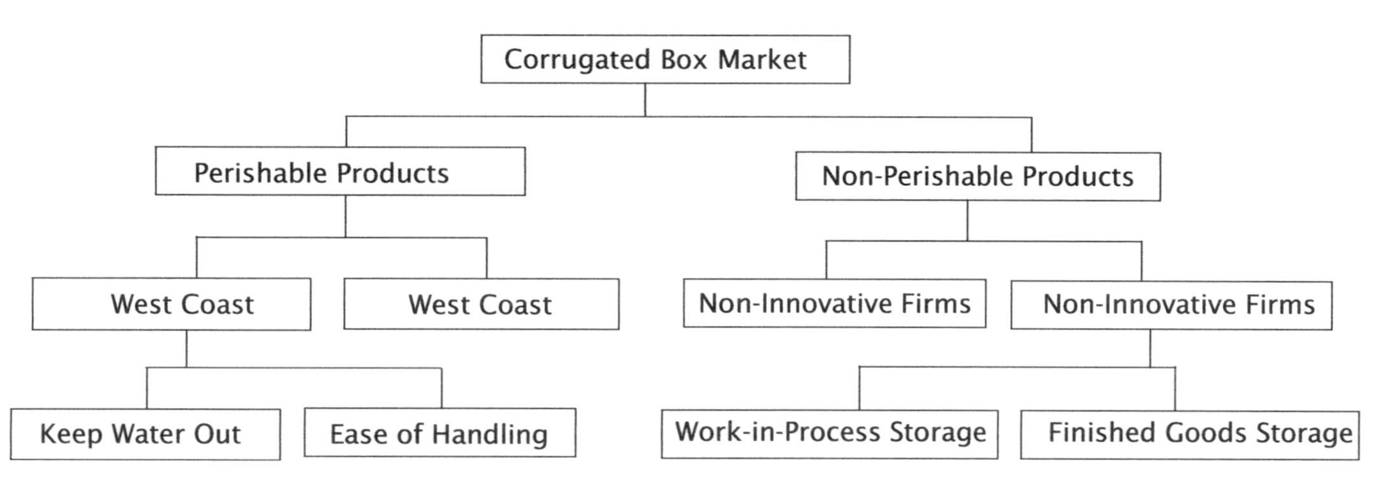

EXHIBIT **4.1.** Breakdown Structure for a Corrugated Box Market

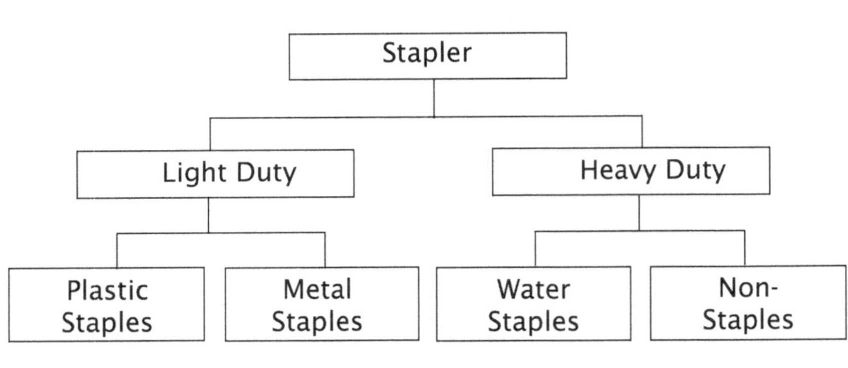

EXHIBIT 4.2. Breakdown Structure for a Stapler Product Opportunity

offers four possible opportunities: (a) a light-duty stapler with plastic staples, (b) a light-duty stapler with metal staples, (c) a heavy-duty stapler that is waterproof, and (d) a heavy-duty stapler that is nonconductive. Naturally, further definition of these opportunities can be undertaken. Also, it should be recognized that market-related information such as potential market/customers could be incorporated into the breakdown structure. Thus, a merging of market and technology structures may bring about the best-defined opportunities.

■ THE PRODUCT DEVELOPMENT CHARTER

Once a set of potential opportunities are identified, the opportunity must be described. One approach is to provide a mission statement for the opportunity via a product development charter (PDC)—also referred to by Crawford (1997) as the product innovation charter. Note that the terminology *product innovation charter* is not adopted here because imitations as well as innovations are viable product development opportunities. A PDC is essentially a general statement identifying what the specific product development initiative is to achieve and the guidelines that need to be followed.

As suggested in Exhibit 4.3, PDCs can be employed at the strategic business-unit level, product platform level, and project level. In all

EXHIBIT **4.3.** The Product Development Charter and Corporate Strategy

cases, the charter should be an extension of the company's overall corporate strategy.

■ ELEMENTS OF A PRODUCT DEVELOPMENT CHARTER

The PDC is most often expressed in paragraph form and comprises four particular sections—although not necessarily equating to four paragraphs. The four sections, which often are combined for legibility, are background, arena, objectives/goals, and special guidelines.

Background provides the rationale for the product development initiative. As part of the background statement, the intended market and/or industry in which the initiative will be focused should be identified. Arena identifies the core competencies of the company and identifies those competencies to be emphasized in the product development initiative. Such competencies could correspond to marketing strength, financial strength, production strength, R&D strength, or a combination of any of these or other key company functions. Objectives/goals outlines the ultimate benchmarks by which the product development initiative will be measured. Objectives are broader statements than goals, but either can be used. Profit, growth, market status, competitiveness, and so on may be recognized. Special guidelines is a "catch-all" category that provides any extra information that should be remembered during the product development initiative. These could include special features that must be included in the new product or specific elements of the marketing plan. Special guidelines also can attune the company to the key success factors of the initiative, such as being first-to-market with state-of-the-art, breakthrough technology or being second-but-better.

Together, these four elements provide a comprehensive statement about the opportunity. One methodology for constructing a PDC is to list information separately in the four categories of background, arena, goals/objectives, and special guidelines. Then, the information can be combined in narrative form to delineate the potential opportunity. For example, consider the opportunity of the light-duty stapler with plastic staples. The following, brief information is listed per category:

Background	*Arena*	*Goals/Objectives*	*Special Guidelines*
• Children can injure themselves with regular household staples	• The company has a core competency in stapler manufacturing	• The company wants a 20% return on investment within 2 years	• Staples should be made of recyclable plastic materials
• Plastic staples are less expensive			

Although it is more brief than normal (more detailed information would be listed), the following PDC can be composed based on this information:

> Children can very easily injure themselves using typical household staplers with metal staples. It is proposed that a new stapler using plastic staples, which are potentially less expensive, be developed. To accomplish this, we want to rely on our core competency as a leader in stapler manufacturing. A 20% return on investment

is expected within 2 years after launch of the product. Particular attention should be paid to plastic staples made of recyclable plastics.

Obviously, more information leads to a longer PDC. The length is not necessarily the issue, however. The overall intent of a PDC is to give enough information to provide an appropriate characterization of the opportunity so that management can decide whether it truly is a valid opportunity to be pursued. Then, it can be used as a guide throughout the entire product development effort.

■ SCREENING PRODUCT DEVELOPMENT CHARTERS

Management must decide on which charters are most valid and, thus, deserving of resources for further development. Decisions concerning selection of PDCs to pursue should be based on market-related and technology-related criteria. A manager or team of managers would use these criteria to grade each charter.

Various criteria can be used to evaluate charters. Twenty sample criteria are offered below, partitioned into the two categories of market-related criteria and technology-related criteria. Each question can be assessed on various scales. For example, a 1 to 5 scale, where 1 = *poor*, 2 = *fair*, 3 = *good*, 4 = *very good*, and 5 = *excellent*, would work well with the following criteria.

Sample Market-Related Criteria

- Market demand for the product
- Market need for the product
- Uniqueness of the product, relative to competitors
- Competitive advantage
- Ability to explain the product to customers
- Ability to demonstrate the product to customers
- Trade channel for the product
- Company's understanding of the product market
- Customer acceptance of the product
- Synergy of the new product with current products offered by the company

- Sample Technology-Related Criteria
- Uniqueness of the technology
- Potential length of life cycle for the technology
- Ability to develop the technology
- Ability to patent the technology
- Ability to keep development costs under control
- Ability to keep development time short
- Ability to manufacture the technology
- Applicability of technology to future products
- Synergy of technology with current company technology base
- Ability to keep to a minimum potential risks associated with the technology

Each company will need to develop its own set of criteria and determine an appropriate scoring methodology to best address its business situation. Those PDCs with higher (more favorable) scores on the given criteria would be deemed acceptable for further consideration in the product development (entire product planning) process. Charters with lower scores would not necessarily be discarded but might be reserved for future consideration or undergo a revision process to further clarify the opportunity.

Key Concepts

- Four sources for opportunities: underused resource, new resource, external mandate, and internal mandate
- Market breakdown structure
- Market segmentation
- Technology breakdown structure
- Product development charter

CHAPTER QUESTIONS

1. What represents an opportunity?
2. What is the difference between market, market segment, and target market?
3. What criteria can be used to validate a market segment?
4. What is the purpose of a product development charter?
5. What are the four elements of a product development charter?
6. What criteria can be employed to screen a product development charter?

CHAPTER
FIVE

CONCEPT GENERATION

Concept generation represents a set of activities that a team/company will complete to amass multiple product concepts. Some call this the ideation stage. Depending on the nature of the product development process and company strategy these concepts may be broad (and unrelated) in nature or narrow in scope. Overall, the purpose of the concept generation stage is to iterate as many concepts as possible, screen these concepts, and then determine the most valid concepts for further development.

A variety of techniques can be employed to generate concepts, and six of them will be discussed in detail in this chapter. Success in applying these techniques depends on various factors, but one important underlying element is creativity. A second important underlying element is an understanding of what makes up a good product concept statement.

■ CREATIVITY

> Creativity is correlated with the ability to withstand the lack of structure, the lack of future, lack of predictability, of control, the tolerance for ambiguity, for planlessness.
>
> —Abraham Maslow, 1998, p. 220

Without creativity, the concept generation process becomes inherently narrow and refined. Creativity affords a broader range of thinking and may make connections that otherwise would be overlooked, leading to better product concepts. Various companies, such as 3M, Lucent Technologies, Motorola, and Sony, have incorporated at least one of the following program elements to stimulate creativity among their workforces:

Free time: Allow employees time to explore and pursue new product ideas within the work week.

Flextime: Allow employees to make their own schedules to capitalize on when employees feel they are most productive—some employees work better in the morning hours, and others work better in the late afternoon.

Special rewards: Offer rewards for innovative thinking and risk taking.

Killer phrases removal: Create a company culture that does not say such things as "cannot be done,""done that before," and "that is too different for our company." Such things stymie creativity.

Bureaucracy reduction: Create a company environment that minimizes paperwork and approval processes for every product planning function. Provide some degree of individual decision making.

Cross-functional teams: Use cross-functional teams to enlighten personnel to multiple perspectives and to cross-fertilize ideas.

■ THE PRODUCT CONCEPT STATEMENT

As one applies one or multiple concept generation techniques, a set of product concepts will emerge. Ultimately, a common product concept will emerge on which a product concept statement can be based. Like the product development charter, a product concept statement serves-to establish a foundation on which to further the product development effort. However, the product concept specifically defines what the product is to be. Three important elements of a product concept need to be considered: form, technology, and benefit. Of these three elements, benefits are the most important element. As previously mentioned, customers buy benefits, not features or form. Thus, specific to each product concept should be the key benefit(s) to be offered by the product. Benefit is defined as the innate need or desire for the product.

Form and technology are the attributes of the given product concept. Form is the view or physical thing created or, in the case of a service, the sequence of steps by which the service is created (styling, industrial design). Technology is the source by which the product is made or the technical features of the product (manufacturing and R&D).

A beverage example is used to illustrate the important roles that each of these three product concept elements plays in formulating a complete product concept. Below are product concepts that only provide one of the three elements (unidimensional product concept statements):

- A cola drink that has a great taste (benefit only)
- A cola drink that has a dark, rich color (form only)
- A cola made by a totally new sweetening process (technology only)

Each of these statements alone does not sound appealing or would not necessarily encourage one to buy the new cola drink. Combining these statements provides the following complete product concept statement:

- A new sweetening process brings forth a cola beverage with a dark and rich color that has great taste (this is form, technology, and benefits)

This statement is much more appealing and robust than the three statements, each standing alone. This shows the importance of developing product concept statements that include elements of form, technology, and benefits. The purpose of such a statement is to ensure that each of these three elements is recognized and incorporated into the next stage of development so that on launch, the product indeed retains and reflects form, technology, and benefits.

■ CONCEPT GENERATION TECHNIQUES

There are many techniques for concept generation. Six general types of techniques are discussed to illustrate the variety. These include need assessment (what does the customer or company want), scenario analysis (futuristic forecasts), group creativity (group innovation), attribute analysis (mechanical approach for obtaining new viewpoints), relationship analysis (force to see new relationships), and lateral search (move away from the product).

Need Assessment

This category of techniques involves understanding current and future needs of the marketplace. Another way to look at need assessment is as an approach for identifying problems in the marketplace and appropriate solutions that the company can offer through its product offerings.

One source of marketplace information is routine market contacts, which can transpire from sales visits and customer service calls. Focus groups with customers as part of ongoing market research can also be used to generate potential ideas for product concepts. Customer complaints and general customer comments are other avenues for market contact, and these are often overlooked.

Note that contacts with customers need to be carefully construed. McQuarrie (1993) offers a popular methodology for conducting customer visits. The key is to realize that the purpose of a customer visit is not to sell customers on the company's products but rather to listen to what customers are saying about what they need. In addition, customer visits should include representation from multiple departments so that all departments can learn from the customer. McQuarrie's methodology for an appropriate customer visit is as follows:

1. *Set objectives:* Indicate the kind of information you want to collect.
2. *Select a sample:* Describe the types of customers to be visited, and estimate the required number of customers.
3. *Compose the visit team:* Identify the individuals from different functional areas who should participate in the visits.

4. *Develop the discussion guide:* Generate the topics and questions to be covered in each visit, organize topics into a sequence, and set priorities.
5. *Conduct the interviews:* Specify roles for team members; seek a loosely structured interaction.
6. *Debrief after each interview:* Assess whether any changes need to be made to the interviews; begin process of analysis.
7. *Analyze, report, and store visit data:* Heed limitations of qualitative research, disseminate reports to interested parties, and archive reports in a customer database.

A second type of need assessment uses experts, who can either be individual consultants or members of an advisory board. Experts may be able to identify future needs and thereby provide intelligence on market direction.

Publications are a source of concepts, too. Key trade and popular press periodicals can serve as references for new concepts as well as market problems. These periodicals also can attune the company to competitor activities through product announcements in these periodicals. Editorials in these periodicals closely align to expert opinion.

Household/industrial panels are usually akin to expert customers. Typically, market research companies maintain their own panels and use them to better understand a particular market with which these panels are familiar.

User observation of current customers can lead to insights into problems and customer preferences. Interestingly, *Business Week* in the early 1990s reported on a customer intelligence system that employed military technology (spy cameras) to monitor the product selection and buying process by final consumers. The visual information included hand motions, eye movements, and product selection. The system was intended to attune companies to how customers shop and potentially to suggest new concepts that might augment and/or facilitate the buying process.

Role playing is another technique for identifying problems and needs. Here, employees attempt to put themselves in the shoes of the customers and work out what problems they have and what solutions they need.

Employees are a good source of concepts, too. In fact, various companies maintain customer suggestion boxes and reward employees with money, should a suggestion eventually become a commercially launched product.

One specific technique that falls across several of the categories is lead user analysis, proposed by von Hippel (1988). As its name suggests, the technique attempts to analyze the needs and wants of lead users. The underlying premise of lead user analysis is that lead users will reflect needs of the main market early on. Thus, if a company can tap into lead users and, identify their needs, then, products that satisfy the main market can be developed expeditiously. Specifically, the tenets of lead user analysis are as follows (von Hippel, 1988, p. 107):

1. Lead users face needs that will be general in the marketplace, but they face them months or years before the bulk of that marketplace encounters them, and
2. Lead users are positioned to benefit significantly by obtaining a solution to those needs.

The lead user methodology is as follows:

1. Specify product market segment
2. Identify trends
3. Identify lead users
4. Develop new product specifications with lead users
5. Test lead user product concept with routine users

Lead user analysis is not necessarily easy to apply. In fact, many companies have found it difficult to identify proper lead users. Assuming that lead users can be identified, Geoffrey Moore (1991) points out in his book *Crossing the Chasm* that lead users sometimes do not reflect the same concerns as the main market and can be misleading in terms of what a market will truly accept. Overall, lead user analysis is a potential technique, but careful use of it is recommended.

Scenario Analysis

Scenario analysis techniques attempt to paint a futuristic scenario and frame potential problems emerging from this scenario. Consequently, new product ideas can be envisioned to solve these problems. In essence, scenario analysis is futuristic forecasting. Two general types of scenario analysis are the extend approach and the leap approach.

The distinction between the extend approach and the leap approach is the starting point. The extend version of scenario analysis starts out in the present and gathers all current trends and facts. The next step is to move out to the future and, based on current trends and facts called "seed trends," speculate about future events and happenings. For example, if we were to employ an extend approach to assess new product concepts for cellular telephones, we would consider current trends of free domestic long-distance, smaller telephones, and longer-life batteries. One possible future consideration based on the trend of free long-distance is free international calling.

In contrast to the extend approach, the leap begins out into the future some given number of years and paints a scenario of what is going on. Future products associated with this scenario are then described. Two variations of the leap approach are a static leap and a dynamic leap. The static leap jumps out into the future and stays out in the future to paint a futuristic scenario. The dynamic leap jumps out into the future and then works back from the future to the present, attempting to connect today's products with future products. For example, assume the leap approach is applied to consider transportation products 50 years in the future. We might envision the use of hydrogen cars, "mag-lev" trains, and battery-powered cars. If we stop there, the leap is static. However, if we work back to the present to plot a course of action to link today's technology to these possible future products, then the leap is dynamic. So if hydrogen cars are of interest, how might today's technology be used to move toward the proliferation of hydrogen cars 50 years from now?

Group Creativity

Group creativity comprises those techniques that stimulate groups to think of new ideas. The most common technique associated with group creativity is brainstorming. Brainstorming is basically an approach to develop as many ideas as possible from a group. Two general guidelines apply to brainstorming. The first is to *defer judgment;* this means that all ideas need to be welcomed, and initial criticism of original ideas is inappropriate. The second guideline is that *quantity breeds quality;* this means that the more ideas, the better; the objective is to put forth all ideas.

To undertake a brainstorming session, the following rules should be followed:

- Brainstorming works best in a small group of 4 to 10 people.
- A target is required. That is, there must be a single defined question or item on which to focus that everybody understands.
- All suggested ideas are publicly recorded; none are edited out.
- Equal opportunity for all group members to express themselves must be ensured.

- All possible answers should be encouraged and actively sought out, including the impractical, wild, or "out-in-left-field" ideas.

Adhering to these rules, brainstorming can proceed according to the following steps.

1. *Review the rules* for brainstorming (stress no criticism).
2. *State the single question or topic,* and make sure everybody understands it. The more specific the question or topic, the better.
3. *Give everyone a turn* in sequence, going around in clockwise order, to state one idea or to "pass" on that round. This ensures that even quieter members are heard and that more dominant individuals do not get all the air time.
4. *Keep going around the team until all ideas are collected* and recorded on flip chart or other large paper (or even a blackboard). Sometimes, a time limit such as 10 minutes creates energy to beat the clock, and if the team agrees, time can be extended in 5-minute increments.
5. *Allow an incubation period,* perhaps overnight. Copies of the ideas might be made and provided to all team members. Or at least the ideas can be left up so that individuals can go back and review them.
6. *Combine, refine, and improve* the exhaustive list of product ideas that is generated during the initial brainstorming sessions. This helps to whittle down the list to a stronger list of ideas. Schnetics, Inc., offers the SCAMPER technique, an acronym for seven questions to aid in refining brainstormed ideas:

   S—What could you substitute? Is there something else that might be better put in this idea's place?
   C—What could you combine? Can any of the ideas be combined?
   A—What could you adapt? Can any of these ideas be adapted together?
   M—What could you magnify, minimize, multiply? Can an idea be broadened or shortened in scope?
   P—What could you put to other uses?
   E—What else? Who else? Where else?
   R—What could you rearrange or reverse?

7. *Poll team members* to vote for ideas they prefer (the team leader should not vote against ideas). If a group of 10 ideas is left, give

team members a certain number of ranked votes that they provide for each of the remaining ideas. This prioritizes the "final" or desirable ideas.

Attribute Analysis

Attribute analysis is a category of techniques that employs product characteristics (attributes) to generate new product ideas. Three approaches within this category are determinant gap analysis, perceptual gap analysis, and similarity/dissimilarity analysis.

Determinant Gap Analysis

The distinction of determinant gap analysis versus perceptual gap analysis is that in the case of determinant gap analysis, attributes are known. Determinant gap analysis starts with key attributes of the potential product idea. Next, the most important attributes or drivers of the marketplace are selected (this can either be from the company's or consumer's perspective). A judgmental approach can then be undertaken to map existing product offerings or potential offerings on the given attributes or dimensions. If a more quantitative approach is desired, scales for each attribute/dimension can be determined. Existing products or potential ideas would then be mapped based on their respective scores for each attribute. The outcome of both approaches is a multidimensional map of the marketplace. Note that typically only the top two or three drivers are used to produce an intelligible map of the marketplace.

Areas on the constructed map where there is a noticeable gap serve as potentially new ideas. However, just because a gap exists does not necessarily suggest a viable new product idea. Judgment is necessary to identify the most appropriate and meaningful gaps.

Determinant gap analysis is referred to as the Attribute Rating (AR) Method because distinct attributes are given and rated. An example of an AR map is provided in Exhibit 5.1, illustrating various tire product offerings. These offerings are organized by a price dimension (high versus low price) and expected mileage dimension (high versus low mileage). For instance, Tire A reflects a high mileage warranty and a high price, but Tire A's price is less than Tire G's price. As shown, there are noticeable gaps for a lower price, lower mileage tire; lower price, higher mileage tire; and a higher price, lower mileage tire. Obviously, among these three gaps, the lower price options represent the more likely options and, thus, are potential new product concepts.

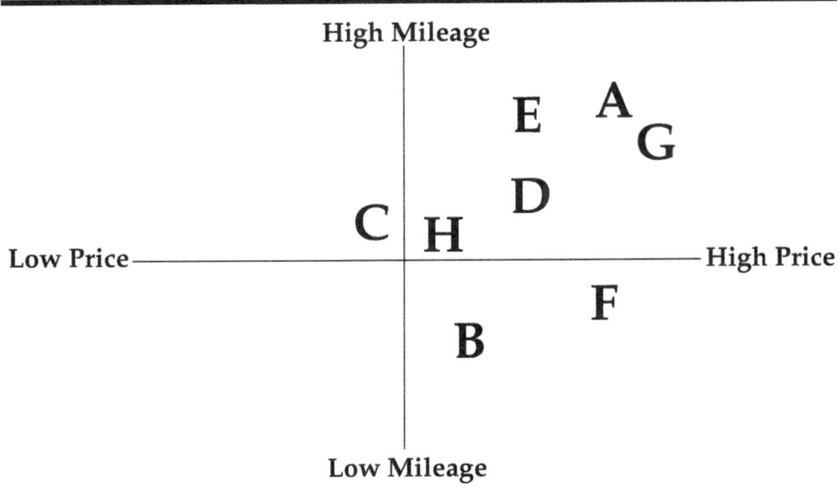

EXHIBIT 5.1. Product Positioning Map, Attribute Rating Method

Should a large set of characteristics describe a particular marketplace or product offering, then, some form of grouping of these characteristics may be appropriate. One technique used in conjunction with determinant gap analysis (AR maps) is factor analysis, which is an advanced statistical technique applicable in the case of larger sample sizes (larger in the sense that there are many respondents/customers who can evaluate each product offering on the given set of characteristics). Factor analysis can be used to group multiple characteristics into broad underlying categories and thereby establish underlying dimensions prevalent within a marketplace. See Hair, Anderson, Tatham, and Black (1998) for a more detailed discussion of factor analysis.

Perceptual Gap Analysis

Perceptual gap analysis is employed when attributes are not known or not easily identified. The methodology for a perceptual gap analysis is to pair all existing products and then make an evaluation of the similarity between the two paired product offerings. After all pairs have been evaluated, a map is constructed in an attempt to illustrate the relationships among all existing products—all existing products are plotted on this map to show their relationships to every other product. If a large sample of respondents/customers is available

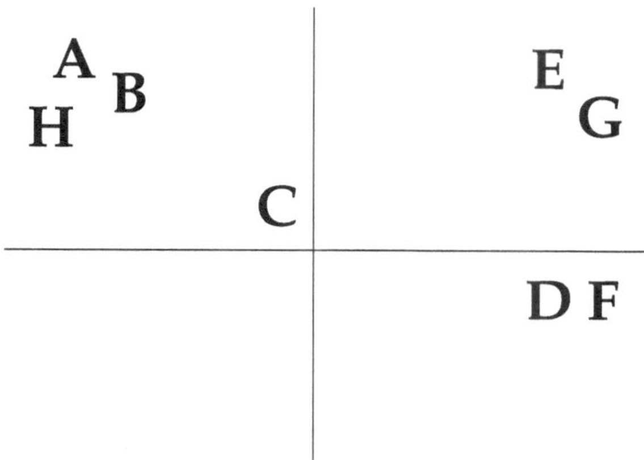

EXHIBIT 5.2. Product Positioning Map, Overall Similarity Method

to evaluate the pairings, then multidimensional scaling, also referred to as MDS, can be used to aggregate all paired comparisons and construct a map. Again, areas on the map where there is a noticeable gap represent potential concepts, but just because a gap exists does not necessarily mean that there is a viable new product idea. Judgment is necessary to identify the most appropriate and meaningful gaps.

Perceptual gap analysis is referred to as the Overall Similarity (OS) method because evaluations are made based on overall similarity between product offerings or potential product offerings. An example of an OS map is provided in Exhibit 5.2, illustrating the various tire product offerings based on their similarities. As shown, Tires E and G are considered similar; Tires D and F are considered similar; Tires A, B, and H are considered similar; and Tire C appears to be unique. Take special note that the axes of the map are not labeled. In this map, there is a noticeable gap in the lower left quadrant. There also appears to be a gap in the center of the map, because only Product C is the competition in this area. To ascertain what these gaps represent, an assessment of the product offerings is made to identify the common characteristics associated with the group offerings, that is, the common characteristic shared by A, B, and H in the upper left quadrant; E and G in the upper right quadrant; and D and F in the lower right quadrant. Identifying common characteristics is not necessarily an easy task, but if achieved, it may present meaningful new product concepts.

Similarity/Dissimilarity Analysis

Similarity/dissimilarity analysis is a variation on gap analysis in which products are evaluated on their similarity/dissimilarity to each other, based on a given set of attributes or characteristics. As in a determinant gap analysis, attributes are given, and as in a perceptual gap analysis, similarity is assessed. However, unlike gap analysis, which is used to identify gaps, similarity/dissimilarity analysis is used to group and classify product offerings to determine the competitive nature of the marketplace for existing or potential product offerings.

Similarity/dissimilarity analysis breaks into two distinct sets of approaches: similarity analysis and dissimilarity analysis. A simple approach for assessing similarity is the use of "yes/no" questions regarding whether a product has a given attribute or not. After all products are evaluated on the same set of attributes, the percentage of similar responses for each of the products is calculated (number of similar attributes divided by the total number of attributes) to represent a similarity index, and then, all indices are summarized in matrix form. Product offerings can then be grouped according to how similar they are to each other.

A similarity analysis is applied to five tire offerings in Exhibit 5.3. Each of the five offerings is evaluated on a yes/no basis across the four attributes of warranty greater than 50,000 miles, steel-belted radial, side reinforced, and high load capacity (that is, the product has this attribute—yes, or does not have this attribute—no). The similarity indices are calculated for the five products, where a higher value signifies greater similarity. For example, the similarity index between product AA and product BB is .75 because the two products match on three out of four attributes. A review of the similarity matrix suggests three possible product groupings: AA and BB as one grouping because of their high similarity index; DD and EE as a second grouping because of their high similarity index; and CC as a third group because it does not load high with either of the previous groupings. As a result of this analysis, a potential product offering against product CC may be worthwhile due to less competition. Note that determination of groupings can be a judgmental exercise.

Dissimilarity analysis focuses on the differences between product offerings. A simple approach is to assess dissimilarity based on a set of

Data

Product	Warranty > 50,000	Steel-Belted Radial	Side Reinforced	High Load Capacity
AA	Y	Y	Y	Y
BB	Y	Y	N	Y
CC	N	Y	Y	N
DD	N	N	N	N
EE	Y	N	N	N

Similarity Matrix

	AA	BB	CC	DD	EE
AA					
BB	0.75				
CC	0.5	0.25			
DD	0	0.25	0.5		
EE	0.25	0.5	0.25	0.75	

Product Similarity Groupings
Group 1: AA, BB
Group 2: DD, EE
Group 3: CC

EXHIBIT **5.3.** Similarity Analysis Example

quantitative questions about attribute characteristics. The answers to these questions are first standardized and then input into a Euclidean distance formula to calculate the distance between the given attributes for each pair of product offerings. A larger distance signifies greater dissimilarity. Euclidean distance values are then organized into matrix form and interpreted as a matrix of dissimilarity indices. Groupings of product offerings are then determined based on these dissimilarity indices.

A dissimilarity analysis is applied to five tire offerings in Exhibit 5.4. Quantitative responses are given for questions concerning the three attributes of mileage warranty, maximum psi, and maximum load capacity. These responses are standardized and then inputted

Original Data

Product	*Warranty*	*Maximum PSI*	*Maximum Load Capacity*
AA	50,000	50	1,201
BB	55,000	50	1,101
CC	48,000	50	1,195
DD	47,500	45	1,045
EE	50,000	45	1,025
Average	50,100	48	1,113.4
Standard Deviation	2966.479395	2.738612788	82.12673134

Standardized Data

Product	*Warranty*	*Maximum PSI*	*Maximum Load Capacity*
AA	−0.075	1.633	2.385
BB	3.694	1.633	−0.338
CC	−1.583	1.633	2.222
DD	−1.960	−2.449	−1.862
EE	−0.075	−2.449	−2.407

Dissimilarity Matrix[a]

	AA	*BB*	*CC*	*DD*	*EE*
AA					
BB	4.649				
CC	1.516	5.864			
DD	6.185	7.138	5.787		
EE	6.295	5.929	6.353	1.962	

Product Similarity Groupings

Group 1: AA, CC
Group 2: DD, EE
Group 3: BB

a. Euclidean Distance Formula $= \sqrt{(x_1 - x_2)^2 + (y_1 - y_2)^2}$

Exhibit 5.4. Dissimilarity Analysis Example

into the Euclidean distance formula $= \sqrt{(x_1 - x_2)^2 + (y_1 - y_2)^2}$ For example, the dissimilarity index between product AA and product BB is $4.649 = \sqrt{(-.075 - 3.694)^2 + (1.633 - 1.633)^2 + (2.385 - (-.338))^2}$. A review of the dissimilarity matrix suggests three possible product groupings: AA and CC as one grouping because of their lower dissimilarity index; DD and EE as a second grouping because of their lower dissimilarity index; and BB as a third group because it reflects higher dissimilarity with the other product offerings. In this analysis, a potential product offering against product BB may be worthwhile due to less competition. Again, determination of groupings can be a judgmental exercise.

Group determination can be done in a more objective fashion by use of cluster analysis. Cluster analysis is an advanced statistical technique that generates item classes or groups. Refer to Hair et al. (1998) for more detailed discussion of cluster analysis.

Relationship Analysis

Relationship analysis is a category of techniques that force relationships between seemingly unrelated issues to discover new product ideas. Like gap analysis, sometimes, these ideas are not feasible, but sometimes, they are indeed potentially viable ideas. The three relationship analysis techniques to be discussed include two-dimensional matrix, morphological analysis, and analogies.

Two-Dimensional Matrix

The two-dimensional matrix approach consists of identifying two key elements in question concerning a product. For example, a Web site-hosting computer might be interested in developing new services. Two key elements might be types of customers and Web-site services. Given three types of Web-site services offered (Web-site development, Web-site hosting, and Web-site promotion)and four types of customers (small business, large business, individual, nonprofit), there are potentially 12 (3 × 4) product ideas (see Exhibit 5.5). Some of these ideas may already be offered by the company, and some ideas may not be feasible. Still, assessing the relationship between Web-site services and customer types may suggest a service that the company has not considered. Naturally, adding to the types of possible Web-site services and potential customers increases the number of product options significantly.

Web-site Service	*Customer Type* Small Business	Large Business	Individual	Nonprofit
Web-site development	1	2	3	4
Web-site hosting	5	6	7	8
Web-site promotion	9	10	11	12

12 possible product concepts:

- Web-site development for small business
- Web-site development for large business
- Web-site development for individuals
- Web-site development for nonprofits
- Web-site hosting for small business
- Web-site hosting for large business
- Web-site hosting for individuals
- Web-site hosting for nonprofits
- Web-site promotion for small business
- • Web-site promotion for large business
- Web-site promotion for individuals
- Web-site promotion for nonprofits

EXHIBIT 5.5. Two-Dimensional Matrix Example

Morphological Analysis

Morphological analysis is a technique that is based on identifying different attributes for a product and identifying multiple levels- for each of the attributes (price could be an attribute, and the different types of prices, e.g., low, moderate, and high, would be levels). Each of the attributes and respective levels are listed, and then each level per attribute is combined with a level from every other attribute to iterate a list of possible product attribute combinations. For example, the previous Web-site services example is augmented to illustrate morphological analysis. Now, as shown in Exhibit 5.6, there are four attributes and various levels associated with each attribute:

Attribute 1: Web-site service offering with the three levels of Web-site development, Web-site hosting, and Web-site promotion

Attribute 2: Customer type with the four levels of small business, large business, individuals, and nonprofit

Web-site Service	*Customer Type*	*Price*	*Graphics*
Web-site development	Small business	Low	Yes
Web-site hosting	Large business	Moderate	No
Web-site promotion	Individual	High	
	Nonprofit		

Total number of possible ideas = 3 × 4 × 3 × 2 = 72

Sample of possible ideas:

- Web-site development for small business at a low price with graphics
- Web-site development for small business at a low price with no graphics
- Web-site development for small business at a moderate price with graphics
- Web-site development for small business at a moderate price with no graphics
- Web-site development for small business at a high price with graphics
- Web-site development for small business at a high price with no graphics
- Web-site development for large business at a low price with graphics
- Web-site development for large business at a low price with no graphics
- Web-site development for large business at a moderate price with graphics
- Web-site development for large business at a moderate price with no graphics
- Web-site development for large business at a high price with graphics
- Web-site development for large business at a high price with no graphics

Exhibit 5.6. Morphological Analysis Example

Attribute 3: Price with the three levels of low, moderate, and high
Attribute 4: Graphics with the two levels of yes or no

Collectively, these four attributes and their respective levels provide 72 new product concepts (3 × 4 × 3 × 2). One possible product concept (combination of attribute levels) is Web-site hosting for small business at a moderate price with graphics. Another combination is Web-site hosting for nonprofits at a low price without graphics. As in the case of the two-dimensional matrix, not all product combinations may be feasible. The overall intent of morphological analysis (as well as the two-dimensional matrix approach) is to force relationships to see if a valid idea exists. Also, note that the technique can explode quickly, especially if there are a lot of dimensions and many levels per dimension. For example, the iteration of four types of attributes and three levels per attribute provides 81 (3 × 3 × 3 × 3 or 3^4) potential product concepts. Adding just one more level to one of the attributes increases the number of potential product concepts to 108 (3 × 3 × 3 × 4)!

Conjoint Analysis (Trade-off Analysis)

One of the difficulties in morphological analysis is discerning which attributes and which levels are more preferred by customers. One way to quantify customer preferences within the guise of a quasi-morphological analysis is trade-off analysis, also referred to as conjoint analysis.

Trade-off analysis is a quantitative technique for calculating the desirability of a particular product's attributes. This, then, can lead to the aggregation of an optimal set of attributes that provides the greatest desirability. The basic approach to conjoint analysis is the iteration of all possible product attribute combinations and a customer's ranking of desirability for the particular product-attribute combination. An average desirability for each product attribute can then be calculated. Aggregation of a set of customer rankings can lead to a determination of overall desirability and preferences for a given set of attributes.

Unfortunately, the technique can become cumbersome when numerous attributes and multiple options per attribute are considered, as previously mentioned. For instance, three attributes and two levels per attribute leads to eight product-attribute combinations. The addition of one more attribute comprising two levels increases the number of product attribute combinations to 16 (doubling the number that a customer will now need to consider). Nonetheless, trade-off analysis can be valuable for identifying the most important attributes for a new product concept.

Consider the example of a cellular telephone with the following three attributes: technology, battery life, and display. Technology has two levels—CDMA and PCS; battery life has two levels—24-hour battery life and 36-hour battery life; and display has three levels—time display, date and time display, and no display. Together, there are 12 possible product combinations for this cellular telephone.

An individual provides the following rankings for these 12 combinations, with No. 1 representing the most preferred combination. Taking these rankings, a desirability score is calculated by subtracting the rank from 13 to make the highest number the most preferable. In this way, higher scores will intuitively correspond to higher desirability:

Technology	*Battery Life*	*Display*	*Rank*	*Desirability*
CDMA	24	Time	8	5
CDMA	24	Time and date	7	6
CDMA	24	None	12	1

Technology	*Battery Life*	*Display*	*Rank*	*Desirability*
CDMA	36	Time	4	9
CDMA	36	Time and date	3	10
CDMA	36	None	10	3
PCS	24	Time	6	7
PCS	24	Time and date	5	8
PCS	24	None	11	2
PCS	36	Time	2	11
PCS	36	Time and Date	1	12
PCS	36	None	9	4

Average desirability of each level is now calculated by averaging the desirability scores of all combinations containing the respective level. For example, the average desirability for CDMA is 5.67, which is the average of all product combinations containing CDMA ([5 + 6 + 1 + 9 + 10 + 3] / 6); the average desirability for PCS is 7.33, which is the average of all product combinations containing PCS ([7 + 8 + 2 + 11 + 12 + 4] / 6). Based on these calculations, it would appear that this individual finds PCS more desirable than CDMA. Similar calculations can be made to determine the average desirability for the remaining levels, and these are shown below.

Although a comparison may be made within each attribute, a comparison across attributes is not appropriate because the inherent variation underlying each attribute may differ. In other words, a 7.33 for PCS may not necessarily mean the same as a 7.33 for a 24-hour battery. Because of this, it is necessary to standardize the average desirability scores. Doing this allows the calculation of "part-worths," which allows a calculation of utility for a given product calculation. Each individual level per attribute has an individual utility value. Summing up these values provides an estimate of the total utility potentially offered by a particular product combination. In the case of the cellular telephone, the overall preference for the cellular telephone can be represented as

$$\text{Preference}_{\text{technology, battery life, display}} = \text{PW}_{\text{technology}} + \text{PW}_{\text{battery life}} + \text{PW}_{\text{display}}$$

where PW means part-worth or utility. To standardize the average desirability scores, the overall average per attribute is first calculated. Each average desirability score per level is subtracted from this average to provide a deviation from the mean score, or what can be termed variation. In the case of technology, the overall desirability score average is 6.5. CDMA is –0.83 deviation from the mean (0.83 below the mean), whereas PCS is +0.83 deviation from the mean (0.83 above the mean). Each deviation from the mean score is squared and summed to provide a sum of squared deviation statistic. In the example, summing up the squared deviations equals 31.44.

Next, a standardizing statistic is calculated by dividing the sum of squared deviation by the total number of levels and then taking the square root of this statistic to put into original units. In the example, there are seven levels, so 31.44 divided by 7 equals 4.49. The square root of this is a standardizing statistic of 2.12. To calculate the part-worth for each level, each deviation score per level is divided by the standardizing statistic. For example, the part-worth for CDMA is calculated as follows: –0.83 / 2.12 = –0.392. Each level's average desirability scores, deviations from the mean scores, and part-worth scores are provided below:

	Average Desirability	*Deviation From the Mean*	*Part-Worth*
Technology			
CDMA	5.6 7	–0.83	–0.392
PCS	7.33	0.83	0.392
Battery life			
24-hour	4.83	–1.67	–0.788
36-hour	8.17	1.67	0.788
Display			
Time	8	1.50	0.708
Time and date	9	2.50	1.179
None	2.5	–4.00	–1.887

Sum of squared deviations = 31.44
Standardizing statistic = 2.12

Note that when there are only two levels, each deviation and part-worth are the positive and negative values of the same number.

Now, using the calculated part-worths, the preference for product combinations can be determined. For example, the total utility for PCS technology, a 36-hour battery, and time and date display is 2.359 (0.392 + 0.788 + 1.179). Calculating the utility for each product combination allows a determination of which combinations are most favorable and which are not so favorable. We can also compare combinations and give relative evaluations; for example, a PCS, 36-hour battery life, time and date display telephone is 0.471 units more valued than a PCS, 36-hour battery life, time display telephone.

Technology	*Battery Life*	*Display*	*Total Part-Worths (Total Preference)*
CDMA	24	Time	–0.472
CDMA	24	Time and date	–0.001
CDMA	24	None	–3.067
CDMA	36	Time	1.104
CDMA	36	Time and date	1.575
CDMA	36	None	–1.491
PCS	24	Time	0.312
PCS	24	Time and date	0.783
PCS	24	None	–2.283
PCS	36	Time	1.888
PCS	36	Time and date	2.359
PCS	36	None	–0.707

Part-worths can also be used to calculate the relative importance of each attribute. In this way, a determination of which attribute is most important to customers can be made. To do this, the range of part-worth scores for each attribute is calculated: The range around technology is 0.784 (or 0.392 to –0.392), the range around battery life is 1.576 (or 0.788 to –0.788), and the range around display is 3.066 (or 1.179 to –1.887). Each individual range for each attribute is divided by the sum of all these ranges to provide a relative importance statistic. For example, technology (0.784 / [0.784 + 1.576 + 3.066]) accounts for 14% of the total preference for this cellular telephone. Battery life accounts for 29% of the total preference for this cellular telephone (1.576 / [0.784 + 1.576 + 3.066]), and display accounts for 57% of the total preference for this cellular telephone (3.066 / [0.784 + 1.576 + 3.066]). This shows that over half of the preference for the cellular telephone under consideration is driven by the display. Thus, greatest attention to the display options would be appropriate.

Of course, the above calculations are based on one individual's rankings. During a conjoint analysis, multiple customers are queried. Overall part-worths and total preference scores can be determined by averaging the part-worths across individuals. For further reading on conjoint analysis, consider Dolan (1993) and Hair et al. (1998).

Lateral Search

Lateral search is a catch-all category of concept generation techniques that do not fit the previously given categories. The overall theme underlying lateral search techniques is to force thinking away from the current product offering or attributes of the current product offering to conceive new product ideas. In short, these techniques attempt to create "out-of-the-box" thinking.

Although numerous techniques are available (refer to Crawford, 1997), four techniques are discussed for illustrative purposes. These include competitor review, avoidance technique, Big Winner technique, and creative stimuli technique.

As the name suggests, a competitor review is a review of what competitors are doing relative to the proposed product offering. In this manner, product attributes, product offerings, and other initiatives that make competitor products popular can be identified and possibly incorporated into a new product concept. A competitor review also can attune thinking to how the respective company can establish a competitive advantage, given current competitor activities.

The avoidance technique is a technique that constantly challenges team members about why they think a certain way. In this manner, the team can better understand why certain preferences exist and how such preferences can be best served. To perform the technique, discussion begins on a particular topic, and then the question "why", or "why not" is posed. This continues until the team is satisfied with the preferences and corresponding ideas generated.

The Big Winner technique attempts to iterate the reasons underlying the success of products, people, things, and so on. The technique begins by listing things that are successful to focus discussion. For example, Tiger Woods could serve as discussion focal point. Next, reasons why this product, person, or thing is successful are iterated (brainstormed). Reasons for Tiger Woods's success may include practice, drive, popularity, and endorsements. These reasons are then discussed to see how such characteristics can be incorporated into a new product concept. For example, how might a tire manufacturer make use of the practice theme to develop a new tire concept? One answer might be a lot of testing. A cellular telephone manufacturer might be able to incorporate drive by developing a strong campaign around its new cellular telephone or, to stretch the idea, the cellular telephone manufacturer could design a telephone explicitly for use while driving (car driving). Anything deemed successful is acceptable; the over-

Amazing	Outer Space
Charity	Participation
Curiosity	Personal
Decorative	Romance
Direct	Security
Education	Showmanship
Efficiency	Sophisticated
Family	Spectacular
Glamorize	Style
Guarantee	Symbolism
Habit	Testimonials
Holiday	Timeliness
Legal	Transportation
Legend	Truth
Magic	Weather
Music	Wild
Mysterious	World

EXHIBIT **5.7.** A Sample of 35 Words That Can Be Used With the Creative Stimuli Technique

NOTE: The above is just a sample. Any adjective or noun can be used as a focal point for simulating new product concept generation.

all intent of the Big Winner technique is to stimulate different ways of bringing elements of success into a new product concept.

The creative stimuli technique is a technique that brainstorms ideas based on a given adjective or noun. Like the Big Winner technique, the creative stimuli technique attempts to connect different ways of making a product by reflecting certain elements of a listed word. The key difference in the case of the creative stimuli technique is that a word, not a success characteristic, is listed and that disconnected words bring about the greatest creativity. For example, if the word *wild* was given in the case of a cellular telephone, thinking would focus on how to make a new product concept wild. Based on this word, the cellular telephone manufacturer might generate new product concepts with wild shapes, wild colors, and/or wild names. Note that the creative stimuli technique is especially useful for ideating on new marketing program ideas. A sample of words for use with the creative stimuli technique is given in Exhibit 5.7.

Key Concepts

- Creativity
- Product concept
- Concept generation techniques: need assessment, scenario analysis, group creativity, attribute analysis, relationship analysis, lateral search
- Similarity/dissimilarity analysis
- Conjoint analysis

Chapter Questions

1. How can one stimulate creativity?
2. What makes up a good product concept statement?
3. Describe the different ways to conduct a need assessment.
4. What is the difference between extend and leap scenario analysis?
5. What are the core principles of brainstorming?
6. What is the difference between determinant and "perceptual gap analysis?
7. What is the purpose of conjoint analysis?
8. What is the purpose of any lateral search technique?

Chapter Six

Concept Evaluation

Once a set of product concepts has been generated, an evaluation of each concept is conducted. The purpose of concept evaluation is to refine the set of concepts to determine those that should continue in the product development process. Naturally, the decision regarding how many concepts can proceed in the product development process will depend on the resources available.

Five general approaches can be used to evaluate concepts. In most cases, these approaches are used together to achieve a broader perspective of which concepts should be continued. These approaches include the product development charter review, concept testing, scoring models, snake plots, and financial analysis.

■ PRODUCT DEVELOPMENT CHARTER REVIEW

In a product development charter (PDC) review, the management team or project team evaluates the respective product concept against the criteria established in the PDC. A product concept that appears to meet the expectations established in the PDC is allowed to proceed into the next product development stage (which is technical development). Ultimately, the decision of "go/no-go" using the PDC review approach is based on managerial intuition and judgment.

■ CONCEPT TESTING

Concept testing incorporates customer opinion into the evaluation process. Thus, concept testing is a process by which customers (potential customers) evaluate a new product concept and give their opinions on whether the concept is something that they might have interest in and would likely buy. Other questions during a concept test can include reasons why the concept is or is not appealing, main strengths of the product concept, key weaknesses of the product concept, and suggestions for improving the proposed product concept.

There are four approaches for conducting a concept test. The first is a narrative concept test. This test represents a text description of the concept being presented to consumers for their opinions. For example, Exhibit 6.1 shows a narrative description of a battery-powered bicycle motor that was used as part of a concept test for this product.

The second type of test is a picture/sketch concept test. In this test, a black and white or color drawing is presented to consumers for their opinions. In choosing between a narrative concept test and a picture concept test, companies should consider whether they would like to show consumers what the product looks like or would rather have consumers attempt to visualize what the product would/should look like. Exhibit 6.1 shows a picture used in conjunction with the narrative description.

The third type of test is a prototype concept test. Here, the consumer is shown and may be able to handle a facsimile of the product; sometimes, a working prototype of the product is shown. The consumer, therefore, witnesses the product firsthand.

The fourth type of test is a virtual reality concept test. In this test, the consumer views a computer image of the product and may interact with the virtual prototype.

Note that new product concepts are typically evaluated through a combination of these four concept tests. For example, a concept test can be staged to observe consumers' evolving opinions as a result of being first exposed to a narrative word description (narrative concept test), then to a picture (picture/sketch concept test), and finally to a working prototype (prototype concept test). Each subsequent test provides additional information to elicit consumer response.

Situation: Concept testing of a battery-powered bicycle motor
Narrative: A lightweight, durable, environmentally safe product that will power your bicycle so you don't have to pedal. The product has a long-life rechargeable battery so you can travel significant distances. It can be easily attached to any standard bicycle. The price for the motor, battery, carrying case, and installation kit is $250.
Picture: Horizontal friction drive motor

Questions Asked:

How interested would you be in buying this product if it were available at any store that sold bicycles? (I would definitely buy, I would probably buy, I might or might not buy, I would probably not buy, I would definitely not buy)

Why would you buy or not buy this product?

How interested are you in a battery-powered motor for a bicycle? (very interested, somewhat interested, not too interested, not interested at all)

What do you see are the product's main strengths?

What do you see are the product's main weaknesses?

If anything could be changed, what do you suggest for improving this proposed product?

Exhibit 6.1. Concept Testing: Examples of Narrative and Picture/Sketch Concept Tests

■ SCORING MODELS

Scoring models comprise lists of criteria and associated rating scales that are generated by the team or established by the company. Each individual product concept is then evaluated on the given criteria by using the given scale. Scores across the list of criteria are summed to provide a total score per concept. Concepts with higher scores are given priority over concepts having lower scores.

The Industrial Research Institute suggests this set of evaluative criteria:

- Cost to do
- Likelihood of technical success
- Profitability
- Size of potential market
- Development time
- Fit with overall corporate objectives and strategies
- The firm's capability to market the product
- Market trends and growth
- The firm's capability to manufacture the product
- Market share expected
- Patent status
- Potential product liability
- Capital investment required

Employing a simple 5-point scale of *very weak on this criterion, weak on this criterion, meets this criterion, strong on this criterion,* and *very strong on this criterion,* a set of new product concepts can be evaluated and compared. Such an evaluation can be performed by a product development team or group of managers. Given the subjective nature of scoring product concepts, the use of multiple people to evaluate concepts leads to a consensus approach for selecting promising new product concepts.

Exhibit 6.2 illustrates a scoring model applied to three new product concepts. As shown, Concept A has the highest score (48) and thus would have priority over Concepts B and C. Should enough funding be available to pursue two product development projects, Concept C (with a score of 46) would be chosen over Concept B (which has a score of 40).

If desired, the criteria in a scoring model can be weighted to emphasize issues critical to new product success. For example, assume that

Criterion	*Concept A*	*Concept B*	*Concept C*
Cost to do	4	2	4
Likelihood of technical success	4	3	3
Profitability	3	3	3
Size of potential market	3	3	2
Development time	3	5	2
Fit with overall corporate objectives and strategies	3	3	4
The firm's capability to market the product	4	5	5
Market trends and growth	4	1	4
The firm's capability to manufacture the product	4	3	3
Market share expected	5	3	5
Patent status	5	3	2
Potential product liability	3	3	4
Capital investment required	3	3	5
	48	40	46

Exhibit 6.2. Scoring Model Example

(Continued)

If weighted criteria are used:

					Weighted Scores		
Criterion	*Weight*	*Concept A*	*Concept B*	*Concept C*	*Concept A*	*Concept B*	*Concept C*
Cost to do	5%	4	2	4	0.200	0.100	0.200
Likelihood of technical success	5%	4	3	3	0.200	0.150	0.150
Profitability	9%	3	3	3	0.270	0.270	0.270
Size of potential market	15%	3	3	2	0.450	0.450	0.300
Development time	22%	3	5	2	0.660	1.100	0.440
Fit with overall corporate objectives and strategies	4%	3	3	4	0.120	0.120	0.160
The firm's capability to market the product	9%	4	5	5	0.360	0.450	0.450
Market trends and growth	5%	4	3	4	0.200	0.150	0.200
The firm's capability to manufacture the product	5%	4	3	3	0.200	0.150	0.150
Market share expected	7%	5	3	5	0.350	0.210	0.350
Patent status	4%	5	3	2	0.200	0.120	0.080
Potential product liability	5%	3	3	4	0.150	0.150	0.200
Capital investment required	5%	3	3	5	0.150	0.150	0.250
		48	42	46	3.51	3.57	3.20

EXHIBIT **6.2.** Continued

time-to-market and market potential are critical to new product success. Weighting these two criteria higher relative to the other criteria would change the previous scoring model's outcome. As shown in Exhibit 6.2, Concept B has a weighted score of 3.57 and would be favored over the other two product concepts. Concept A, with a weighted score of 3.51, would be favored over Concept C, which has a weighted score of 3.20.

Various approaches can be used to determine criteria weights. One approach for determining a criterion's weight is managerial judgment, that is, managers decide which criteria will be given greater importance. The derived weights are, therefore, subjective in nature. A statistical approach is another way to calculate appropriate weights. In particular, correlations or regression (e.g., multiple linear regression or logit regression) can be used to determine coefficients (weights) for each of the criteria. In the case of logit regression, historical data of the scoring model scores and the project outcome, that is, project success or project failure, would be tabulated. Through the use of logit regression with project success (or project failure) as the dependent variable, the criteria important to success and failure would be identified. Assuming that a satisfactory regression model can be constructed, criteria weights would be derived from the standardized coefficients.

■ SNAKE PLOTS

Snake plots are an extension of the scoring model approach. For each product concept, the unweighted score per criterion is plotted. Therefore, by plotting the scoring profiles of multiple product concepts, a comparison of product concepts can be made regarding which profile is most reasonable or appealing. Typically, a favorable profile would be one with a more stable profile so long as an acceptable minimum score is achieved. A profile could also be considered favorable if a product concept has a higher score on certain desirable criteria. For example, Exhibit 6.3 shows a snake plot of the scoring data in Exhibit 6.2. As shown, Concept A's profile is 3 or higher across all the given criteria, whereas Concept B's profile falls below a score of 3 once. If the desire was to meet all the given criteria—and a score of 3 represents *meets the given criterion*—these snake plots indicate that Concept A should be given a higher priority, followed by Concept B.

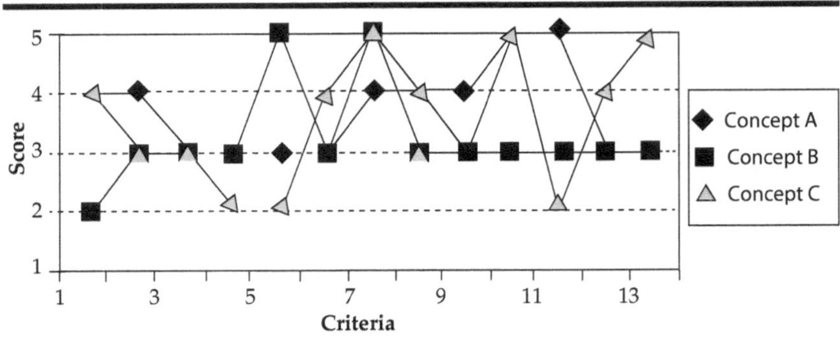

EXHIBIT **6.3.** Snake Plot Example (Using Exhibit 6.2 Data)

FINANCIAL ANALYSIS

Although this is an early stage in the product development process, most upper-level managers will desire a financial analysis of a particular product concept to determine whether it would prove a profitable venture. There are multiple ways to calculate financial impact. Two ways discussed below are the ATAR model and ECV approach.

ATAR Model

A simple approach is the ATAR model, where ATAR stands for awareness, trial, availability, and repeat purchase (Crawford, 1997). This approach is typically referred to as a breakdown approach because an aggregate market size number is broken down by the percentage of awareness in the market due to promotion, percentage of trial by consumers, percentage of availability in existing distribution channels, and percentage of consumers who will buy again, multiplied by how much will be bought in a given time period. For example, assume that a new adult daily vitamin is being marketed to a city with an adult population of 1 million (total market size = 1 million); the proposed advertising and promotion plan will contact 90% of this population (awareness = 90%); market research suggests that about 30% of adults will try the product (trial = 30%); about half of the retailers in the city will provide shelf space for the new product (availability = 50%); market research suggests one out of four adults indicated they would continue to buy the vitamin (repeat purchase = 25%); and the 30-tablet bottle would be purchased monthly (number bought per year = 12). The ATAR model calculates that a market potential of 405,000 bottles exists (1,000,000 × .9 × .3 × .5 × .25 × 12). The ATAR model also can be used to estimate profit by multiplying the number of bottles (i.e., units sold) by the margin per unit (price minus cost per unit). If the margin was $2 per bottle, the potential for total market profit would equal $810,000. Exhibit 6.4 illustrates the above discussion of the ATAR model.

Note that the ATAR model does not factor in competition and thus should be viewed as estimating total market potential. One way to compensate for this limitation is to estimate the company's market penetration rate and apply this to the ATAR model's market forecast. In the above example, a market penetration rate of 20% would suggest a sales level of 81,000 bottles per year. Multiplying this by the margin suggests a profit of $162,000 per year. Refer to Exhibit 6.4.

Also, note that the ATAR model can be modified to meet specific characteristics of a given market, be it a final consumer market or a business-to-business market. For example, assume that a car theft-deterrent device is being targeted to rental car agencies in Atlanta. The following assumptions are made: there are 30,000 rental cars in the Atlanta market (total market size = 30,000); the top 10 rental car companies, owning about 80% of these cars, will receive literature on the product (awareness = 80%); one out of four companies have expressed an interest in trying the product (trial = 25%); 60% of these companies will be able to purchase equipment outside of their normal procurement process (availability = 60%); and only one device is needed per car. Given these assumptions, the ATAR model suggests a total market potential of 3,600 units. If a penetration rate of 10% was achieved, only 360 devices would be sold on an annual basis.

A third issue with the ATAR model is the lack of consideration for research and development (R&D) and other costs incurred to get the product concept to market. Hence, the total cost of the project should be estimated, including such costs as development cost (e.g., hours, capital), prototype and pilot costs, manufacturing costs for tooling, scale-up, and ongoing manufacturing, marketing costs (e.g., advertising, packaging, promotion), pricing, anticipated sales, and payback measures (e.g., return on investment, profit contribution, anticipated margin). Using the ATAR model to estimate revenue, then subtracting the estimated total cost of the project, provides an estimate of the

	Awareness	*Trial*	*Availability*	*Repeat Purchase*	*Number Bought Per Year*		*Market Potential*	*Market Share*		*Forecast*	
1 million	0.9	0.3	0.5	0.25	12	=	405,000	0.2	=	81,000	Original Model
1 million	0.91	0.3	0.5	0.25	12	=	409,500	0.2	=	81,900	900
1 million	0.9	0.31	0.5	0.25	12	-	418,500	0.2	=	83,700	2,700
1 million	0.9	0.3	0.51	0.25	12		413,100	0.2	=	82,620	1,620
1 million	0.9	0.3	0.5	0.26	12	-	421,200	0.2	=	84,240	3,240
1 million	0.9	0.3	0.5	0.25	13	=	438,750	0.2	=	87,750	6,750

900	1-unit (%) change in awareness
2,700	1-unit (%) change in trial
1,620	1-unit (%) change in availability
3,240	1-unit (%) change in repeat sales
6,750	1 unit (%) change in number bought

Exhibit 6.4. An Example of the ATAR Model

product concept's profitability. If the product development project should exceed a 1-year time horizon, a net present-value methodology should be used to estimate the profitability.

Cost figures can be used in a break-even analysis, as well. The formula for determining break-even is fixed costs divided by price minus variable costs (i.e., fixed costs / [price - variable costs]). The break-even analysis will indicate what break-even point (in units or dollars) is needed to ensure profitability. The use of the ATAR model will indicate what the total market potential is, whether the break-even point falls within this potential, and if so, what is the necessary penetration rate in the market—too high a penetration rate may indicate the project is too costly or will not generate enough revenue. In the case of the car theft-deterrent device, a budget of $225,000 was expected for development and commercialization costs. Treating these as fixed costs and considering that the device will be priced at $250 and cost $175 to produce, the break-even point is 3,000 units ($225,000 / [$250–$175]). Assuming that the penetration rate is indeed 10% and only 360 units are sold per year (as previously calculated), it is obvious that the product concept will not be profitable in the first year nor in subsequent years (in fact, the break-even calculation does not take into account additional funding for marketing costs in Year 2 and beyond). Assuming that the market potential is correctly calculated to be 3,600, a market penetration rate (market share) of 83% would be necessary. An 83% market penetration rate is improbable.

Some companies have realized that identifying a specific percentage for each of the components in the ATAR model cannot be done accurately. Thus, they focus on the model components themselves to get a better understanding of the variability for each of the ATAR model components (percentage awareness, percentage trial, percentage availability, percentage repeat purchase, number bought per year) and investigate how fluctuations in each of the components can influence the overall market estimate. Indeed, some companies perform a sensitivity analysis on each of the model components to isolate the critical model components, also referred to as critical assumptions. In doing this., some companies will focus more resources on getting better control or understanding of these critical assumptions to achieve a more accurate market forecast. For example, a sensitivity analysis of the components in the vitamin product ATAR model indicate that a 1-unit increase in the market size will translate into a .081 increase in market demand, a 1% increase in awareness will translate into a 900-unit increase, a 1% increase in trial will translate into a 2,700-unit increase, a 1% increase in availability will translate into a 1,620-unit increase, a 1% increase in repeat purchase will translate into a 3,240-unit increase, and a 1-unit increase in number bought per year will translate into a 6,750-unit increase. This simple sensitivity analysis shows that number bought per year is the most critical assumption, followed by percentage repeat purchase and then percentage trial. Special care to confirm estimates of these three components would be prudent to ensure a more accurate forecast. Refer to Exhibit 6.4.

ECV Approach

Cooper, Edgett, and Kleinschmidt (1998) point out that a strict net present value approach (cost estimation approach) may unfairly penalize certain types of new product concepts and that the net present value approach does not take into consideration various options that may arise during a product concept's development. A probabilistic approach can, therefore, be employed to evaluate product concepts as part of a company's portfolio management process.

The specific approach to be discussed calculates the expected commercial value (ECV) of a particular product concept, using a decision-tree methodology. This methodology incorporates the probability of technical success and the probability of commercial success to estimate the overall expected commercial worth of a particular product concept. The formula is as follows:

$$ECV = [(NPV \times P_{cs} - C) \times P_{ts} - D],$$

where ECV is the expected commercial value of the product concept, NPV is the net present value of the product concept's future earnings discounted to the present, P_{cs} is the probability of commercial success (given technical success), C is commercialization costs, P_{ts} is the probability of technical success, and D is development costs (remaining in the project). Exhibit 6.5 illustrates this formula via the decision-tree framework. Note that this formula can be modified to reflect more than the two given decision points (technical success and commercial success) if a more detailed analysis is desired.

Exhibit 6.6 provides a numerical example to illustrate the ECV approach. Product Concepts A, B, and C are considered. As shown, Concept C reflects the highest ECV ($7.9 million), even though it does not have the highest NPV This illustrates how the probabilities of technical success and commercial success can affect the consideration of product concepts. In fact, Concept B, which had the highest NPV, reflected the lowest ECV.

Cooper et al. (1998) are quick to point out that the ECV approach is predicated on estimates for probabilities of technical success and

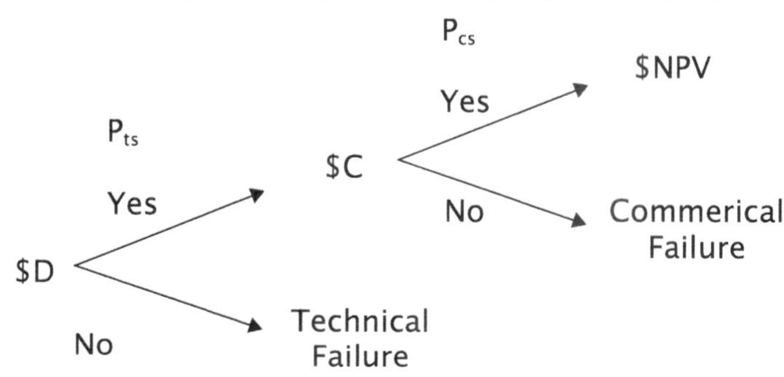

$\$ECV = [NPV \times P_{cs} - C) \times P_{ts} - D]$
where
$ECV = Expected Commercial Value of the Project
$D = Development Costs Remaining in the Project
Pts = Probability of Technical Success
$C = Commercialization (Launch) Costs
Pcs = Probability of Commercial Success
$NPV = Net Present Value of the Project's Future Earnings

EXHIBIT **6.5.** The ECV Decision Tree Framework

SOURCE: From *Portfolio Management for New Products,* by Robert G. Cooper, Scott J. Edgett, and Elko J. Kleinschmidt. Copyright © 1998 by R. G. Cooper, S. J. Edgett, & E. J. Kleinschmidt. Reprinted by permission of Perseus Books Publishers, a member of Perseus Books, LLC.
NOTE: $\$ECV = (\$NPV\ P_{cs} - \$C)\ P_{ts} - \$D$ where $ECV = Expected Commercial Value of the project; $D = Development Costs remaining in the project; P_{ts} = Probability of Technical Success; $C = Commercialization (Launch) Costs; P_{cs} = Probability of Commercial Success; $NPV = Net Present Value of the project's future earnings.

com-mercial success and that inaccurate estimates of these probabilities will lead to an erroneous ECV calculation. Four recommended approaches for calculating these probabilities are (a) Delphi consensus approach, (b) matrix approach, (c) scoring model, and/or (d) NewProd model. In the Delphi consensus approach, each manager anonymously submits his or her probability estimates, which are then compiled and reported to each of the managers. Discussion about the numbers usually will take place if there are significant differences across the estimates, and then, subsequent rounds of anonymous probability estimates will ensue. The process ends when consensus on the numbers is reached.

The matrix approach consists of documentation in two-dimensional matrices that specify probability of technical success across different

Product Concept	*Net Present Value of the Project's Future Earnings ($NPV)*	*Probability of Technical Success (Pts)*	*Probability of Commercial Success (Pcs)*	*Development Costs ($D)*	*Commercialization (Launch) Costs ($C)*	*Expected Commercial Value of the Project ($ ECV)*
A	30	0.8	0.5	3	4	5.8
B	45	0.5	0.4	5	4	2
C	35	0.7	0.6	4	4	7.9

Exhibit 6.6. An Example of the ECV Approach

SOURCE: From *Portfolio Management for New Products,* by Robert G. Cooper, Scott J. Edgett, and Elko J. Kleinschmidt. Copyright © 1998 by R. G. Cooper, S. J. Edgett, & E. J. Kleinschmidt. Reprinted by permission of Perseus Books Publishers, a member of Perseus Books, LLC.

NOTE: $\$ECV = (\$NPV \times P_{cs} - \$C) \times Pts - \$D$

scenarios and probability of commercial success across different scenarios. Such probabilities are calculated from company experience and intuition and serve as standards to be used by all product development projects in that company. Exhibit 6.7 shows an example of the matrix approach.

The scoring model approach is a more detailed version of the matrix approach. A scoring model comprising key criteria is provided. In this case, the scores across these criteria are summed and compared to a given standard score to indicate the probabilities for technical success and commercial success.

The last approach, NewProd, is a proprietary model developed by Dr. Robert Cooper (1993). The model is an empirically based computer model that is customized to a company situation. Responses from a team of company representatives answering a series of 30 questions are loaded into the NewProd computer model, these data are compared to profiles within the model, and then, a prediction of success or failure is given.

In using any of the above approaches for estimating probabilities, it must be realized that any derived probability is an estimate. Thus, there will often be inaccuracy. Still, a systematic approach to estimating a probability should lead to a better estimate than a guess. Furthermore, seldom can one assume that any new product concept has a 100% chance of technical success and 100% chance of commercial success. The use of probabilities in evaluating new product concepts is an attempt to get a more realistic perspective and a better prioritization of new product concepts.

■ CONCLUSION

The goal of the concept generation stage is to select a promising set of product concepts that can be further developed. Typically, the final concepts are elaborated in what is called a product protocol, which will be discussed at the beginning of the next chapter. The product protocol is used to direct the technical development stage, which is where intangible concepts become tangible and closer to eventual launch. As for those concepts that did not successfully traverse the concept evaluation phase, better companies typically place these concepts into an idea bank, where they can be accessed in the future should a similar concept arise, providing background information to enhance the newer concept.

Commercial Success Probabilities*

Market Type		*Probability Score*	
Current	0.6	0.7	0.8
New to company	0.1	0.2	0.6
New to the world	0.05	0.1	0.2
	Low	Moderate	High
		Competitive Advantage	

Definitions:

Low Competitive Advantage = Minor cost reduction or product improvement; new product will not overcome significant switching costs.

Moderate Competitive Advantage = Product should be able to provide a great enough benefit to stimulate some switching behavior in absence of other factors.

High Competitive Advantage = Benefit should be able to stimulate significant levels of switching behavior, given the current competitive environment.

Technical Success Probabilities*

Likelihood That the Process Will Work Successfully		*Probability Score*	
High	0.4	0.7	0.8
Moderate	0.3	0.5	0.6
Low	0.2	0.2	0.3
	Low	Moderate	Low
		Likelihood That the Product Will Work Successfully	

Definitions:

High = Prototype in hand demonstrating all necessary characteristics, performance close to optimal.

Moderate = Prototype not yet ready, but strong likelihood that the technology will perform as expected.

Low = Technology not well established; uncertainty over whether technology will perform as expected or whether the technology is feasible.

*Note that the above probabilities are given for illustrative purposes only and do not represent industry benchmarks.

Exhibit 6.7. The Use of Scoring Models for Determining Probabilities of Commercial and Technical Success (adapted from Cooper et al., 1998)

Key Concepts

- Product development charter review
- Concept testing
- Scoring models
- Snake plots
- ATAR model
- ECV approach

Chapter Questions

1. What is the purpose of concept testing?
2. What are the four types of concept testing?
3. How would one construct a scoring model?
4. What is the purpose of a snake plot?
5. What are the key components of the ATAR model?
6. Why would one recommend the ECV approach over a strict net present value approach?

Chapter Seven

Technical Development

The technical development stage represents the point in the product development process at which a tangible new product emerges or where the specifics of a service to be delivered are determined. Although characterized as a single stage, multiple sets of activities are conducted under the technical development umbrella. The technical development stage, therefore, may have various substages related to detailed product design, manufacturing engineering, and market plan development.

■ THE PRODUCT PROTOCOL

In most cases, some version of a product protocol (i.e., product definition) is employed to drive all activities in the technical development stage. A product protocol would be constructed for a particular product concept after it has been selected for continued development. Construction of the product protocol may occur at the end of the concept generation stage after concept evaluation, or it may occur at the beginning of the technical development stage. In either case, the product protocol is an important guiding document because it specifies what should be ultimately developed, to match what was initially intended to be developed.

By definition, a protocol is a signed document containing a record of the points on which agreement has been reached by negotiating parties. A product protocol, therefore, represents the points of agreement for product specifications and deliverables; it reflects that all departments and senior management have agreed on the product specifications and deliverables. In addition to identifying product specifications and deliverables (not all deliverables can be known, but critical deliverables are assumed to be known), the product protocol communicates essentials to all team members and lays out what each department will provide to deliver the final product to the customer. The product protocol also establishes clear boundaries for development cycle time and provides definitions of product success so that proper measures/metrics can be used.

One approach to constructing a product protocol is to address 12 distinct elements (Crawford, 1997). In this way, the product protocol would be a document comprising 12 distinct paragraphs or sections. The recommended elements are as follows:

1. *Target market:* Who is the intended purchaser of the product?
2. *Product positioning:* How is the product to be positioned in the market relative to existing company offerings and competitor offerings?
3. *Product attributes:* Describe the technology and form of the product in specific product functions and features. Attributes are typically viewed by the development staff as product specifications, which represent a precise description of what the product has to do. This description is typically technical in nature comprising a *metric* and a *target value.* The metric represents the specific function or feature to be built into the product, and the target value represents the boundary conditions for building that function/feature into the product. Using a laptop as an example, weight would be a metric, and "no more than three pounds" would be the value. A target value can be expressed other ways. Generally, there are five ways in which to set target values for metrics:

   At least X: These specifications establish targets for the lower bound on a metric, but higher is still better. Example: The range for a new electric car (metric) must be at least 50 miles (target value)

At most X: These specifications establish targets for the upper bound on a metric, with smaller values being better. Example: the weight of a new cellular phone (cellular) can be no more than 8 ounces (target value).

Between X and Y: These specifications establish both upper and lower bounds for the value of the metric. Example: the page count for a new book (metric) can range from 200 to 250 pages (target value).

Exactly X: These specifications establish a target of a particular value of a metric, with any deviation degrading performance. Example: The duration of a new movie (metric) must be 90 minutes (target value).

A set of discrete values: Some metrics will have values corresponding to several discrete choices. Example: Case sizes for a new beverage product (metric) can come in counts of 6 or 12 (target value).

Other ways: These include customer opinion, internal research/judgment/experimentation, and competitive benchmarking. It also should be recognized that .specifications are established at least twice. As Ulrich and Eppinger (1995) suggest, there are initial target specifications and refined target specifications.

4. *Competitive comparisons:* What are competitors currently doing?
5. *Augmentation dimensions:* How is the product to be differentiated? What is the product's competitive advantage?
6. *Timing:* What is the product development schedule? What dates need to be met?
7. *Marketing requirements:* Describe any special marketing issues.
8. *Financial requirements:* Describe any special financial issues.
9. *Production requirements:* Describe any special production issues.
10. *Regulatory requirements:* Describe any special regulatory/legal considerations.
11. *Corporate strategy requirements:* What core competencies are to be emphasized in developing the product?
12. *Potholes:* Do there appear to be any foreseeable problems in developing this product?

Exhibit 7.1 shows a sample product protocol for a trash disposal/recycling system for home use.

Sample Product Protocol for a Trash Disposal/Recycling System for Home Use

1. *Target market:*
   Ultimate: Top 30% of income group in cities of over 100,000 with upscale lifestyle
   Intermediate: Stakeholders in building industry for homes over $300,000, especially developers, architects, builders, bankers, and regulators
2. *Product positioning:*
   A convenient, mess-free method for recycling items in the home
3. Product attributes:
   The system must automate trash disposal in a home environment with recycling (separating trash, compacting, placing bags outside, and rebagging empty bins and notifying user when the bag supply is running low) at a factory cost not to exceed $800
   The system must be clean, ventilated, and odor-free. The user will want an easy-to-use appliance. Rodents, pets, and angry neighbors could become a problem if odors exist
   Installation must be simple. Distributors and other installation personnel must have favorable experience in installations
   The system must be safe enough for operation by children of school age
   The entire working unit must not be larger than twice a 22-cubic foot refrigerator
4. *Competitive comparisons:*
   None—first of its kind
5. *Augmentation dimensions:*
   Financing will be available
   Generous warranty
   Competent installation service and fast/competent postinstallation service
   Education about recycling and about the product will be essential
6. *Timing:*
   Being right overrides getting to market fast. However, window will not be open for more than 2 years
7. *Marketing requirements:*
   Marketing announcement must be made at national builders shows and environmental shows
   A new channel structure will be needed for the intermediate target market, but it will eventually collapse into the regular channel
   Small, select sales force will be needed for introduction
   To capitalize on announcement value, 50 installations during the first 4 months are needed
8. *Financial requirements:*
   Development and introductory period losses cannot exceed $20 million
   Break-even is expected by end of second year on the market
   The project must achieve a 5-year net present value of zero, based on a 35% cost of capital

EXHIBIT 7.1. Example of a Product Protocol

EXHIBIT 7.1. Continued

9. *Production requirements:*
   Once the product is launched, there must be no interruptions of supply
   Quality standards must be met without exceptions
10. *Regulatory requirements:*
   Regulations are from many sources and vary by states and localities
   There are multiple stakeholders. A clear understanding of each stakeholder and his or her role is needed
11. *Corporate strategy requirements:*
   Corporate strategy is driving this project, and upper management is committed to this project
   The company seeks a diversification of markets, enhanced reputation for innovativeness, and sustainable margins higher than those in current markets
12. *Potholes:*
   This project has massive pothole potential because of its newness. There is concern regarding (a) obtaining regulatory approval, (b) accomplishing the $800 cost constraint, and (c) getting fast market acceptance for early installations

THEMES UNDERLYING ENGINEERING-RELATED ACTIVITIES

One of the prevalent themes underlying engineering-related activities during the technical development stage is *design for excellence* or DFX. DFX represents a philosophy in which careful consideration is given to cost-effective operations, distribution, installation, service, and customer use of the product. Bralla (1996) formally defines DFX as

> a knowledge-based approach that attempts to design products that maximize all desirable characteristics—such as high quality, reliability, serviceability, safety, user friendliness, environmental friendliness, and time-to-market—in a product design, while at the same time, minimizing lifetime costs, including manufacturing costs. (pp. 22–23)

DFX should, therefore, be recognized as a philosophy that not only underlies engineering-related activities during the technical development stage but also should pervade all departmental activities (engineering departments plus all other departments) throughout the entire product development process.

Below are themes inherent in the DFX philosophy.

Ensure that the product functions and performs in the way it is intended.

Design the product to protect consumers and society in general from harm when the product is used. Bralla's (1996) guidelines to ensure product safety include

- Design products to be fail-safe
- Allow for human error
- Avoid sharp corners
- Provide guards or covers over sharp blades and similar elements
- Make sure repair, service, or maintenance pose no safety hazards
- Provide clearances between moving parts and other elements to avoid shearing or crushing points in which hands or other parts of the operators body might be caught or injured
- Arrange controls so that the operator does not have to stand or reach them in an unnatural, awkward position
- Anticipate the environment in which the product will be used and provide safeguards against those environmental factors that could create safety hazards
- Ground electrical products properly
- Use electrical interlocks in circuits with potentially injurious voltage so that unless a guard is in proper position, the circuit is open and no current will flow
- Make small components bulky enough so that they cannot be accidentally swallowed by children
- Make the product from high-impact or resilient materials so that if the product is dropped or otherwise broken, neither sharp edges, sharp points, nor small fragments that are potentially swallowable by small children will result
- Give special attention to the strength of all parts whose failure might result in injury to the operator
- Do not use paints or other finishing materials with more than 6% content of heavy metals
- Incorporate warning devices that become actuated if any hazardous materials in the product are released or if dangerous components are exposed

- Make sure point-of-operation guards are convenient and do not interfere with the operator's movement or affect the output of the product
- Check that plastic bags used in packaging are not too thin
- Minimize, as much as possible, the use of flammable materials including packaging material
- Eliminate cuts from paper edges by serrating edges
- Make markings, especially those for safety warnings, very clear, concise, and long-lasting
- Avoid the use of hazardous materials, including those that are a hazard when burned, recycled, or discarded
- Develop products that do not require heavy or prolonged operation to avoid the kinds of user actions that can lead to cumulative trauma disorders such as carpal tunnel syndrome
- Do not design parts with unguarded projections that can catch body members or clothing

The product should have quality and be perceived as having quality. This recognizes that quality is both objective and perceived. Often, a product's commercial success is predicated on the quality customers perceive. Thus, it is important to view quality as whatever consumers judge it to be. To do this, customer surveys can be used to investigate customer satisfaction with the product and post-sales service. Objective quality is predominantly an internal measure of quality and more product-focused and cost-focused. Minimizing design costs and production costs indicates internal company quality.

Company quality initiatives are often reflective of a total quality management (TQM) program. Such a program stresses that quality must be designed into the product rather than tested for at the end of the production process. TQM guidelines include

- A strong orientation toward the customer in matters of quality
- Emphasis on quality as a total commitment for all employees of all functions at all levels in the organization
- A striving for error-free production
- Use of statistical quality-control data and other factual methods rather than intuition to control quality
- Prevention of product defects rather than reaction after they occur
- Continuous improvement

The product should be reliable. Although related to quality, reliability is defined as "the probability that a product will perform satisfactorily for a specified period of time under a stated set of conditions" (Baffa, 1996, p. 165). Explicit in this definition are the notions that reliability is probabilistic in nature and predicated on satisfactory performance, that it is time-based, and that it is bounded by specific operating conditions. It is probabilistic in nature because it is usually expressed as a fraction or percentage showing the likelihood that a product, a product component, or a product subcomponent will successfully operate over a given period of time. Determining what is successful operation corresponds to the notion of satisfactory performance. Thus, to assess reliability, it is necessary to establish what indicates satisfactory (successful) performance. Time is critical to the notion of reliability because the time factor must be known to assess the probability that the product (and its components and subcomponents) can last that long. Time also is typically used to translate reliability into observable measures such as mean time-to failure and mean time between failures. Using a time factor, reliability can be plotted to create a failure-rate curve, also referred to as the bathtub curve. This curve illustrates a higher rate of initial failures during the "debugging" stage; a lower, constant rate during the product's expected life; and an increasing rate of failure at the end of the product's life during the "wearout" stage (see Exhibit 7.2). Naturally, specific operating conditions such as temperature, humidity, vibration, and so on when a product is functioning, stored, and transported will affect what the failure-rate curve looks like, and thus, consideration of operating conditions is necessary to evaluate reliability.

The product should be designed to account for manufacturing issues and to minimize manufacturing problems, manufacturing cycle time, and manufacturing costs. To do this, various programs can be employed including design for assembly, design for manufacturability, design for manufacturability and assembly, group technology, and synchronized manufacturing.

Two themes of design for manufacturability are that (a) maximum savings occur when a part is eliminated or combined with another, rather than just being simplified; and (b) final product assembly often is a high labor cost in a typical cost structure, and assembly support is a high overhead item. These two themes pervade the following design for manufacturability recommendations:

- Minimize the number of parts; if possible, eliminate parts, especially fasteners

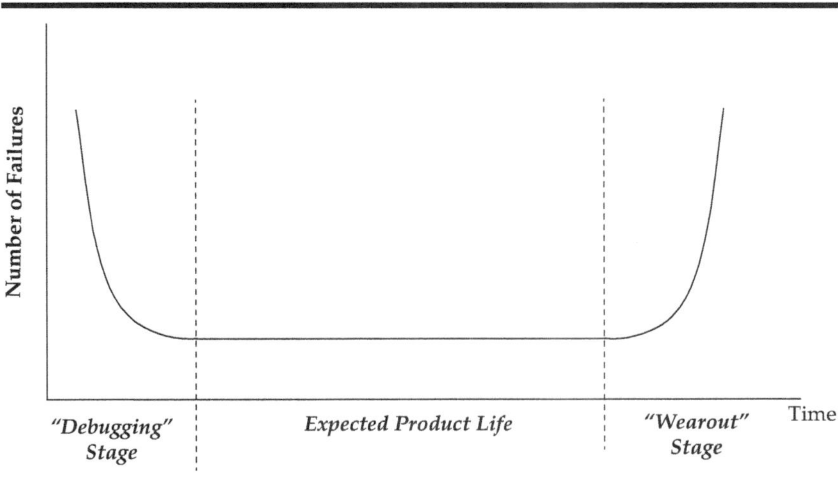

EXHIBIT 7.2. Failure Rate Curve

NOTE: Failure rates are high initially, usually due to manufacturing defects; then, they level off to a low rate until the third stage, when components begin to wear out (Bralla, 1996, p. 168).

- Attempt to use plastics to provide snap fits, and combine parts that would be otherwise separate
- Use parts such as integral hinges, springs, cams, and bearings
- Attempt to eliminate steps requiring machining operations
- Standardize parts
- Use materials that can be processed
- Fit the product design to the present manufacturing process
- Design each part to be easy to make
- Design for the expected production quantity
- Design parts so that they fit together easily
- Minimize the number of production equipment adjustments that have to be made

The product should be designed to minimize its impact on the environment as a result of pollutants, disposal, and so on. Bralla's (1996) guidelines for environmental friendliness include

- Avoid as much as possible the use of toxic materials in the product and its manufacturing process
- Design the product and its components so they can be reused, refurbished, or recycled

- Minimize the number of parts
- Minimize the amount of material in the product
- Avoid the use of separate fasteners, if possible
- Use the fewest number of fasteners
- Design the product to be easily disassembled, even if some parts are corroded
- Minimize the number of different materials in a product
- Choose materials that are compatible and can be recycled together
- Avoid the use of composite materials such as glass or metal-reinforced plastics
- Standardize components to aid in eventual refurbishing of products
- Use molded-in nomenclature rather than labels or separate nameplates for product identification
- Use modular designs to simplify assembly and disassembly
- Wherever feasible, identify the material from which the part is made right on the part
- Make separation points between parts as clearly visible as possible so that disassembly and recycling are made easier
- Avoid designs that require spray-painted finishes
- Provide predetermined break areas, if needed, to allow easy separation of fasteners that may be incompatible with the recycling stream
- Use a woven-metal mesh instead of metal-filled material for welding thermoplastics; this is more likely to be recyclable
- Design the product to use recycled materials from other sources

The product should be designed so that if returned for service, such service can be enacted easily, quickly, and efficiently. Such service corresponds to both regular maintenance and repair situations. Bralla's (1996) guidelines for serviceability include

- Increase the reliability of the overall product to reduce service requirements
- Design the product so that components that will require periodic maintenance and those prone to wear or failure are easily visible and accessible
- Design all high-mortality parts, or those that need replacement or removal for service to other parts, for easy detachment and re-

placement, for example, quick disconnects or snap fits for quick disassembly

- Design high-mortality parts so that they can be replaced without removing other parts or disturbing their adjustment
- Design with field replacement in mind
- When tools are required, use standard, commonly available tools
- Consider the use of modules—assemblies containing all components needed for a particular function—which are easily replaced when necessary and easily tested to verify their operability. A module is a group of components and subassemblies performing a particular function and packaged together in a self-contained unit so that they can be installed or replaced as one unit at the same time
- Design the product for easy testability:
  - As much as possible, design the product and its components so that tests can be made with standard instruments
  - Incorporate built-in test capability and if possible, built-in self-testing devices in the product
  - Make the tests themselves easy and standardized, capable of being performed in the field
  - Provide accessibility for test probes, for example, prominent test points or access holes for test probes
  - Make modules testable while still assembled to the product
- Use standard commercial parts as much as possible to further ensure their interchangeability and to simplify the problem of field stocking of replacement parts
- Provide malfunction annunciation, that is, design the product so that indicators inform the operator that the equipment is malfunctioning and indicate which component is malfunctioning
- Make sure that parts that may require replacement during service are clearly identified with part numbers or other essential reference designations
- Design replacements parts to prevent their incorrect insertion during maintenance
- Design for fault isolation
- Use the minimum number of screw head types and sizes in fasteners or portions of the product
- Provide anticipated spare parts with the product
- When access covers cannot be removed, make sure that they are self-supporting when open

- Make sure repair, service, or maintenance tasks pose no safety hazards, for example, sharp corners, burrs
- Incorporate automatic timing or counting devices in the product to signal the need for replacement of high wear or depletable parts
- Provide clear and complete preventive maintenance manuals or instructions as part of the engineering specifications for the product
- Provide room for drainage of fluids that must be periodically changed; make sure drainage plugs are accessible
- Ensure that components that are apt to be replaced, or are adjacent to those that are, are not too fragile

The product should be designed with the user in mind, including considerations relating to understanding how to properly install and operate the product. Bralla's (1996) guidelines for user friendliness include

- Fit the product to the user's physical attributes and knowledge
- Simplify the structure of the user's tasks
- Make the controls and their functions obvious
- Use mappings so that the operator understands what the controls do
- Use constraints to prevent incorrect actions
- Provide user feedback
- Display operating information clearly
- Make controls easy to handle
- Anticipate human errors
- Avoid awkward and extreme motions for the user
- Standardize arrangements and systems

The product should be appealing to customers and users. Realize that, at times, the customer and user are distinct and that different aspects of the product may appeal to each party. The classic example is diapers, where the customer is the parent and the baby is the user. Considerations of price and absorbability may be important to parents, whereas the feel of the diaper may be most important to the baby. Both sets of considerations are deserving and therefore necessary to consider.

Product accessories, attachments, and peripheral functions of the product should be given careful consideration. Particular attention should be paid to too many extraneous accessories, attachments, or peripheral functions, which unnecessarily increase product price and may make the product more difficult to use (Nussbaum & Neff, 1991).

Product development speed is crucial. Efforts to minimize design, tool-up, and manufacture of the product should be given top consideration. Bralla's (1996) guidelines for minimizing time-to-market include:

- Use standard components rather than ones specially designed for the application
- Use standard and existing systems, procedures, and materials
- Use modules, especially if they are from existing products.
- Don't redesign more than necessary
- Design conservatively
- Design to do it right the first time
- Design for processes that do not require long tooling lead times or could be made with standard available tooling

DFX Computer Systems

To facilitate DFX activities, various computer systems exist. These include computer-aided-design (CAD), computer-aided-manufacturing (CAM), and computer-aided-engineering (CAE). Another emerging technology is stereolithography, which is a computer-based system that takes a CAD drawing of a discrete part, translates it, and creates a three-dimensional prototype by guiding a laser through a resin material that hardens into the respective part. Stereolithography and other related technologies represent key technologies for rapid prototyping.

■ KEY TECHNIQUES USED TO AID TECHNICAL DEVELOPMENT: QUALITY FUNCTION DEPLOYMENT

One of the more popular techniques used in conjunction with DFX is quality function deployment (QFD). Developed in the 1960s for use in Japan's Kobe shipyards, QFD was later adopted by the Japanese and U.S. automobile industries and, subsequently, by other industries. The attractive objective of the QFD methodology is that it purposely links customer needs with technical specifications in an attempt to create an optimal product configuration.

The original QFD methodology comprises four stages of evaluation, beginning at a top level with the linkage between customer benefits sought and product specifications. The next three levels detail product specifications down to the level of parts specifications and further down to the lev§l of manufacturing process specifications (see Exhibit 7.3). In most cases, companies have found that managing the QFD process across these four stages is extremely complex and time-consuming. Thus, most companies find the most expeditious approach is to focus on the top level of evaluation, which links customer benefits sought to product specifications (technical specifications). This level is commonly referred to as the "House of Quality" (Hauser & Clausing, 1988).

The House of Quality illustrates the relationships between the Voice of the Customer (VOC) and the Voice of the Engineer (VOE), where the VOC emphasizes what the customer wants to get out of using the product or product benefits and the VOE delineates the technical characteristics of the product. This is accomplished via a matrix approach where the VOC is located on the rows of the matrix and the VOE is located in the columns of the matrix (see Exhibit 7.4). For example, a customer describing a pencil may state a need for it not to easily roll when placed on a hard surface, whereas an engineer may look at a similar consideration by looking at pencil hexagonality (note that a typical customer would not use the terminology of hexagonality). The matrix indicates a strong relationship between these two issues, and thus, hexagonality should be a design consideration if reducing the roll of a pencil is deemed a priority.

VOC information is collected through VOC studies. Three important pieces of information are collected during a VOC study: (a) the customer needs/benefits sought, (b) the importance of each of these needs/benefits relative to each other, and (c) evaluations of the company's and competitors' current offerings in satisfying these needs/benefits. For many companies, this in itself provides an ample amount of information. Thus, many companies choose not to perform a full QFD analysis but rather analyze the ample amount of data collected during a VOC study to clarify what specific needs/benefits customers have. This information is then used to frame the product's technical specifications. Other companies take the next step with VOC data and attempt a match with technical data, thereby applying the QFD methodology.

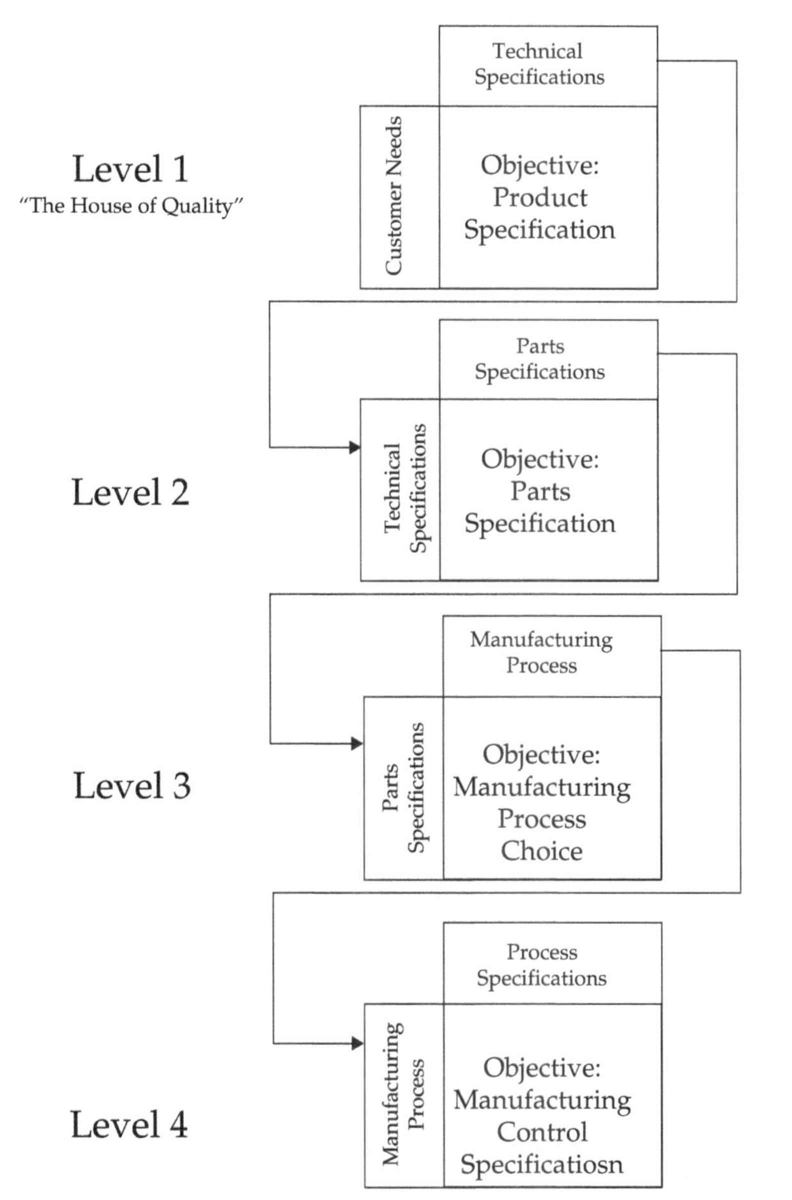

EXHIBIT 7.3. The Four Stages of Quality Function Deployment

A-1 Pencil

Engineering Parameters

Customer Needs	length ▲	time between sharpening ▲	lead dust generated ▼	hexagonality ▲		rate of importance	company now	competitor x	competitor y	plan	ratio of improvement	sales points	absolute wt.	demanded wt.
Easy to hold	O 42			O 42		3	4	3	3	4	1	1	3.0	14%
Does not Smear		O 69	O 207			4	5	4	5	5	1	1.2	4.8	23%
Point lasts	△ 44	◎ 396	O 132			5	4	5	3	5	1.25	1.5	9.4	44%
Does not roll	△ 19			◎ 171		3	3	3	3	4	1.33	1	4.0	19%
Total	105	465	339	213	1122						Total		21.2	100%
%	9%	41%	30%	19%	100%									
company now	5″	3pgs	3g	70%										
competitor x	5″	5pgs	2g	80%										
competitor y	4″	2.5pgs	4g	60%										
plan	5.5″	6pgs	2g	80%										

Main Correlations
◎ 9 = strong correlation
O 3 = some correlation
△ 1 = possible correlation

Sales Points = 1.5, 1.2, or 1

EXHIBIT 7.4. The "House of Quality" Matrix

VOE data represent specific technical characteristics (technical specifications) of the product. Such characteristics may derive from the product protocol or correspond to those characteristics that can be readily tested. In addition to specifying technical characteristics, VOE data will indicate a desired course of action for each respective characteristic in terms of reducing or increasing the magnitude of this characteristic. For example, the engineering team for a new car, in specifying the technical characteristic of weight, may indicate a desire to reduce weight. The third element of VOE data is specifying the relationships between each of the technical characteristics, that is, how would reducing car weight affect wind resistance. These relationships are specified in a matrix above the technical characteristics called the "trade-off roof." Both negative and positive correlations between the technical specifications are indicated. A fourth possible element that may be included in VOE data is the benchmarking of the company's product with competitors' products on the given technical characteristics. Such benchmarking provides quantitative benchmarks on each of the technical characteristics.

Exhibit 7.4 illustrates the QFD methodology in the case of a pencil. Customer needs (VOC data) are listed on the rows, and technical specifications (VOE data) are given in the columns. Four customer needs are specified: easy to hold, does not smear, point lasts, and does not roll. Each of these needs is rated on importance using a 5-point scale where 1 is *not important* and 5 is *very important,* in the column following the technical specifications. The needs are also evaluated across the company's and its top competitors' products using a 5-point scale, where 1 is *very weak on this need* and 5 is *very strong on this need.* As shown, "point lasts" is the most important need (rate of importance = 5), but the company is evaluated as being below Competitor X on this need but above Competitor Y. The column after the competitor evaluation data is the plan. The plan represents what the company wants customers to perceive. The plan is, therefore, a management decision. The next column, ratio of improvement, is the calculation of plan divided by the company's position now. Given that the company scored a 4 on "point lasts," it has set a plan of 5, which leads to a 1.25 (or 5/4) ratio of improvement. This can be interpreted as meaning that the company wants to improve perceptions of "point lasts" by 25% (note that a ratio of 1 would represent 0% or no change). Sales points are incremental bumps to particular needs that management or the sales force believes are necessary to create a competitive advantage. In the given example, three sales points are possible: a score of 1 (no bump), a score of 1.2 (slight bump), or a score of 1.5 (bump). Absolute weight is calculated by multiplying the rate of importance by the ratio of improvement by the sales points. "Point lasts" has an absolute weight of 9.4(5 × 1.25 × 1.5). Demanded weight is the relative percentage of the absolute weight to the total absolute weight. In the example, the total absolute weight is 21.2 (the sum of the absolute weights for easy to hold, does not smear, point lasts, and does not roll). The demanded weight for "point lasts" is, therefore, .44 or 44% (9.4 / 21.2). The use of demanded weight allows for the interpretation that 44% of product demand is based on the point lasting. Note that some QFD methodologies prefer not to use the sales point system because it is argued that only the customer should dictate how needs are weighted. The sales point system is used in the present example because it can be used to emphasize needs that may become more important in the future (as will be discussed later). Also note that the series of calculations provides a way of prioritizing customer needs, which can then be presented to engineering. In certain situations, the prioritizing of customer needs is sufficient to drive technical development, and this is why many companies do not apply the full QFD methodology.

Following the prioritizing of customer needs, the relationships between each of the customer needs and technical characteristics are examined. In most cases, a intense discussion is held between marketing and engineering personnel to clarify these relationships. This highlights the key benefit of QFD as a tool for facilitating interdepartmental communication. Assuming that consensus is reached, which may take time, the correlation between the respective need and characteristic is listed. In the given example, three types of correlations can be listed: a weak correlation, which is given the weight of 1; some correlation, which is given the weight of 3; and a strong correlation, which is given the weight of 9. Using these weights, the relationships between each customer and technical specification can be weighted accordingly by multiplying the weight of the relationship by the demanded weight for the respective customer need. For example, the relationship between "point lasts" and "time between sharpenings" is indicated to be a strong correlation, which is a weight of 9. Multiplying this weight by the "point lasts" demand weight of 44% equals a score of 396. Completing the calculations across all cells and then totaling the columns provides a total score for each technical specification. Taking the relative percentage of each column to the total score suggests how much demand is predicated on the respective technical characteristic. For example, "time between sharpenings" has a score of 465, which represents 41% of the total score. This can be loosely interpreted as suggesting that 41% of product demand is predicated on addressing the "time between sharpenings" characteristic. At this point, engineering has a priority list for which technical characteristics to focus on during development. The respective engineering benchmarks serve as milestones to drive the technical development process.

The Theory of Innovative Problem Solving (TIPS/TRIZ)

One issue that can arise in the QFD methodology is contradictions between technical characteristics. For example, the greater the "time between sharpenings," the more "lead dust generated"—even though greater time between sharpenings and less lead dust are desirable. One approach is to favor the higher weighted characteristic, a methodology called the Theory of Innovative Problem Solving (TIPS) that has emerged from Russia, where it is called TRIZ (the Russian equivalent of the Theory of Innovative Problem Solving).

TRIZ was developed by Genrich Altshuller as part of a World War II initiative to develop new military technology for the Soviet Union. The purpose of this initiative was to review patents around the world to discern new military opportunities. Altshuller found certain distinct principles that could be used to solve certain distinct problems. He subsequently developed a matrix linking 40 common problems or contradictions and specifying the principles used to resolve these contradictions. TRIZ (TIPS) is, therefore, being used by companies to identify potential principles for resolving technical contradictions. Note that TRIZ does not offer a specific solution but rather a class of solutions, which the company needs to investigate. In the case of the contradiction between "time between sharpenings" and "lead dust generated," it is possible to classify the first as a "time of action of a stationary object" problem and the second as an "amount of substance" problem. Resolving a contradiction between these two problem areas may be achieved by looking at the principles of local quality, transformation properties, and porous materials. Local quality principles encompass considerations that (a) an object or outside environment can make a transition from homogeneous to heterogeneous structure, (b) different parts of an object should carry out different functions, and (c) each part of an object should be placed in conditions that are most favorable for its operation. Principles of transformation properties encompass (a) changing the physical state of the system,

(b) changing the concentration or density, (c) changing the degree of flexibility, and (d) changing the temperature or volume. And porous materials principles include (a) making an object porous, or using supplementary porous elements (inserts, covers, etc.) and (b) if an object is already porous, filling pores in advance with some substance. Based on these principles and their elements, a possible solution to the contradiction may be conceived. This briefly illustrates how the TRIZ methodology can be applied. See Altshuller (1997) for further reading.

The Kano Model

Another consideration in performing the QFD methodology is to go beyond developing products that just satisfy customers' needs to develop products that delight customers. Based on the Kano model proposed by Dr. Noriaki Kano in the 1980s, three types of product attributes or features can be designed into a product to satisfy customers and to work toward delighting them: assumed features, expected features, and delighting features. As shown in Exhibit 7.5, the degree to which assumed features, expected features, and delighting features are incorporated into a product will have different effects on customer satisfaction.

Assumed features are basic product attributes that customers equate with the particular product. As shown, assumed features do not drive customer satisfaction but rather minimize customer dissatisfaction. As more and more assumed features are designed into the product, a potential customer will be less and less dissatisfied but never satisfied.

Expected features are product attributes that are expected in the product. The distinction of expected features is that they have a linear relationship with customer satisfaction: If the expected features are better than customers' expectations, customers will be satisfied.

Delighting features are unexpected product attributes that surpass customers' expectations for what typically would be delivered in the product or service. Of course, such unexpected product attributes would need to be perceived as adding value to the product and not just being superfluous.

For a case example, the Kano model is applied to the service provided by the American Automobile Association (AAA). An assumed feature would be that if a customer calls for a tow truck because of a flat tire, AAA will answer the telephone and send out a tow truck for

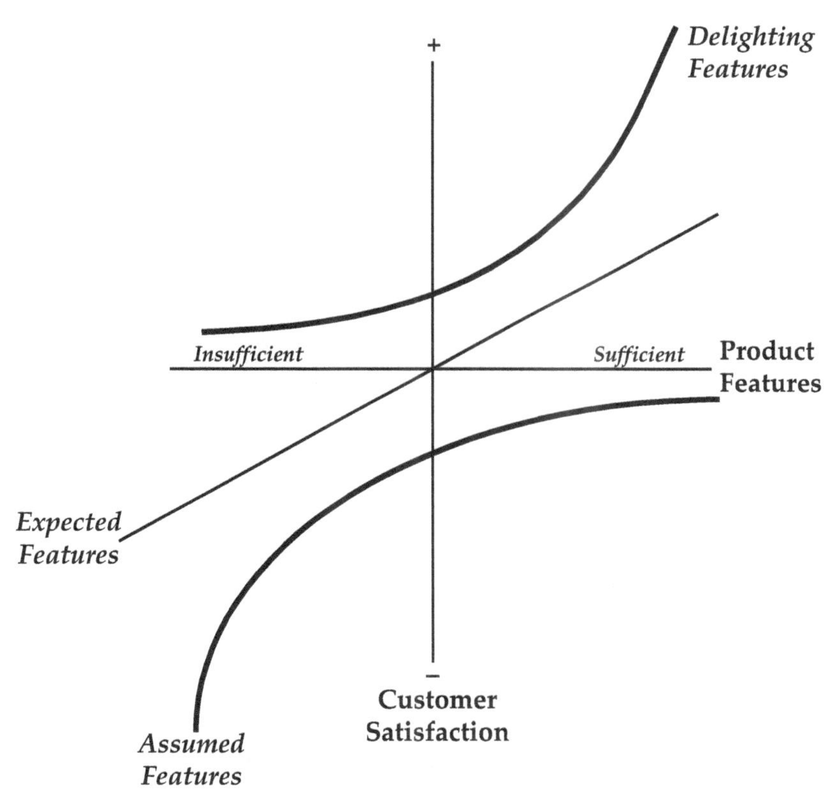

EXHIBIT 7.5. The Kano Model

roadside assistance. This is a basic service that AAA members pay for and would assume to be a standard feature. An expected feature would be the time in which the tow truck arrives to the customer. The sooner the tow truck arrives on the scene, the more satisfied the customer will be (as defined, expected features have a linear relationship with customer satisfaction). Naturally, the customer having a flat tire would expect the tire to be repaired (or the car towed for repair). However, if the tow truck personnel not only fixed the flat tire but, in the same time, washed the car and changed the oil at no extra charge, the customer would most likely be very delighted; this would represent a delighting feature.

An approach for incorporating the Kano model into the QFD methodology is to use sales points. That is, the weights of 1,1.2, and 1.5 can be used to represent assumed, expected, and delighting features, respectively. Determining which features are which would require a process of customer interviews, managerial judgment, and company experience. Note that in using the Kano model, features identified as delighting in a current version of a product may be expected features in the next version of product. Thus, it is recommended that only a few delighting features be used in each product design; otherwise, customers will expect or even assume these features in future product versions. It is also possible that building too many delighting features into the product may make it too costly for customers to afford.

■ PRODUCT USE TESTING

After the product concept becomes tangible, questions surrounding whether the product meets the given product protocol may arise. This includes the primary question of whether the product actually works. Product use testing (also known as use testing or field testing) is, therefore, employed to evaluate a product's functional performance and to examine the product protocol characteristics. Three specific types of product-use testing are possible.

Alpha testing: In-house testing where employees serve as the basis for testing. The advantages of alpha testing are that it is often less expensive, and competitors are not tipped to the new product. The disadvantage is that employees may not necessarily reflect customer views.

Beta testing: Seeing if the product works in customer operations. The basis for testing is, therefore, the customer site. The advantage of beta testing is that the customer provides insight into the product and its functioning. The disadvantage is that competitors can learn about the new product, and the sample customers chosen for the test may not necessarily reflect the total market.

Gamma testing: Longer-term test where the product is put through extensive use by the customer. Gamma testing is predominantly used by pharmaceutical companies due to the regulatory issues surrounding medicinal drugs. In most cases, companies will only pursue alpha and beta testing.

Overall, product use testing can be a beneficial exercise, even though there are risks. In particular, product use testing can provide customers' first impressions of the product. Being attuned to first impressions can help to ensure that the product is perceived as intended and is understandable to customers. Product use testing also can provide early use experiences and determine if the product is used as intended. In addition, product use testing can determine if the product is being used for unintended (possibly, incorrect) purposes and if there are inherent benefits that were not expected. All this information can be assessed, and a determination can be made of how well the new product meets the protocol. This information also can be assessed to help determine the potential success of the product and what is necessary for properly marketing the product.

Structuring a Product Use Test

Crawford (1997) provides a detailed structure for conducting a product use test. This structure contains five testing dimensions: test objectives, test group characteristics, product usage considerations, product form considerations, and measurement and analysis considerations. Prior to conducting a product use test, a written plan outlining the product use test by these dimensions would be beneficial.

The first dimension, test objectives, specifies what the company wants/needs to learn by performing the product use test. The focus of the objectives will be to include the elements in the product protocol. Other key issues not necessarily given in the product protocol but considered important by the development team or management should be listed, too.

The second dimension, test group characteristics, concerns test group composition, mode of contact, company disclosure, and degree of product explanation to be given. Test group composition involves the issue of whether customers and/or noncustomers should serve as the test group. Noncustomers could include experts, industry opinion leaders, and employees. Mode of contact includes the choice of mail or personal interaction, individual or group setting, and central testing location (e.g., in-house at the company or at a market research facility) or multiple testing locations (e.g., at customer sites or multiple market research facilities). Company disclosure would pertain to whether users should be given the company name and the brand. It is possible that such information may introduce halo effects. That is, users' perceptions of the company and brand name will bias their views of the new product. The last issue is the degree of product explanation to be given. Should customers be given the new product without any explanation of use to see if they can figure out how to use the product? Should customers be given a limited amount of information to start them? Or should full information be given? Degree of product explanation will depend on the objectives of the test.

The third dimension, product usage considerations, concerns the degree of control to be given to users during the test, number of usage exposures to be allowed, and duration of each product use experience. Degree of control pertains to whether the company should control the users' experience with the product during the test (e.g., a laboratory setting) or users should be given freedom to use the product as they wish. Related to this is whether the users' experience with the product should be supervised or unsupervised. Another consideration is how many exposures to the product should be allowed. A monadic test would represent a one-time experience, whereas a sequential monadic test would represent a series of single experiences. A third consideration is the duration of each users' experience with the product. For example, the experience could be timed, or the experience could be as long as the user wishes.

The fourth dimension, product form considerations, concerns the nature of the product to be given to users during the test. One issue in this dimension is the form of the product. Should the product be the best single product possible, or should multiple variations of the product be provided? Another issue concerning product form is the source of the product. Possible sources include engineering prototype, batch production, pilot production, and final production. Naturally, an engineering prototype may not be as refined as the product emerging from final production runs.

The fifth dimension, measurement and analysis, concerns the recording and assessment of test results. One issue is the mode for recording user reactions. Options for recording user reactions include paper documentation, audiotape, and videotape. With regard to paper documentation, some considerations are whether a standard form/questionnaire should be used or just note taking. A designation of whether the user or a test attendant will fill out the paperwork or talk to the audiotape or videotape needs to be made. Another issue is a designation of norms for the product use test. That is, the criteria for a good test should be designated, assuming that comparative information from previous product use tests is available. A final issue concerns whether measurement and analysis should be performed in-house or by a consulting agency (i.e., should the product use test rely on internal versus external expertise).

■ SOME FINAL COMMENTS ABOUT PRODUCT USE TESTING

Product testing does not always go as planned. Sometimes, customers/users will provide contrary evidence or even conflicting data. In response to this situation, product planners should not change the data just because results were not what they expected. Rather, product planners need to examine the data closely to determine what is wrong or conflicting and then answer the question why. More important, product planners should be alert to strange results. Such results might indicate that a problem situation exists.

In a few select situations, a product use test would not be performed. Reasons might be time pressures or a fear of alerting competitors to the new product. In such a situation, the company would naturally continue toward launch, but special attention would be given to constructing a thorough set of contingency plans in case problems did arise. Overall, some type of product use testing is highly recommended to proof the product before launch.

KEY CONCEPTS

- Product protocol
- Design for Excellence (DFX)
- Quality Function Deployment (QFD)
- Theory of Innovative Problem Solving (TRIZ/TIPS)
- Kano model
- Product use testing

Chapter Questions

1. What is the purpose of a product protocol?
2. What elements are recommended in a product protocol?
3. What is Design for Excellence (DFX)?
4. What are the general themes of the DFX philosophy?
5. What is the purpose of Quality Function Deployment (QFD)?
6. What are the components of a Voice of the Customer (VOC) study?
7. What is the purpose of the theory of innovative problem solving (TRIZ/TIPS)?
8. What three types of attributes or features are distinguished by the Kano Model?
9. What is the purpose of product use testing?
10. What are the important dimensions in setting up a product use test?

Chapter Eight

Market Planning

Another stream of activities within the technical development stage is market plan development. A subtle distinction between the present set of activities and those activities discussed in the previous chapter is that market plan development is not officially finalized until product launch, whereas, for the most part, the product's engineering design is finalized prior to initiating launch activities.

Market planning can be envisioned as a process involving two distinct sets of activities: the situation analysis and marketing mix development. The situation analysis involves an assessment of the 3Cs: company issues, competitor issues, and customer issues. Marketing mix development involves identification and integration of the most appropriate product issues, place (distribution) issues, promotion issues, and price issues. Together the 3Cs (company, competition, customer) and 4Ps (product, place, promotion, price) represent a framework for market plan development, where the 3Cs orient the 4Ps and the 4Ps represent the company's offering to the marketplace (refer to Exhibit 8.1).

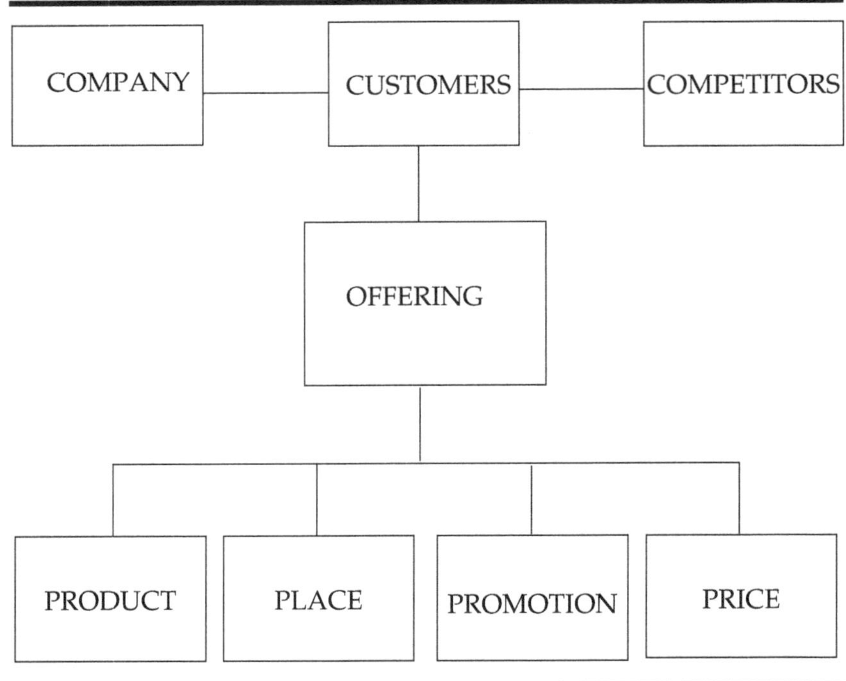

EXHIBIT **8.1.** A Market Planning Framework: The 3Cs and 4Ps

■ THE SITUATION ANALYSIS

The purpose of the situation analysis is to assess competitors and customers within a given marketplace, as well as evaluate the ability of the company to compete against these competitors and provide offerings to satisfy customer needs. Various types of analyses can be performed as part of the situation analysis, including an industry analysis, competitor analysis, company analysis, customer analysis, and sales analysis. Note that both internal and external data sources will be needed to properly conduct these analyses. A listing of possible external data sources is provided in Appendix A.

Industry Analysis

The purpose of an industry analysis is to assess the forces that affect doing business in a given marketplace. In this way, the company can

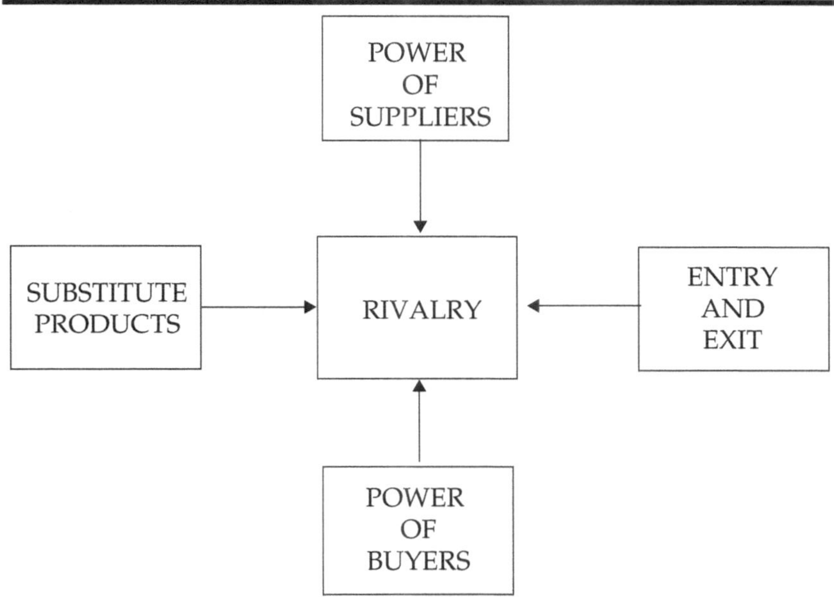

EXHIBIT **8.2.** Porter's Five Forces Model

determine whether the market is attractive enough to launch the particular product being developed.

One popular framework for conducting an industry analysis is Michael Porter's (1980) Five Forces Model. The five forces include the power of buyers, power of suppliers, threat of substitute products, barriers to entry and exit, and competitive rivalry (see Exhibit 8.2). In general, a more attractive market would reflect low levels of each of these five forces. The following characteristics are indications of high levels for each of the respective forces:

High bargaining power of the buyer exists when

- The buyer accounts for a large percentage of the industry's output
- The product is undifferentiated
- Buyers are earning low profits
- There is a threat by the buyer to backwards integrate
- The buyer has full information

High bargaining power of the supplier exists when

- Suppliers are highly concentrated (only a few firms dominate the market)
- There is no substitute for the product supplied
- The supplier has differentiated its product and/or built-in switching costs

High pressure from substitute products exists when

- Valid, similarly priced substitutes are available
- New and better technologies are emerging

High (strong) barriers to market entry and exit exist when

- There are economies of scale
- Products are highly differentiated
- There are extensive capital requirements
- There are high switching costs
- A distribution network is necessary for success

Intense rivalry exists when

- There are many balanced competitors
- Market growth is slow
- Fixed costs are high
- Products are not well differentiated

In addition to these five forces, an industry analysis should consider environmental factors and market-specific factors. An assessment of environmental factors would consider the technological, economic, social, political, and regulatory environments. The technological environment pertains to emerging technologies that could influence or replace current marketplace technologies, including product technologies and manufacturing technologies. The economic environment pertains to inflation rates and monetary fluctuations that could influence the market cost structure and/or customer demand. The social environment pertains to trends in demographics and psychographics (consumer lifestyles, values, attitudes) within the marketplace that would influence customer preferences and demand. The political environment pertains to the influence of local, state, national, and international politics on a company's ability to sell a product and the consumers' ability to buy the product; applicable taxes and tariffs are also considered. Related to the political environment is the regulatory environment, the laws and regulations under which a product is to be developed, marketed, and purchased.

Market-specific factors are factors that describe the nature of market demand for a given product and the nature of profitability in satisfying such demand. Several factors that should be considered include market size, market growth, market life cycle, seasonality, cyclicity, marketing mix drivers, and profitability. Market size concerns the amount of potential demand for the product, given in terms of potential customers, unit sales potential, and/or revenue potential. Market growth is the rate at which the number of customers, unit sales, and/or revenue will increase (or possibly decrease) over time. Market life cycle recognizes that the market is new and, thus, an uncertain market; growing and, thus, a booming market; mature and, thus, a stable but competitive market; or declining and, thus, a questionable market. Seasonality pertains to the distinct buying patterns within a given year, whereas cyclicity pertains to the possible repetitive economic patterns for a given market over 2 years. Marketing mix drivers indicate the sensitivity of demand within the given market to particular elements of the marketing mix, that is, a price-sensitive market, a promotion-sensitive market, a technology-driven features market, and so on. And profitability indicates the profit potential of the given market or the degree to which current companies are profitable in the marketplace. One way of suggesting profitability is to identify the current or potential margin rate.

Combining Porter's model components with environmental factors and market-specific factors, an industry analysis can be performed by indicating whether conditions on a particular factor are favorable or attractive for entering the market with the new product. As shown in Exhibit 8.3, attractiveness can be simply noted as a plus or minus for each factor. A market with a majority of pluses is more attractive and more opportunistic for the new product.

Competitor Analyses

In analyzing competitors, two types of analyses can be performed. The first is employed to identify immediate competitors and potential competitors. A second type can then be employed to assess the abilities of the most immediate competitors to formulate competitive strategies.

Market Factors	*Competitive Factors*	*Environmental Factors*
Size (+)	Power of Buyers (–)	Technological (–)
Growth (0)	Power of suppliers (–)	Economic (0)
Life cycle stage (0)	Rivalry (–)	Social (+)
Cyclicity (0)	Substitutes (+)	Political (+)
Seasonality (0)	Entries and exits (+)	Regulatory (0)
Financial ratios (0)		

With five + scores (favorable market situation), seven 0 scores (neutral market situation), and four - scores (unfavorable market situation), this market is attractive: The pluses outnumber the minuses.

EXHIBIT **8.3.** Evaluating Market Attractiveness

Identifying Competitors

One approach to identifying immediate and potential competitors is to consider four levels of competition: product form competition, product category competition, generic competition, and budget competition (Lehmann & Winer, 1997). Product form competition is the most specific view of competition, with competitors being those products/companies in the product category that are going after the same segment with essentially the same product features. Product category competition is a broader view of competition representing those products with similar features. Generic competition focuses on substitutable product categories, that is, those products or services fulfilling the same customer need. Budget competition is the broadest view of competition, where all products and services competing for the same customer dollars are identified as competitors. Aside from identifying competitors, the model can be used to identify potential complementary products as well. For example, bundling the product with a budget competitor may result in a better new product. Note, however, that identifying all budget competitors is difficult and complex due to the many potential competitors that may exist.

These four levels of competition are illustrated using the case example of videocassette recorders (VCRs) (see Exhibit 8.4). Assuming that the product being developed is a four-head VCR, its immediate competitors would be other four-head VCRs, representing product form competition. Product category competition would result from

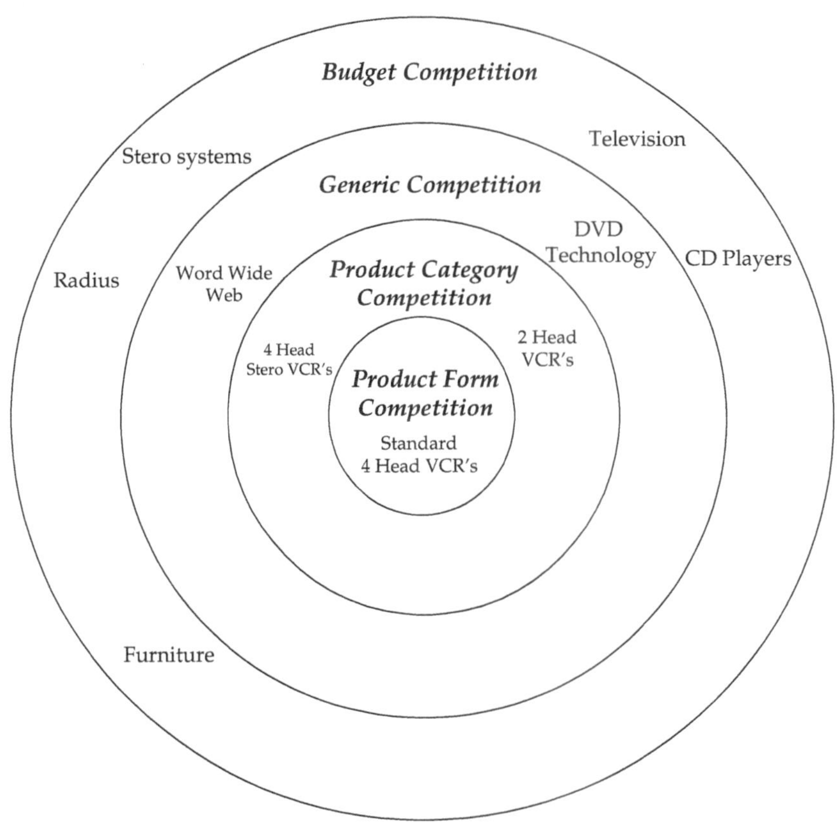

EXHIBIT **8.4.** Evaluating the Four Levels of Competition: A Videocassette Recorder Example

other types of VCRs, including four-head stereo VCRs and two-head VCRs (basically, all remaining types of VCRs). Generic competition would include DVD technology and World Wide Web applications—all potential substitutes for video recorders (although DVD technology presently cannot record). Potential budget competition could include television, stereo systems, CD players, radios, and even furniture; these all represent items that a potential VCR customer could buy with the same amount of money. Bundling product form and budget competition characteristics could suggest a potential product that integrates a television and VCR (which currently exists) or a full stereo system that includes a VCR (which also exists).

In addition to structuring competition, the four levels of competition can be useful in providing market definitions. In the VCR example, product form competition can be defined as a standard four-head VCR with the benefits of playing VHS tapes and recording television shows. Product form competitors would include other four-head VCR manufacturers, such as Sony, JVC, and Mitsubishi. Product category competitors would most likely be other four-head VCRs with additional features such as stereo and higher quality recording. The benefits at the product category level would be higher quality playing and recording capabilities. Generic competition would most likely be DVD players for an advanced movie-watching audience desiring a movie theater-quality television experience. By going through this exercise of creating definitions and establishing benefits, a greater understanding of the market may be achieved. It is acknowledged that the VCR example is fairly intuitive. In other markets, creating distinct definitions may not be so easy for the lines between products/ services are not as clear. A second point is that the process of arriving at a market definition is subjective in nature, and thus, different individuals (work teams) may arrive at different market definitions and identified benefits. Nevertheless, arriving at a market definition is important, for it provides a basis on which the company can build a market plan and launch the product.

After defining the market, it is also valuable to consider how different market segments may appeal to different competitors. In this way, it may be found that what seems to be an immediate competitor is not in fact. For illustrative purposes, the market segments of college students, single with income, double income with no kids, and families are identified in Exhibit 8.5. As shown, among college students and families, the standard four-head VCR would compete against other four-head VCRs, but not DVD. However, DVDs would be more of a competitor in higher-income markets, for example, single-income households and double-income households with no kids. Constructing a table like the one in Exhibit 8.5 may be based on analytical market research or managerial intuition. Again, the value in undertaking this exercise is to provide market understanding and a basis on which the company can build a market plan and launch the product.

Assessing Competitor Abilities

Once a set of immediate and potential competitors is identified, an assessment of their abilities should be undertaken to determine their

	College Students	Singles	Married (No Children)	Families
Standard four-head VCR	x			x
Other four-head VCRs	x	x	x	x
DVD		x	x	

EXHIBIT 8.5. Competition Across Market Segments

threat to the company. One approach is proposed by Lehmann and Winer (1997), who put forth the following five types of abilities:

- The ability to conceive and design (patent issues, research labs capabilities, R&D funding, technology strategy, development capabilities)
- The ability to produce (manufacturing capabilities, process flexibility, suppliers, plant locations, economies of scale)
- The ability to market (distribution network, advertising effectiveness, sales force effectiveness, marketing budget, customer service)
- The ability to manage (corporate culture, decision-making capabilities, number of employees, top management reputation, level of bureaucracy)
- The ability to finance (long-term debt, short-term debt, liquidity, profitability, revenue)

In a fashion similar to the previous industry analysis, pluses and minuses can be used across criteria associated with each-of the above abilities to determine the strengths and weaknesses of a particular competitor. Exhibit 8.6 illustrates a case example. Again, company intuition and judgment are elements of this analysis.

Company Analysis

While a company is assessing competitors, Lehmann and Winer (1997) recommend that the company also evaluate itself on the list of abilities to see how it compares against competitors. Based on this assessment, strategies for marketing the product can be detailed capital-

	Competitor A	*Competitor B*	*The Company*
Ability to conceive and design	+	+	0
Ability to produce	0	0	+
Ability to finance	0	0	–
Ability to market	+	+	0
Ability to manage	–	–	+

Based on this assessment, there appears to be some degree of parity in the marketplace across the five types of abilities.

EXHIBIT 8.6. Assessing Competitor Abilities

izing on company strengths and minimizing company weaknesses. This is one way of analyzing the company.

A broader analysis can be achieved with a SWOT (strengths, weaknesses, opportunities, threats) analysis. As implied by the name, the SWOT analysis identifies areas on which to capitalize and other areas to avoid. Thus, the SWOT analysis goes beyond delineating a company's abilities by pointing out potential opportunities and threats presented by these abilities (or lack of abilities). (See Exhibit 8.7.)

Customer Analysis

The purpose of a customer analysis is to clarify the market segments and identify the target market(s) for the product being developed. This analysis is critical to market plan development because any marketing plan is predicated on serving a target market. Failure to identify a segment and then a specific target market will lead to a badly specified (and in most cases, an ineffective) marketing plan.

Market Segmentation

The market breakdown structure proposed in Chapter 4 is one approach for segmenting the market. Other approaches range from judgmental techniques to sophisticated statistical analyses. Two approaches that fall somewhere in the middle are use of similarity

Potential Internal Strengths	*Potential Internal Weaknesses*	*Potential External Opportunities*	*Potential External Threats*
• Core competencies in key areas	• No clear strategic direction	• Serve additional customer groups	• Entry of lower-cost foreign competitors
• Adequate financial resources	• Obsolete facilities	• Enter new markets or segments	• Rising sales of substitute products
• Well thought of by buyers	• Subpar profitability	• Expand product line to meet broader range of customer needs	• Slower market growth
• An acknowledged market leader	• Lack of managerial depth and talent	• Diversify into related products	• Adverse shifts in foreign exchange rates and trade policies of foreign governments
• Well-conceived functional area strategies	• Missing key skills or competencies	• Vertical integration (forward or backward)	• Costly regulatory requirements
• Access to economies of scale	• Poor track record in implementing strategy	• Falling trade barriers in attractive foreign markets	• Vulnerability to recession and business cycle
• Insulated from strong competitive pressures	• Plagued with internal operating problems	• Complacency among rival firms	• Growing bargaining of customers and/or suppliers
• Proprietary technology	• Falling behind in research and development	• Market growth	• Changing buyer needs and tastes
• Cost advantages	• Too narrow a product line	• Others?	• Adverse demographic changes
• Better advertising campaigns	• Weak market image		• Others?
• Product innovation skills	• Weak distribution network		
• Proven management	• Below average marketing skills		
• Ahead on experience curve	• Unable to finance needed changes in strategy		
• Better manufacturing capabilities	• Higher overall unit costs relative to key competitors		
• Superior technological skills	• Others?		
• Others?			

NOTE: These issues should be considered while performing a company SWOT (strength, weaknesses, opportunities, and threat) analysis (adapted from Peter & Donnelly, 1998).

EXHIBIT **8.7.** SWOT Analysis

and/or dissimilarity indices, akin to the methodology discussed in Chapter 5. These two approaches are easy to apply and can provide meaningful insight. In fact, these approaches can be employed to validate a market breakdown structure.

In the case of a customer analysis, the similarity index reflects the degree of similarity between customer attributes. Again, using the simple methodology previously discussed, key customer/market characteristics are listed, and customers are evaluated on whether they reflect or do not reflect these characteristics (this can be done in the presence of the customer or without the customer). Each customer is then compared with other customers to reveal the number of matched characteristics. The ratio of matched characteristics to total number of characteristics is calculated. A matrix containing these ratios is then generated to identify and group customers. Each group conceivably represents a market segment, or if specific enough, a target market.

An example is presented in Exhibit 8.8. Assume seven business copier customers are evaluated on the four characteristics of (a) downtown location, (b) high copier usage, (c) interest in service plan, and (d) single division structure. Yes or no answers to whether a respective customer reflected the given characteristic can be employed and provide a raw data matrix, as shown in Exhibit 8.8. Similarity indices for each pair of customers are then calculated using the given formula of number of matched characteristics divided by the total number of characteristics (refer to the matrix of similarity in Exhibit 8.8). Each similarity index between two customers would indicate the percentage of "same" characteristics: between the two. For example, Customers A and B reflect the exact same characteristics and, thus, have a similarity index of 1. Customers A and C have only two characteristics in common, a similarity index of 0.5.

The next step would be to group similar customers into segments. Given that the seven companies are current customers, these segments would potentially represent distinct target markets. Decisions concerning how to group customers can be made by use of a simple heuristic (e.g., group two customers if they are more than 50% similar) or cluster analysis (a sophisticated statistical analysis technique). Using the heuristic approach, three distinct segments or potential target markets can be identified: (A, B), (D, F), and (C, E, G). Note that use of a different heuristic can lead to a different set of segments. Thus, the heuristic approach is judgmental in nature with regard to identifying not only the segments but also what the segments represent. In the

Data

Customer	*Downtown Location*	*High Copier Usage*	*Interested in Service Plan*	*Single Division*
A	*Y*	*N*	*Y*	*Y*
B	*Y*	*N*	*Y*	*Y*
C	*N*	*N*	*Y*	*N*
D	*Y*	*N*	*N*	*Y*
E	*Y*	*N*	*Y*	*N*
F	*Y*	*N*	*N*	*Y*
G	*Y*	*N*	*Y*	*N*

Similarity Matrix

	A	B	C	D	E	F
A						
B	1					
C	0.5	0.5				
D	0.75	0.75	0.25			
E	0.75	0.75	0.75	0.5		
F	0.75	0.75	0.25	1	0.5	
G	0.75	0.75	0.75	0.5	1	0.5

Similarity Groupings
Customer Segment 1: A, B
Customer Segment 2: D, F
Customer Segment 3: C, E, G

EXHIBIT **8.8.** Market Segmentation Using Similarity Analysis

current example, it is speculated that (A, B) represent customers interested in a service plan, (D, F) represent customers not interested in a service plan, and (C, E, G) represent customers that are multidivision enterprises interested in a service plan. The benefit of segmentation is to give insight into how to tailor a marketing plan to best serve the needs of customers. These results, therefore, suggest three separate plans: one targeted at satisfying single division firms interested in a service plan, one targeted at satisfying single division firms *not* interested in a service plan, and a third targeted at satisfying multiple division firms interested in a service plan.

A second approach to segmentation is the dissimilarity index. The simple methodology of listing key quantitative, demographic information about customers (again, this can be done with the customer or without the customer), standardizing the data, and then calculating Euclidean distances is employed to calculate the distance or dissimilarity between customers. A matrix containing dissimilarity indices is then constructed so similar customers can be identified and grouped together. Each group would then conceivably represent a market segment, or if specific enough, a target market.

For example, assume four business copier customers are evaluated on the three characteristics of (a) number of years in business, (b) distance from downtown, and (c) number of copiers used in business. The raw data are presented in Exhibit 8.9 along with the subsequent dissimilarity indices based on standardized data and Euclidean distance. The next step is to group customers with low dissimilarity ratings into segments. Once again, because the four companies are current customers, these segments would potentially represent distinct target markets. Also, as with the similarity indices matrix, decisions concerning how to group customers can be made by use of a simple heuristic (e.g., group two customers if their dissimilarity index is less than 2) or cluster analysis (a sophisticated statistical analysis technique). Using the heuristic approach, three distinct segments or potential target markets are identified: (A, D), (B), and (C). (A, D) appear to represent companies that have been in business for 20 years and have five copiers. B represents companies away from downtown. And C represents downtown companies in business for 21 years with four copiers. Again, the use of a different heuristic could lead to a different classification of customers.

Characterizing the Market

After distinct market segments are identified, it is necessary to describe each of the segments and establish a profile. Lehmann and Winer (1997) offer eight general questions that are useful in establishing such a profile:

Original Data

Customer	*Age of Business (Years)*	*Distance (Miles) From Downtown*	*Number of Copiers Used in Business*
A	20	1	5
B	21	5	3
C	21	0	4
D	20	0	5
Average	20.5	1.5	4.25
Standard Deviation	0.577	2.380	0.957

Standardized Data

Customer	*Age of Business (Years)*	*Distance (Miles) From Downtown*	*Number of Copiers Used in Business*
A	–1.73	–0.42	1.57
B	1.73	2.94	–2.61
C	1.73	–1.26	–0.52
D	–1.73	–1.26	1.57

Dissimilarity Matrix[a]

	A	B	C
A			
B	6.38		
C	4.13	4.69	
D	0.84	6.86	4.05

Groupings:
Customer Segment 1: A, D
Customer Segment 2: B
Customer Segment 3: C

a. Euclidean distance formula $= \sqrt{(x_1 - x_2)^2 + (y_1 - y_2)^2 + (z_1 - z_2)^2}$

EXHIBIT **8.9.** Market Segmentation Using Dissimilarity Analysis

Who is the customer and user? Use demographics (gender, age, education, income, and so on) and psychographics (lifestyles, attitudes, and so on) to construct customer and user profiles.

What does the customer buy? Assess important product/service characteristics and typical quantity purchased.

Where does the customer buy? List and describe purchase locations.

When does the customer buy? Discover and analyze the time of day/week/month/year when purchases are made, as well as special situations surrounding when a purchase is made (e.g., on sale versus regular price).

How does the customer choose to buy what they buy? Identify key elements of the customer decision-making process like opinion leaders, purchase influences, and information sources.

What is value to the customer? Learn what benefits customers are seeking and how they link these benefits to product/service attributes.

Will a customer buy again and why? Determine the likelihood of repurchase by examining customer satisfaction drivers, customer complaints, and repurchase drivers.

Are customers sensitive to marketing mix elements? If yes, which ones? Examine customer sensitivity to product issues, distribution issues, promotion issues (including advertising, publicity, sales force, and special promotions), and price.

Answering these eight questions will help to identify which market segments (target markets) are most favorable and, thus, should be pursued. In addition, answering these eight questions should help identify the marketing mix activities that will be important to driving market awareness, market acceptance, and purchase.

Sales Analysis

Unlike the previous analyses, a sales analysis is focused on intracompany data. Specifically, a sales analysis examines sales of existing products to identify demand patterns. A sales analysis also can pinpoint profitable versus less profitable products.

Companies can undertake various analyses of sales data. One analysis is to investigate the demand history of products to ascertain their average level of sales, sales variability, sales trend (upward/growing sales or downward/declining sales), and sales seasonality.

Such an analysis can be based on statistical analysis of a time series of data, that is, typically, a stream of 2 to 3 years (or longer) of monthly sales product data. The mean or average can be calculated on the data time series to indicate the sales level; standard deviation and coefficient of variation (mean divided by the standard deviation) can be used to indicate sales variability; a simple time series regression where sales are regressed onto time can be used to indicate trend; and the autocorrelation between month/quarters in a given year to previous years can be used to suggest possible seasonality Exhibit 8.10 illustrates various sales patterns as part of a sales analysis, including no trend, no seasonality (a level data pattern); trend, no seasonality (trended data); no trend and seasonality (seasonal data); and trend and seasonality.

A second useful analysis is to examine the margin per product. One way to conduct this analysis is to compare unit volume to revenue over time. If the pattern of unit volume is distinctly different than revenue, the company may need to investigate, especially if (a) the revenue line is decreasing while unit volume is increasing, or (b) revenue is decreasing at a faster rate than the rate of unit volume.

■ MARKETING OBJECTIVES

Having conducting the various analyses composing a situation analysis, it is necessary to outline marketing objectives and goals prior to framing marketing mix activities. The reason a situation analysis should be conducted prior to outlining objectives and goals is that such analysis can be useful in outlining appropriate objectives and realistic goals.

Objectives can be defined as general statements concerning what the company wants to be or achieve. Such statements can relate to financial criteria or nonfinancial criteria such as image, innovativeness, and market standing. The following are examples of marketing objectives:

- To be the market leader
- To provide technologically innovative products
- To remain profitable
- To continue to increase sales
- To stand out with customer service

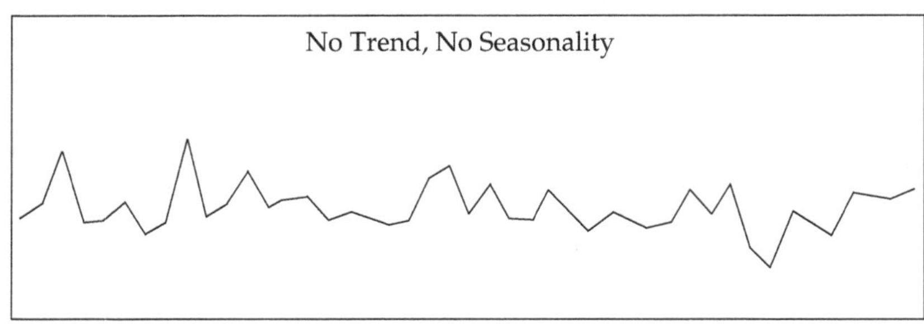

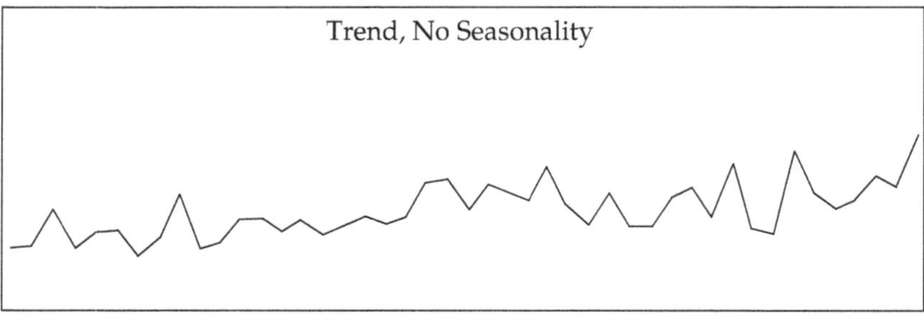

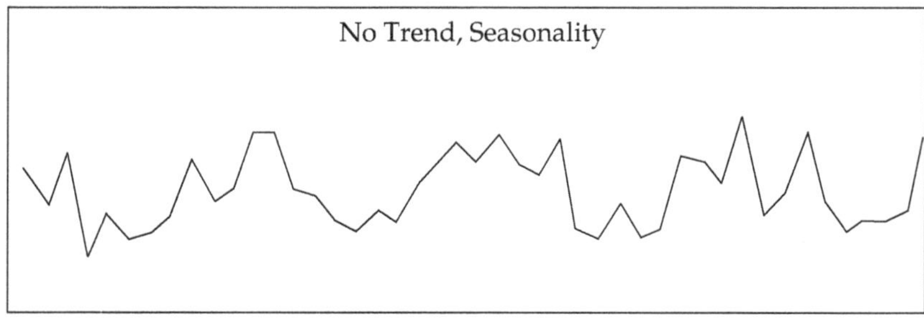

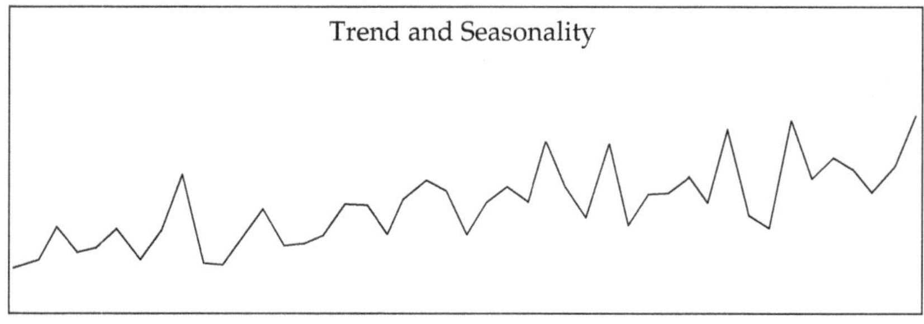

EXHIBIT **8.10.** Sales Pattern Recognition

Goals are similar to objectives and are very much linked to them. The distinction of goals versus objectives is that goals are specific, measurable, time-specific criteria on which the achievement of objectives is measured. That is, objectives are broken down into specific, measurable criteria that are given as benchmarks to be achieved within a given time period. The following are examples of marketing goals:

- A minimum unit sales volume of 100,000 units per quarter
- A 10% increase in year 2000 sales
- A 5% increase in customer satisfaction ratings
- The introduction of five new products by year 2001

Only when marketing management and upper management agree on the objectives and goals that will guide the product development project can work begin on assimilating appropriate marketing mix activities.

■ MARKETING MIX ACTIVITIES

The assimilation of marketing mix activities is called the marketing strategy process. This is because decisions concerning marketing mix activities have budget implications and, thus, strategic ramifications for the company.

The marketing mix, however, is only one element of marketing strategy. The other critical element is the identification of the target market or target markets to be served. In fact, identification of target market(s) must precede the identification of appropriate marketing mix activities. Failure to do so prohibits the tailoring of marketing mix activities and, in a broader sense, leads to an undefined or ill-defined marketing strategy.

Assuming that the target market is specified, four particular elements of the marketing mix need to be addressed: product issues, place (distribution) issues, promotion issues, and price issues. In general, product issues concern providing an offering that encapsulates customer needs and wants, place issues address availability of the product, promotion issues communicate the product to the customer, and price represents the cost to the customer. Many issues are conceivably associated with each of these Ps, as illustrated in Exhibit 8.11.

	Product	*Place*	*Promotion*	*Price*
Objective	*Customer needs and wants*	*Convenience*	*Communication*	*Cost to the customer*
Activities	• Variety	• Channels	• Advertising	• Price
	• Quality	• Coverage	• Sales force	• Discounts
	• Design	• Assortment	• Publicity	• Allowances
	• Style	• Locations	• Special promotions	• Payment plans
	• Brand	• Inventory	• Direct marketing	• Competition
	• Packaging	• Transportation		• Costs
	• Size			
	• Support			
	• Warranty			

EXHIBIT **8.11.** Marketing Mix Activities

Among the host of issues that deserve consideration, a sample of key issues inherent to each of the Ps are now detailed.

Key Product Issues

Positioning: The product's standing relative to other competitors' products, as well as other company products.

Product attributes: Product benefits, features, functions, and form.

Branding: Considerations of brand name, brand mark, trade character, trademark, trade dress.

- Brand name—A word, letter, number, letters, or group of words that can be spoken (e.g., Charmin, Sprint)
- Brand mark—A symbol, design, or distinctive coloring of lettering that cannot be spoken (e.g., Prudential's Rock, Traveler's Umbrella)

- Trade character—A brand mark that is personified (e.g., McDonald's Ronald McDonald, Disney's Mickey Mouse, Morton's Umbrella Girl)
- Trademark—A brand name, a brand mark, trade character, or combination thereof that is given legal protection
- Trade dress—The color of the product and/or its packaging, which distinguishes the product in the marketplace (e.g., Kodak film packaging is gold, Fuji film packaging is green)

Note that a good brand name should be recognizable, short, easy to remember, easy to pronounce, easy to spell, and markedly different from other similar products. If the intent is to eventually trademark the brand name, then, by law, the particular name cannot be immoral or misleading, cannot be too descriptive, cannot imply characteristics that the product does not possess, and should not be confusingly similar to any existing trademarks.

Packaging: Considerations of primary packaging, secondary packaging, and tertiary packaging for purposes of product containment, protection, safety, and display, as well as to assist the customer/user.

- Primary packaging—A product's immediate packaging (e.g., the bottle that holds the aspirin)
- Secondary packaging—The container for multiple units of the product (e.g., the box/carton containing multiple bottles of aspirin that the retail store receives)
- Tertiary packaging—The pallet or slip sheet on which multiple boxes/cartons are secured and shipped (e.g., multiple boxes/cartons of aspirin are placed onto a pallet; strapped, shrink-wrapped, or stretch-wrapped together, and then shipped to a distribution center serving individual retail stores)

Key Distribution Issues

Channel type: Consumer versus business-to-business.

Channel structure: Direct (manufacturer direct to the customer) versus indirect (through channel intermediaries).

Distribution strategy: Exclusive, selective, or intensive distribution strategy.

Exclusive: Offer the product in only a very few distribution outlets
Selective: Offer the product in more than just a few distribution outlets, but not all outlets
Intensive: Offer the product in as many distribution outlets as possible

Physical distribution/transportation: Physical distribution/transportation options include rail, motor carrier, waterway, air, and pipeline

Key Promotion Issues

Advertising: A promotional message paid for by a sponsoring organization. Key advertising issues include objective, theme, and media.

Objective: awareness, reminder, change attitudes about product use, change perception about importance of brand attributes, change beliefs about brand, attitude reinforcements, corporate/product line image branding
Theme: Creative message to be promoted via the advertising
Media: Newspapers, television, radio, direct mail, outdoor, magazines, Internet, and so on

Publicity: A promotional message *not* paid for by a sponsoring organization; thus, it is not under the control of the sponsoring organization. Publicity includes activities related to public relations, press relations, and government relations for purposes of awareness, credibility, and relationship-building.

Personal selling: Direct contact with the purchaser for purposes of prospecting for new business, information gathering, communicating with the customer, taking orders, and/or managing accounts. Key personal selling issues include the following:

Sales force organization: Decisions related to sales force size and territory design
Sales force responsibilities: Identification of sales managers and sales force supervision; sales force reporting structure
Incentives/bonuses: Compensation package; incentives to encourage selling of a new product versus current products
Support materials: New product literature (e.g., brochures, handouts), other promotional materials

Support staff: Account management, customer database management, sales force automation functions, other support resources

Special Promotions: A diverse set of customer incentives for stimulating purchase in the short term. Includes coupons, samples, point-of-purchase displays, rebates, two-for-one bundling, contests, premiums (gifts), and so on.

Key Pricing Issues

Pricing strategy: Premium, parity, or penetration pricing strategy.

Premium: Charge a higher price for the product for purposes of image or greater margin to recoup development costs (also known as a price-skimming strategy)
Parity: Charge a price that is equivalent to current competitors in the marketplace
Penetration: Charge a lower price to encourage higher sales volume

Bases for price calculation: Considerations of how the price will be calculated, including the product cost to the manufacturer (cost focus), range of prices that customers are willing to pay (customer focus), and current price of similar offers (competitor focus). Typically, all of these bases should be used in determining a product's market price.

■ ESTIMATING THE MARKETING STRATEGY BUDGET

The next step after composing the marketing strategy is to calculate the budget necessary to implement the respective strategy. This is important because, in many cases, what may appear to be the best strategy can turn out to be cost-prohibitive. In those cases where the budget exceeds management expectations, a process of weighing the costs and benefits of each marketing mix activity is undertaken to construct an acceptable marketing strategy.

The ATAR model discussed in Chapter 6 can be used to determine whether the budget is acceptable. Expected sales revenue from the new product can be calculated and compared to the budget in the form of a profit and loss statement. Obviously, if the budget exceeds the expected sales revenue, a revised marketing strategy is in order. This can mean one of two things: (a) a revised marketing mix or (b) a new target market and corresponding marketing mix. For example, assume that market potential is estimated to be 5 million, a 20% share is estimated, and the product selling price is $1.80; sales revenue is calculated to be $1,800,000. The corresponding marketing strategy to achieve this 20% share is estimated at $1,650,000, which includes $750,000 for advertising and promotion, $800,000 for sales force and distribution initiatives, and $100,000 for other marketing activities such as market research. Profit is, therefore, $150,000 or about a 9% rate of return on expenditures. Given this information, management would need to decide whether the estimated profit is in line with company policy and thus acceptable. Otherwise, a new strategy would be necessary, assuming that the company would still want to commercialize the product.

To help in estimating marketing costs, Exhibit 8.12 presents generic costs associated with various promotional activities.

■ MARKETING STRATEGY CONTROL

After an acceptable budget is constructed, it is necessary to determine the metrics by which the success of the proposed marketing strategy will be measured. This helps to track the product and ensure that the strategy is indeed on budget and on course to meeting objectives and goals.

Appropriate metrics to employ are ones that are directly linked to the given objectives and goals. For instance, if profitability is a key goal, then profitability, not sales revenue, should be tracked. In addition, how a particular metric is to be measured should be specified. So if market share is to be tracked, then a definition of market share will be useful, that is, total category market share, total subcategory market share, segment market share, and so on.

Overall, each metric should help in evaluating the performance of the respective marketing strategy across the given objectives and goals. If a metric is below expectations or a predetermined target value, then a course of action remedying the situation will be necessary. Action may include increasing the budget to emphasize a particular marketing mix element or revising the proposed set of marketing mix activities. If the product performs poorly across each metric

Marketing Mix Activity	*Cost*	*Advantages*	*Limitations*
Newspapers	$45,900 for one page weekday, *Chicago Tribune*	Flexibility, timeliness, good local market coverage, broad acceptance, high believability	Short life, poor reproduction quality, small "pass-along" audience
Television	$1,900 for 30 seconds of prime time in Chicago (does not include development cost of ad)	Combines sight, sound, and motion; appealing to the senses; high attention; high reach	High absolute cost, high clutter, fleeting exposure, less audience selectivity
Direct mail	$1,520 for the names and addresses of 40,000 veterinarians	Audience selectivity, flexibility, no ad competition within the same medium, personalization	Relatively high cost, "junk mail" image
Radio	$400 for one minute during commuting hours in Chicago	Mass use, high geographic and demographic selectivity, low cost	Audio presentation only, lower attention than television, non-standardized rate structures, fleeting exposure
Magazines	$126,755 for one page, four-color ad in *Newsweek*	High geographic and demographic selectivity, credibility and prestige, high-quality reproduction, long life, good pass-along readership	Long ad purchase lead time, some waste circulation, no guarantee of position
Outdoor advertising	$25,500 per month for 71 billboards in metropolitan Chicago	Flexibility, high repeat exposure, rel-atively low cost, low competition	No audience selectivity, creative limitations
Internet banner advertising	Advertising packages start at $1,000 to $1,500 and go up	Visual, high attention, high reach	High clutter, fleeting exposure, less audience selectivity

EXHIBIT **8.12.** A Sample of Costs and Attributes for Various Marketing Mix Activities (adapted from Kotler, 1997)

for a given period of time—even after several marketing mix revisions—this may be an indication that the product is poorly conceived and/or market demand has shifted, and the product should be removed from the marketplace.

KEY CONCEPTS

- Market planning
- Situation analysis: industry analysis, competitor analysis, company analysis, customer analysis, sales analysis
- Marketing objectives
- Marketing mix: Product, place, promotion, price
- Marketing budget

CHAPTER QUESTIONS

1. What two distinct activities make up market planning?
2. What factors should be examined during an industry analysis?
3. What are the four levels of competitors?
4. What types of questions should a customer analysis answer?
5. What are appropriate marketing objectives and goals?
6. What would be considered a key product issue? A key place (distribution) issue? A key promotion issue? A key price issue?
7. How should one construct and control a marketing budget?

CHAPTER NINE

COMMERCIALIZATION AND LAUNCH

At the end of the technical development stage, the developed product and its marketing plan are assessed. If everything is in order and approval is given, the product enters the last stage of product development, which consists of initiatives that commercialize and ultimately launch the product. Characteristically, this stage is called the commercialization stage.

Various activities will be undertaken in this stage. Market testing, launch preparation, and new-product forecasting are common activities.

■ MARKET TESTING

Market testing is used to evaluate the marketing plan. Although much of the marketing plan will be set, market testing is useful for refining the marketing plan to ensure that it is comprehensible to the marketplace. Market testing also can be useful for identifying problems in the marketing plan, which would lead to its revision. Feedback from market testing can be used to calculate revenue and unit volume sales forecasts as well.

In general, market testing can be broken down into three categories of techniques: the pseudo sale, controlled sale, and full-scale test. The distinctions between these categories are what is sold (or not sold) and the extent of the selling effort (exclusive versus selective distribution). The pseudo sale is not a real selling situation, whereas the controlled sale and full scale are. Pseudo and controlled sale market testing are targeted to an exclusive customer base, whereas full-scale market testing is a selective or even intensive distribution scenario.

Pseudo Sale

Pseudo sale market testing involves artificial selling situations that are akin to role-playing or hypothetical selling situations. Thus, the actual product is not available for sale. There are basically two types of pseudo sale market-testing techniques: the speculative sale and premarket testing.

Speculative sales rely on the sales force and are typically associated with business-to-business products. During a speculative sale situation, a salesperson approaches a customer, makes a full pitch about the product, and then sees if the customer would likely buy the product. Situations that are well-suited to the speculative method include

1. Where industrial firms have close downstream relationships with key buyers
2. Where new products are technical, entrenched within a firm's expertise, where little reaction is needed from the marketplace
3. Where the venture has little risk, and thus, a costlier method is not defendable
4. Where a firm has a tight patent
5. Where the item is new, and key diagnostics are needed

Premarket testing is typical of shopping mall intercepts, where a market research firm surveys shoppers at a shopping center or mall. Premarket testing is, therefore, more appropriate for consumer product goods and services. Typically, participants during a premarket test are asked to provide demographic information, answer various investigative questions, and provide feedback on one or more hypothetical products. Sometimes, advertising samples will be shown. The survey information is summarized and can be incorporated into proprietary market research models, such as BASES II, ASSESSOR, LITMUS, and ESP, to create new-product forecasts. Overall, premarket testing attempts to predict the likelihood of commercial success for a given new product.

Controlled Sale

The second category of market-testing techniques is the controlled sale. The distinction of the controlled sale category is that the product is available for purchase in an exclusive market setting. There are basically three types of controlled sale market-testing techniques: informal selling, direct marketing, and minimarkets.

Informal selling is typically performed at trade shows, where salespeople can show the product, informally approach customers, make the pitch, and see if the customer will actually buy the product.

Direct marketing focuses selling efforts on a particular market segment or target market; this segment or target market receives information about the product and has the opportunity to purchase the product. For example, some catalog shopping companies may add a new product to a special catalog that is only sent to a particular segment/target market; the response that this new product generates in this market segment/target market is evaluated. A variation on this approach is to use "vapor" products. For example, one shoe manufacturer adds high-resolution computer-aided drawings of new product concepts to its catalog—these renderings look just like photographs. The policy is that a new shoe will only be produced when a certain number of orders come in; otherwise, the customer is informed that the product is "out-of-stock," and another option is offered.

The third technique is minimarkets, where only certain stores in a specific geographic location sell the product and are supported with promotional materials. For example, when Black and Decker introduced a new version of its snakelight, only certain Ace Hardware stores supported by in-store advertising sold the product initially to gauge interest in the product.

Full-Scale Test

The third category of market-testing techniques is the full-scale test. This means actually selling the product in a selective or intensive distribution environment. Two techniques associated with full-scale market testing are test marketing and rollout.

Test marketing is mostly used to fine-tune the product and the marketing campaign. It is an extensive initiative where a representative piece of the market receives the total marketing program. In many cases, test marketing is applied on a city-by-city basis. One of the benefits of test marketing is that it provides an abundant supply of information and can verify production capabilities. However, test marketing is not without problems: It is expensive, competitors can affect results by introducing new promotions or pricing strategies, and there is always the risk that the test-market city will not reflect the behavior of the overall market.

The second full-scale technique is rollout, which represents an actual launching of the product. A rollout is when a subset of the intended target market receives the product; the company then slowly introduces the new product to other parts of the target market until the entire market is receiving it. In many cases, a rollout will be geographic in nature, with the smallest region receiving the product first, followed by other regions in a predetermined order, often smallest to largest. This going from smallest to largest regions allows production to increase gradually to meet the demands of larger regions and the overall total market. Serving smaller regions initially helps keep volume down and offers the manufacturing operation time to work any problems out of the system. Rollout, too, has risks: Full production capabilities must be ready, channel members must accept the product, competitors will respond, and rollouts tend not to get media attention to the same degree that national launches do.

Conceivably, the three types of market testing may be employed in tandem. The key in using each of the techniques is to carefully examine the market-testing results, determine if refinements or revisions are necessary, and then effect such changes. In sum, market testing will help to signal if the product and corresponding marketing plan is indeed market acceptable and ready for launch.

■ UNDERSTANDING THE LAUNCH PHENOMENON

Assuming that all signals indicate a "go," efforts to launch the product begin. These efforts can comprise a variety of activities, all requiring proper management. Overall, such activities aim to increase awareness, trial, availability, and repeat purchase—akin to the previously discussed ATAR model. Prescriptions for addressing these issues are as follows:

Get awareness: Let customers know about the company and what it is offering. A key way of getting awareness is through pre-announcing.

Get trial: Encourage customers to try the product, through promotions that generate self-interest or interest that is vicarious in nature (trying the product because others have tried the product). Barriers to trial that must be overcome include

- Lack of interest in the product
- Lack of belief in the product
- Rejection of something negative about the product
- Complacency about the product
- Competition
- Doubts about trying the product
- Lack of usage opportunities
- Product cost
- Customer loyalty to other products
- Customers' perceived risk of rejection or product failure

Ensure availability: Make sure that distributors, dealers, and resellers can offer your product to the market. Trade discounts and incentives are often used as a way to ensure availability in the channel.

Get repeat purchases: Encourage customers to purchase again, if possible. Promotions are popular mechanisms in the final consumer channel, whereas contracts may be useful for getting repurchase in business-to-business channels.

The ATAR model is an extension of diffusion theory (see Rogers, 1995), which offers an understanding of the launch phenomenon. By definition, diffusion is the accumulation of all individual adoption processes. Adoption is the process that an individual (or group/business) undergoes in making a decision about whether or not to purchase a new product.

Rogers's work indicates that, in general, consumers (individual or business-to-business) will go through a five-stage process:

1. Knowledge—The customer receives physical or social stimuli
2. Persuasion—The customer weighs risks versus benefits
3. Decision—Adoption or rejection by the customer

Note that there are two types of rejection: active rejection (when the customer considers adoption and may even try the product but decide not to adopt) and passive rejection (when the customer never considers use of the product; also referred to as nonadoption).

4. Implementation—The actual purchase and use of the product
5. Confirmation—Customers seek reinforcement of the innovation decision to reduce possible cognitive dissonance (i.e., second thoughts about the purchase)

Rogers's (1995) research has found that five key product characteristics can facilitate the adoption process, and thus, facilitate the overall diffusion process. The prescription is to consider how the new product can reflect these characteristics or how the characteristics can be integrated into the product design and/or marketing plan. In short, a new product needs to

Reflect a relative advantage: The new product must be superior to current product offerings

Have compatibility with the customer's environment: The product needs to fit with current product usage and customer activity

Minimize complexity: The product should be easy to understand and not confusing

Be divisible (Trial-ability): If possible, the innovation should be divided into trial samples; have trial opportunities available

Be communicable (Observability): The product should be easy to communicate, not only in terms of its promotion, but also in terms of customer word-of-mouth; it should be possible to observe the product publicly

Rogers's (1995) work also illustrates that adoption occurs at different points in time for different types of customers. Specifically, Rogers indicates that there are five types of customers with respect to adoption of new products: the innovators (or lead users as previously mentioned), generally composing 2.5% of the market; early adopters, composing 13.5% of the market; early majority, composing 34% of the market; late majority, composing another 34% of the market; and laggards, composing 16% of the market. (See Exhibit 9.1.)

These percentages can be useful not only for conceptualizing market segments, but also for estimating market penetration (market diffusion) of discontinuous innovations. For example, if forecasts for a new emerging technology suggest a market potential of 100,000 units, conceivably only the innovators and early adopters will purchase the

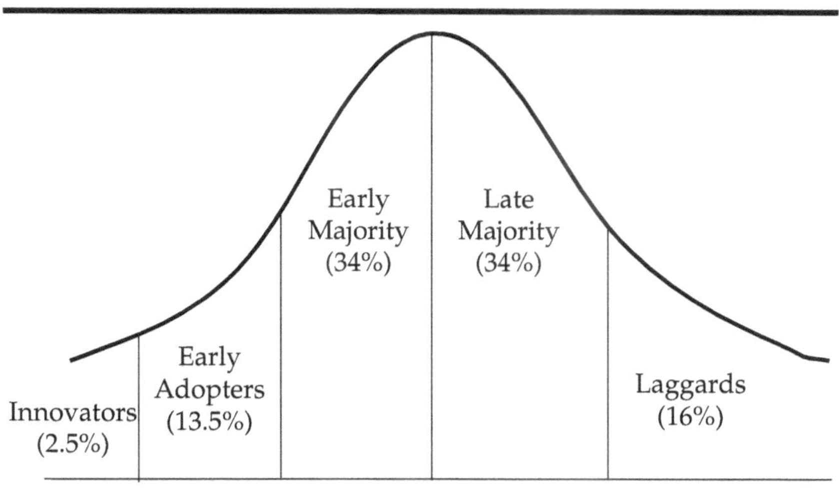

EXHIBIT 9.1 Customer Types Associated with Product Diffusion

product in the first year. Hence, market potential may be really only 16% of 100,000 units, or 16,000 units. From this, a company market penetration rate of 20% will only generate 3,200 unit sales.

Another way to look at these relative percentages is to total them and generate a cumulative percentage curve. As shown in Exhibit 9.2, this curve takes the shape of an S and, thus, is commonly referred to as the S-curve or diffusion curve. The purpose of this curve is to understand the rate of diffusion that a new product will have within the marketplace. In particular, it predicts the point in time when 50% of consumers in the market will adopt the product (50% represents a majority of the market, comprising innovators, early adopters, and the early majority). This point is called the *inflection point* or the point at which the rate of diffusion (market growth) is increasing at a diminishing rate. Prior to the inflection point, the rate of diffusion is increasing at an increasing rate. Overall, the S-curve is helpful in planning strategy on how to expedite customer purchases of the product to penetrate most of the market as soon as possible. In other words, the S-curve can suggest different scenarios based on different rates of diffusion and help identify which scenario is most preferred and most likely to occur.

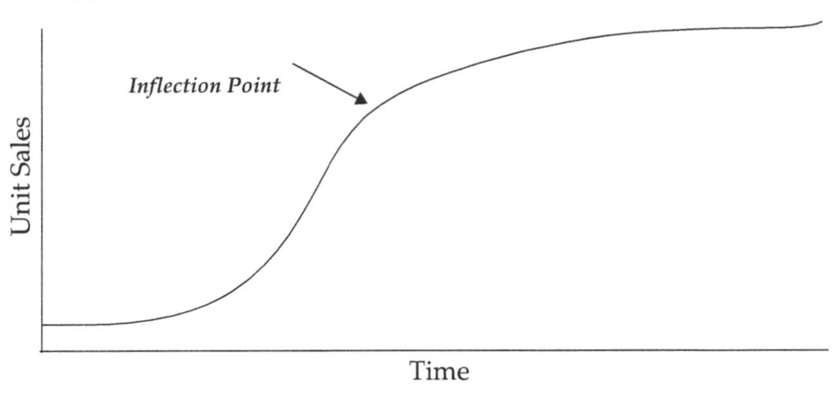

EXHIBIT **9.2.** The S-Curve

■ THE LAUNCH CYCLE

Assuming that all signals indicate a "go," the launch cycle begins. By definition, the launch of a product proceeds in four phases: (a) prelaunch preparation, (b) announcement, (c) beachhead, and (d) early growth. (See Exhibit 9.3.)

Prelaunch preparation comprises the activities that precede the point at which the product is officially offered for sale in the market. These activities typically include making pre-announcements (public company statements about the pending launch of the product), building marketing capability, establishing service capability, promoting the new product via public relations, and filling the distribution pipeline. Together, these activities have the purpose of building excitement and ensuring that the company is ready to meet market demand.

The second phase is announcement. Announcement is the point at which the product is officially offered to the complete market. With the announcement, all decisions are finalized.

The third phase is beachhead. Here, efforts focus on achieving market awareness and generating an initial stream of sales.

The fourth phase of launch is early growth. Usually, sales grow as interest in the new product grows. If sales are not growing, a decision needs to be made quickly. In general, there are five decision options: (a) increase spending, (b) revise the launch/marketing strategy, (c) revise the product (a costly, time-consuming, and potentially risky

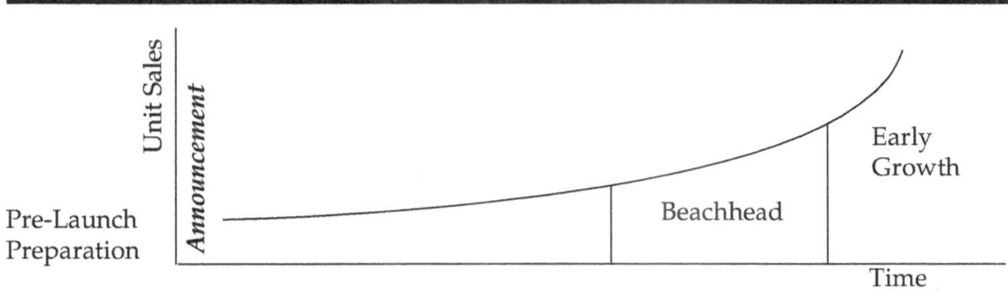

EXHIBIT **9.3.** The Launch Cycle

en-deavor), (d) pull the product temporarily from the marketplace (a risky option, which often does not to lead to success the second time around), or (e) abandon the product (given the amount of resources expended during the product development process, this option should be considered last). Note that Options 1 and 2 should be considered initially. If these two options do not work, then Options 3, 4, and 5 should be considered, with Option 5 representing the last resort/final option.

Prelaunch Preparation: Launch Control Protocol

One tool that is useful during prelaunch preparation is the launch control protocol. Like the product protocol during the technical development phase, the launch protocol is used to monitor and control activities during the launch cycle. Specifically, the launch control protocol identifies key deliverables or success measures during product launch. Such measures correspond to a variety of issues, including sales volume, profitability, market awareness, or other designated issues. Along with these success measures, the launch control protocol establishes trigger points to indicate when action needs to be taken. The launch control protocol further specifies what type of action should be taken to avoid unnecessary confusion during launch.

Constructing a launch control protocol is done in four steps. First, potential problems that might occur during a particular product's launch are identified. Three ways to identify such problems include reviewing the situation analysis from the marketing plan to outline potential threats, looking at the company's product launch history to indicate problems from previous product launches, and role-playing.

Role-playing, in which employees represent various channel members and competitors, is especially powerful for revealing problems. One company found that after several iterations of a role-playing exercise, a list of foreseeable problems had been created, and remedies had been established for these problems. As it turned out, the company was able to stay one step ahead of competitors because they had foreseen competitor responses and potential market problems.

The second step in a launch control protocol is to select the problems that should be monitored and controlled. Selection should be based on the potential impact of the problem on the commercial success of the product. Problems that could severely hamper success should be selected.

The third step in a launch control protocol is to design a system for monitoring and controlling each of the selected problems. To do this, it is necessary, first, to identify a measurable variable that corresponds to the problem. For example, if a selected problem is"sales lower than expected," two possible variables to measure would be unit sales volume or revenue sales volume. Thus, it is necessary to specify which variable is most appropriate to get at the selected problem: unit sales, revenue sales, or both. In addition to identifying the measurable variable, it is necessary to identify the trigger point for that variable. If "sales lower than expected" is the problem, what would represent a situation of lower than expected: unit sales less than 100,000 units? Revenue sales less than $1 million? The boundary at which a problem exists should be specified.

The fourth step in a launch control protocol is to develop remedies or contingency plans for each of the selected problems. Essentially, these remedies or contingency plans set out a course of action that the company can undertake in the event that the problem arises.

Exhibit 9.4 presents a sample of a launch control protocol. As shown, the problem of "overall sales lower than expected"is tracked by unit shipments, with the trigger point of less than 1,000 unit shipments per month signifying a problem. The remedy for the problem is implementation of an instantaneous redeemable coupon campaign.

During preparation of the launch control protocol, some consideration should be given to unforeseen and untrackable problems. Obviously, these will be difficult to conceive. In a good launch control protocol, contingencies (courses of action) are specified regarding what to do if something not specified in the launch control protocol occurs. In this way, the launch team knows ahead of time what can be done if something averse does happen.

Potential Problem	*Tracking*	*Contingency Plan*
Customers are not making trial purchases of the new product	Look at point-of-purchase reports; At minimum, 100 purchases per retail outlet are expected	Install point-of-purchase displays
Overall sales volume is lower than expected	Track monthly unit shipments; shipments of less than 1,000 per month signify a problem	Implement a instantaneous redeemable coupon campaign
Competitor has similar new product	Difficult to track, but conduct surveys with retailers and final consumers	Offer two-for-one program; consider bundling new product with other products

EXHIBIT **9.4.** The Launch Control Protocol

Plotting the Launch Process

Another tool that is useful during launch is construction of a path diagram to spell out the launch cycle. A path diagram portrays the activities to be undertaken during the launch cycle to assure that all activities are performed and that the launch is on time. A path diagram specifically illustrates the network of activities during launch, with each distinct activity represented by a node (circle) and the order in which these activities must be undertaken represented by arrows (the arrow points in the direction activities should proceed).

To construct a path diagram, all the launch activities to be undertaken should be listed. Next, the launch activities are organized into sets of activities, where each set represents the sequencing of activities within the given set. Those activities that do not need to be sequenced and/or are not predicated on any other launch activity serve as their own set. For example, 10 launch activities are listed: do pilot production, approve advertising copy, produce brochures, purchase air time for advertising, train sales force, procure raw materials, build initial finished goods inventory, hire advertising agency, prepare final production, and notify key accounts of pending new product. These activities are organized into three sets of activities and ordered accordingly:

Manufacturing-related activities: procure raw materials → pilot production → prepare final production → build initial finished goods inventory

Promotion-related activities: hire advertising agency → approve advertising copy →purchase air time for advertising → produce brochures

Sales-related activities: train sales force → notify key accounts of pending new product

These three sets of activities are then combined into the path diagram presented in Exhibit 9.5. A key benefit of this diagram is to identify critical activities, which lead to other necessary activities. Also, the diagram helps to identify activities that can be undertaken in the event that a particular critical activity is not yet completed. For example, in Exhibit 9.5, it is apparent that hiring an advertising agency is critical to all promotion-related activities. However, a delay in purchasing air time for advertising does not prevent the company from producing brochures, which can occur simultaneously.

Once a path diagram is completed, it can serve as a road map for the launch cycle. A path diagram also can be used in two advanced forms of scheduling analyses: Critical Path Method (CPM) and Program Evaluation and Review Technique (PERT). Both techniques are similar in their logical structure; however, CPM is deterministic in nature. A specific time to complete each activity is given, and based on this information, a set of critical activities (called the critical path) is identified. In short, the critical path represents those launch activities where there is no slack time (scheduling flexibility); that is, these activities cannot be delayed, or the overall launch will be delayed. PERT is probabilistic in nature and provides optimistic, most likely, and pessimistic times of completion for a given launch activity and the overall launch cycle. Based on these times, it can be reasonably determined if the launch will be on time, early, or late. For more information on CPM and PERT, refer to the *Project Management Handbook* (Pinto, 1998).

■ NEW-PRODUCT FORECASTING

New-product forecasting techniques are another set of tools that are used during the launch cycle, as well as earlier in the product development process. During the launch cycle, a company's production and

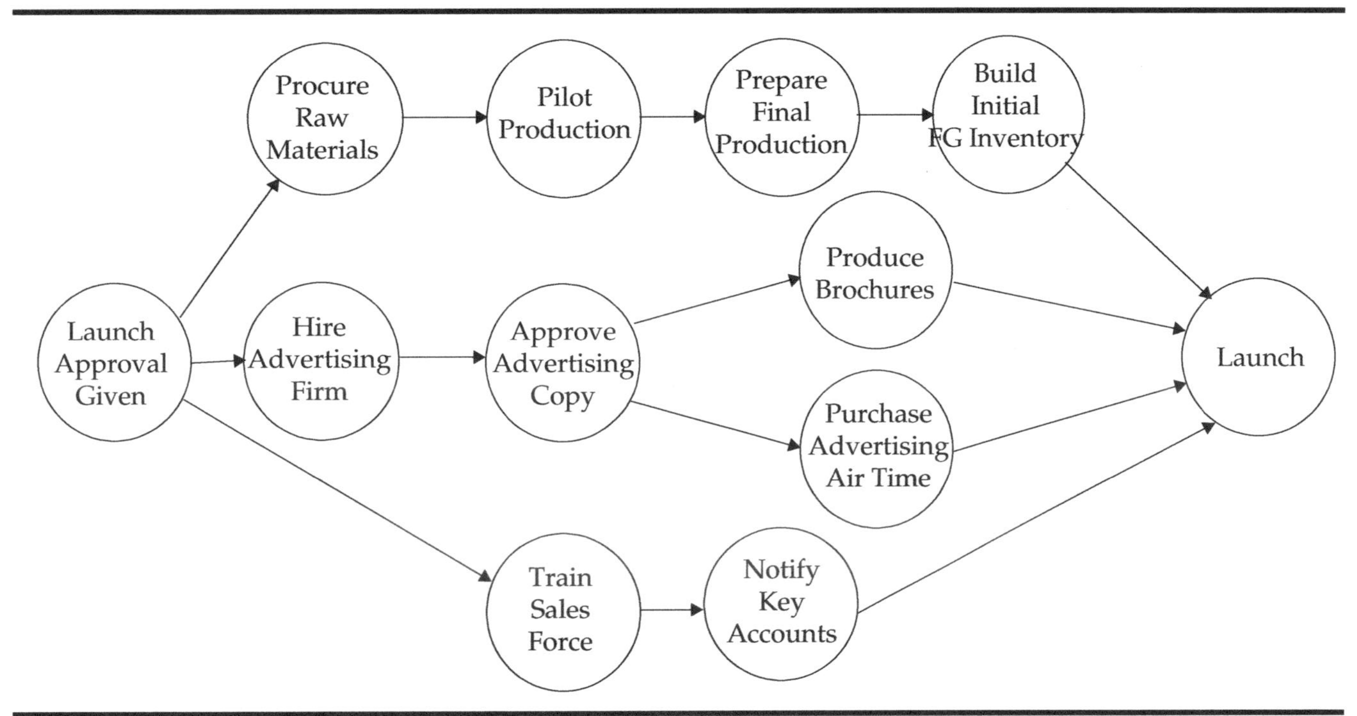

EXHIBIT **9.5.** Critical Path Model

distribution systems will use these forecasts to prepare for launch. Thus, new-product forecasts during the launch cycle should be as accurate as possible.

A variety of techniques are possible for new-product forecasting. These are listed in Exhibit 9.6. Based on a study that benchmarked new-product forecasting practices (Kahn, 2000), the more popular new-product forecasting techniques are customer/market research, jury of executive opinion, sales force composite method, and looks-like analysis (see Exhibit 9.7). In fact, these techniques appear to be used in similar ways, regardless of the type of new product.

However, when forecasting for new products in current markets—cost improvements, product improvements, and line extensions—companies tend to make greater use of trend line analysis, experience curves, moving average, exponential smoothing techniques, and regression, all of which require some degree of product sales history and/or existing market data. When forecasting for new markets—market extensions, new category entries, and new-to-the-world products—companies tend to make greater use of the market analysis model, scenario analysis, and simulation, all of which are useful what-if analytical tools. Overall, it would appear that whereas some companies take analytical steps toward understanding the market, most companies still prefer to use less sophisticated forecasting techniques.

Further analysis, however, indicates that the companies satisfied with their new-product forecasting process employ more analytical techniques for new-product forecasting and conduct a greater degree of customer/market research (see Exhibit 9.8). In addition, companies satisfied with their new-product forecasting process are less likely to be solely reliant on qualitative techniques such as jury of executive opinion, looks-like analysis, and sales force composite method.

It is important to realize that even with multiple techniques, new-product forecasting is typically not accurate. Indeed, many forecasters attribute high forecast error (low forecast accuracy) to having minimal data on which to develop a forecast and limited time for analysis. Benchmarking of new-product forecasting practices (Kahn, 2000) indicates that the average new-product forecasting accuracy is 57%, with cost improvement and product improvement forecasts 65% accurate, line extensions 61% accurate, market extensions 54% accurate, and new-to-the-company/new-to-the-world products 46% accurate (see Exhibit 9.9). The average forecast horizons for these forecasts are 19 months for cost improvements/product improvements, 21 months for line extensions, 21 months for market extensions, and 36 months for new-to-the-company/new-to-the-world.

Box-Jenkins techniques: Box-Jenkins techniques represent a set of advanced statistical approaches to forecasting that incorporate key elements of both time series and regression model building. Three basic activities (or stages) are considered: (a) identifying the model, (b) determining the model's parameters, and (c) testing/applying the model. Critical in using any Box-Jenkins technique is understanding the concepts of autocorrelation and differencing.

Customer/market research: Customer/market research represents typical market research activities. Customer feedback on current and/or new products is collected to forecast customer demand patterns.

Decision trees: Decision trees are a probabilistic approach to forecasting. Various contingencies and their associated probability of occurring are determined. Conditional probabilities are then calculated, and the most probable events are identified.

Delphi method: The Delphi forecasting method is based on subjective expert opinion gathered through several structured and anonymous rounds of written interviews. After each successive round, consolidated feedback is given to the respondents, and the forecast is further refined. The objective of the Delphi method is to capture the advantages of multiple experts in a committee, while minimizing the effects of social pressure to agree with the majority, ego pressure to stick with one's original forecast despite new information, the influence of a repetitive argument, and the influence of a dominant individual.

Diffusion models: Diffusion models estimate the growth rate of product Sales by considering various factors that influence consumers adopting a product. These models are typically employed for new-product forecasting.

Experience curves: Forecasting using experience curves assumes that as the cumulative production volume for a product rises, the cost of producing each unit falls according to a predictable curve. The slope of the line depends on the nature of the product and the manufacturing process.

Expert systems: Expert systems are typically computer-based heuristics or rules for forecasting. These rules are determined by interviewing forecasting experts and then constructing "if-then" statements. Forecasts are generated by going through the various applicable if-then statements until all statements have been considered:

Exponential smoothing techniques: Exponential smoothing techniques, develop forecasts by addressing the forecast components of level, trend, seasonality, and cycle. The weights or smoothing coefficients for each of these components are determined statistically and are applied to smooth previous period information.

Jury of executive opinion: This forecast is achieved by the ad hoc combination of the opinions and predictions of informed executives and experts.

Linear regression: Regression analysis is a statistical methodology that assesses the relation between one or more managerial variables and sales. As the name suggests, linear regression assumes that those relationships are linear.

(Continued)

EXHIBIT **9.6.** New-Product Forecasting Techniques

EXHIBIT **9.6.** Continued

Looks-like analysis (analogous forecasting): Looks-like analysis attempts to map sales of other products onto the product being forecast. Typically, looks-like analysis is employed for new-product forecasting to determine what new-product sales might be, given previous product introductions.

Market analysis models (ATAR model, assumption-based models): Market analysis models attempt to model the behavior of the relevant market environment by breaking the market down into market drivers. Then, by assuming values for these drivers, forecasts are generated.

Moving average: A forecasting technique that averages only a specified number of previous sales periods.

Neural networks: Neural Networks are advanced statistical models that attempt to decipher patterns in a particular sales time-series. In most cases, the models are proprietary.

Nonlinear regression: Regression analysis is a statistical methodology that uses the relation between one or more managerial variables and sales. Nonlinear regression does not assume that those relationships are linear.

Precursor method (correlation method): Precursor curve forecasting is a form of forecasting by analogy. A correlation is determined between the product to be forecast and other products. The product reflecting the highest correlation with the product to be forecast is selected as an analogous product. Once this product is identified, forecasts are made by assuming that the new product will follow the same pattern as the analogous product.

Sales force composite: The sales force composite method is a "bottom-up" forecasting technique. Individuals (typically salespeople) provide their forecasts. These forecasts are then aggregated to calculate product line forecasts.

Scenario analysis: This type of analysis involves the development of scenarios to predict what sales might be. Two types of scenario analysis include normative and exploratory approaches. The normative approach leaps out to the future and works back to determine what should be done to achieve what is expected to occur. The exploratory approach starts in the present and moves out to the future based on current trends.

Simulation: Simulation represents an approach to incorporate market forces into a decision model. "What-if" scenarios are then considered. Normally, simulation is computer-based. A typical simulation model is Monte Carlo simulation, which employs randomly generated events to drive the model and assess outcomes.

Trend line analysis: The objective of trend line analysis is to fit a line to a set of data. This can be done either graphically or mathematically.

Forecasting Technique	*Cost Improvements/ Product Improvements*	*Line Extensions*	*Market Extensions*	*New-to-the-Company/ New-to-the-World*
Box-Jenkins techniques (ARMA/ARIMA)	2	1	1	0
Customer/market research	33	37	37	51
Decision trees	6	2	4	7
Delphi method	6	5	4	7
Diffusion models	0	1	1	2
Experience curves	10	7	5	5
Expert systems	4	2	2	1
Exponential smoothing techniques	7	10	7	4
Jury of executive opinion	30	27	29	39
Linear regression	6	6	4	1
Looks-like analysis	17	22	20	25
Market analysis models (includes ATAR model)	5	5	6	11
Moving average	14	11	9	8
Neural networks	0	0	1	0
Nonlinear regression	1	1	2	1
Precursor curves (correlation method)	0	1	0	0
Sales force composite	26	31	26	27
Scenario analysis	6	8	10	14
Simulation	1	3	4	5
Trend line analysis	17	14	12	10

EXHIBIT 9.7. New-Product Forecasting Technique Use (Percentage of Respondents)

Forecasting Technique	*Satisfied With the Process*	*Dissatisfied With the Process*	*Statistical Difference at* Δ*.05*
Box-Jenkins techniques (ARMA/ARIMA)	3	0	Yes
Customer/market research	48	37	Yes
Decision trees	7	3	Yes
Delphi method	5	4	
Diffusion models	2	1	
Experience curves	11	6	Yes
Expert systems	7	2	Yes
Exponential smoothing techniques	14	6	Yes
Jury of executive opinion	24	32	Yes
Linear regression	13	3	Yes
Looks-like analysis	15	22	Yes
Market analysis models (includes ATR model)	9	6	Yes
Moving average	11	9	
Neural networks	1	0	Yes
Nonlinear regression	6	0	Yes
Precursor curves (correlation method)	2	0	Yes
Sales force composite	19	31	Yes
Scenario analysis	15	6	Yes
Simulation	11	0	Yes
Trend line analysis	15	13	

EXHIBIT **9.8.** New-Product Forecasting Technique Usage by Those Satisfied Versus Dissatisfied With Their New-Product Forecasting Process (Percentage of Respondents)

A better and more satisfying approach to new-product forecasting requires the following elements (see Kahn, 2000):

- Involvement of technical business functions such as market research, R&D, and sales forecasting in the new-product forecasting process

	Average Percentage Accuracy Achieved (Standard Deviation, Sample Size)	*Forecast Horizon in Months (Standard Deviation, Sample Size)*
Cost improvements / product improvements	65.09 (*sd* = 24.9, *n* = 74)	18.93 (*sd* = 14.8, *n* =90)
Line extensions	61.20 (*sd* = 23.1, *n* = 45)	20.70 (*sd* = 19.7, *n* =70)
Market extensions	54.10 (*sd* = 24.1, *n* = 42)	21.11 (*sd* = 17.2, *n* =66)
New-to-the-company / new-to-the-world	45.93 (*sd* = 26.6, n = 56)	36.11 (*sd* = 36.8, *n* =82)

EXHIBIT **9.9.** New-Product Forecasting Accuracy Achieved

- Customer/market research studies to obtain a view from outside the company and to provide customer/market information on which to base new-product forecasts
- More sophisticated, analytical techniques such as experience curves, exponential smoothing, linear regression, moving average, scenario analysis, and simulation in conjunction with qualitative techniques, such as jury of executive opinion, looks-like analysis, and sales force composites
- Good interdepartmental communication, especially with the marketing and sales departments

According to research, companies that are more successful at the new-product forecasting process go through a reconciliation of new-product forecasts based on multiple techniques, including both analytical/quantitative and qualitative/judgmental techniques. In addition, these companies recognize that new-product forecasting is an error-prone endeavor, and that expecting precision is not realistic. Consequently, companies more successful at new-product forecasting believe that a new-product forecast should be given in terms of a range rather than in terms of a specific number (Kahn, 2000).

KEY CONCEPTS

- Market testing
- Launch
- Diffusion of innovations
- The launch cycle
- Launch control protocol
- Launch scheduling: path diagrams, critical path method (CPM), program evaluation review technique (PERT)
- New-product forecasting

CHAPTER QUESTIONS

1. What is the purpose of market testing?
2. What are the different ways to conduct market testing?
3. What is the difference between diffusion and adoption?
4. What are the five stages customers typically go through in buying a new product?
5. What are the five key characteristics that facilitate the adoption of innovations?
6. What is launch? What are the four stages of the launch cycle?
7. How is a launch control protocol constructed?
8. What is the difference between the critical path method (CPM) and program evaluation review technique (PERT)?
9. What are the various techniques that can be used for new-product forecasting?

Chapter Ten

Life Cycle Management

After launch, the product begins what is termed the *product life cycle.* At this point, the product development team is no longer responsible for the product, and a product management team takes over (in many cases, this transition in responsibility takes place before launch).

The product management team focuses on the life cycle management of the product: that is, ensuring that the product reaches its full potential as a particular product item or emerging product line in the company's product mix. Associated with reaching this potential are decisions concerning fine-tuning the product's marketing strategy, defending against competitors, and continuously innovating the product, if feasible. Brand management considerations also persist after product launch.

■ THE PRODUCT LIFE CYCLE

The product life cycle is a concept that attempts to describe a product's unit sales postlaunch through its eventual termination. The curve parallels the diffusion or S-curve, suggesting product diffusion into the marketplace.

The theory underlying the product life cycle is that unit sales will move through four distinct product life cycle stages: introduction, growth, maturity, and decline (see Exhibit 10.1). The introduction stage represents the launch cycle. Here, sales slowly emerge as the company tries to establish a beachhead and then early growth. The focus of the marketing effort is to create awareness and get trial. During the growth stage, sales rise steadily, and the focus is to maximize market share. The maturity stage represents a leveling of sales and a focus on maximizing profit and maintaining market share. The decline stage is the final stage, characterized by decreasing unit sales. Correspondingly, the marketing strategy is to reduce marketing expenditures and harvest the product.

The product life cycle also can be used to describe the possible development of an emerging market. In particular, the framework suggests that competition will be low in the introduction stage but fierce during the growth stage, as competitors see the growth potential of the respective market. During the maturity stage, a reduction in the number of competitors through company mergers, acquisitions, and market departures will occur. Market share, at this point, is mostly determined, with intense efforts needed to make headway in securing additional market share. The decline stage represents a declining number of competitors as companies leave the market.

It is important to use the product life cycle concept as a guideline and not a definitive model. Various companies have inappropriately used the product life cycle, incorrectly determined that their product was declining, pulled resources from the product, and prematurely terminated their product. In one case, a toothpaste manufacturer saw sales decline over a period and concluded, based on the product life cycle, that the product was in the decline stage. Consequently, the company reduced the amount of resources going to the product, which contributed to a further reduction in sales. The manufacturer then sold off the product to another company. This company refreshed the marketing campaign, put ample marketing resources into the product, and grew the market (Dhalla & Yuspeh, 1976). It is necessary to keep in mind that

- The stages of the product life cycle, time span of the entire life cycle, and shape of the life cycle will vary by product.
- External factors can affect the performance of a product, which may shorten or lengthen its life cycle.
- A company can influence a product's life cycle.
- Events in the product life cycle can he a self-fulfilling prophecy; a tendency to believe something will happen may lead to doing

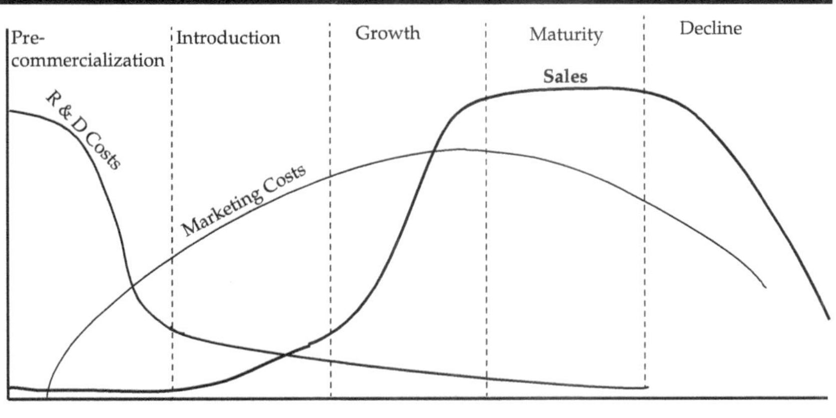

EXHIBIT **10.1** The Product Life Cycle

things that ensure it will happen; that is, if sales are expected to decline and the promotion budget is reduced, this, in turn, will typically reduce sales.

Another issue is the variations of the product life cycle curve, depending on the level of analysis to be performed. The product form and product class levels reflect a view based on, respectively, form and product type. The generic need level offers an overall industry view. For example, an herbal tea manufacturer can see three different perspectives when using the product life cycle concept, depending on the level of analysis that provides the focal perspective. From the beverage industry view, an analyst for the company may see a mature market. Using tea as the product class, the analyst may see a slight declining market. But at the herbal tea level, the market suggests a growth situation. This highlights a need for proper definition of the market to be analyzed and careful interpretation of the product life cycle curve.

Overall, the product life cycle should be viewed as a managerial planning tool and not a market forecasting tool. The product life cycle can provide insight into possible changing consumer composition, competition, and support requirements, as well as what may be a balanced portfolio based on these market dynamics. It should, therefore, be designated as a tool for developing strategy (see Exhibit 10.2) and not a tool for making unit sales predictions.

	Product Life Cycle Stage			
	Introduction	*Growth*	*Maturity*	*Decline*
Market Characteristics:				
Sales	Low sales	Rapidly rising sales	Peak sales	Declining sales
Costs	High cost per customer	Average cost per customer	Low cost per customer	Low cost per customer
Profits	Negative	Rising profits	High profits	Declining profits
Customers	Innovators	Early adopters	Middle majority	Laggards
Competitors	Few	Growing number	Stable number beginning to decline	Declining number
Strategic Considerations:				
Marketing objectives	Create product awareness and trial	Maximize market share	Maximize profits while defending market share	Reduce expenditures and milk the brand
Product strategies	Offer a basic product	Offer product extensions, service, warranty	Diversify brand and models	Phase out weak items
Distribution strategies	Build selective distribution	Build intensive distribution	Build more intensive distribution	Go selective; phase out unprofitable outlets
Promotion strategies	Build product awareness among early adopters and dealers; use heavy sales promotions to entice trial	Build awareness and interest in mass market; reduce sales promotions to take advantage of heavy consumer demand	Stress brand differences and benefits; increase sales promotions to encourage brand switching	Reduce promotion activity to the level needed to retain hard-core loyal customers
Price strategies	Charge cost-plus	Price to penetrate market	Price to match or beat competitors	Cut price

SOURCE: *Kotler*, 1997.

EXHIBIT 10.2. Strategic-Considerations Across the Traditional Product Life Cycle

■ STRATEGIC CONSIDERATIONS DURING THE MATURITY STAGE

In conjunction with any analysis that may be done using product life cycle, a company will need to decide on a strategy to enact late in the growth stage that will carry into the maturity stage. In particular, three strategic options may be enacted.

The first strategy is a maintenance strategy. This strategy focuses on fine-tuning the marketing mix to ensure product profitability. Thus, minor changes are made to the marketing mix to minimize marketing expenses to keep costs low and sustain a reasonable margin.

The second strategy is a defense strategy. With this strategy, the focus is on an issue perceived to be important from the customer perspective, for example, price, product quality, or service quality. In this way, the product differentiates itself from competitors by being superior on this important issue. A comment about this strategy is the great risk in using price as a differential advantage—price is the easiest marketing mix element to copy, and most of the time, someone is willing to match price.

The third strategy is an innovation strategy. This strategy emphasizes new products as a way to sustain a competitive advantage. These new products include flankers or line extensions, new uses/users or market extensions, and/or significant innovations (next-generation or new-to-the-world products). Note that product improvements are associated with the first two strategies. The flanker option is a common approach but can lead to product proliferation (too many similar products). The significant innovations option is a valid but risky endeavor because it makes the current product obsolete; however, the adage behind this latter option goes as follows: "If you're going to have cannibals, might as well keep the cannibals in the family."

■ PRODUCT FAMILIES, PRODUCT PLATFORMS, AND THE PRODUCT MIX MAP

Product families are a life cycle management consideration if the respective company decides to expand beyond a single product offering. Such a decision may derive from an interest in expanding width or depth of a product line or from an inherent need to introduce next-generation products to keep up with the technological pace in the industry. Moreover, once a decision to expand is made, consideration is also given to the notion of product platforms and product families.

Product platforms are typically an underlying basis for a product family. Product platforms provide a common foundation on which new products (line extensions or next-generation products) can be built. Specifically, product platforms represent the sharing of essential design elements and critical components by a set of products to make production, distribution, and service processes more effective and efficient. For example, Chrysler used the same basic car frame, suspension, and drive train for the Chrysler Concorde, Eagle Vision, and Dodge Intrepid, thereby reducing Chrysler's overall production costs. Chrysler later introduced its New Yorker model based on a longer version of the platform (Meyer & Utterback, 1993).

By definition, product families are "products that share a common platform but have specific features and functionality required by different sets of customers" (Meyer & Utterback, 1993). Thus, a product family can be conceived as serving a market segment or set of market segments, whereas the individual products within the family serve specific target markets within the segment(s). In terms of the product mix hierarchy, product families are an assortment of similar product lines that, in turn, include an assortment of similar product items. Similarity, in this case, would be based on the common platform used across the product lines, and each of the individual features and functionalities would designate the individual items within each line. The assortment of product families would represent the company's product mix.

The use of product families is driven by a need for greater effectiveness and efficiencies in the manufacturing process. Among other things, effectiveness and efficiencies stem from (a) less inventorying of specialized parts because products would share parts, (b) less production downtime related to production line turnover because products would share common processing steps, and (c) greater customer responsiveness. In the latter, the standard product platform allows staging of the production process so that some of the manufacturing process takes place up-front, and tailoring of the product takes place only when an order is received. Product families also offer the benefit of providing structure to a complex product mix. These or other reasons encourage use of a product family structure.

With respect to structure, mapping of the product mix can help identify product family groupings, identify gaps in product lines, and illustrate the product development history of the company. Product mix maps also can suggest core competencies of a company by linking the structure of the product mix and product successes, based on the assumptions that successes reflect where the company is strongest.

To build a product mix map, the company or a particular company strategic business unit (SBU) would list its current product items. These items would then be grouped according to product line. Taking each product line, the historical product offerings of the line would be listed in chronological order to show a perspective of product development for the line. This would, then, be repeated across the other product lines. Next, similar product lines could be grouped based on various characteristics to suggest a possible product family. Those products sharing a common platform would characteristically be a product family. On completion, the map would show the structure of the product mix and historical perspective of how each of the lines developed. Other data can be used in conjunction with the product mix map, such as market segments served by each product line, to offer a market perspective when assessing each potential product family.

Exhibit 10.3 presents an example of a product mix map for a hypothetical shoe manufacturer. The map shows an evolution of the product mix from an even distribution of business and casual shoes to a greater number of casual shoes, suggesting an inherent company focus toward the casual shoe market.

■ BRAND MANAGEMENT

A third area during life cycle management is brand management, which is being increasingly recognized as a key element of life cycle management as well as product launch. The driver of brand management's emerging recognition is the fact that the brand can help customers interpret and process information about the product, feel more confident in their decision to buy the product, and/or feel more satisfied after purchase. Because of this, brands offer much value to companies in improving the efficiency and effectiveness of marketing campaigns. As the product moves to other life cycle stages, brands can offer a strong competitive advantage, provide a basis for an improved profit margin, solidify brand loyalty, and assist in developing other new products via brand extensions.

Although simplified in the marketing plan discussion as considerations of brand name, brand mark, trade character, trademark, and trade dress, brand management is much more.

Brand management focuses on the establishment and maintenance of, if not growth of, brand equity.

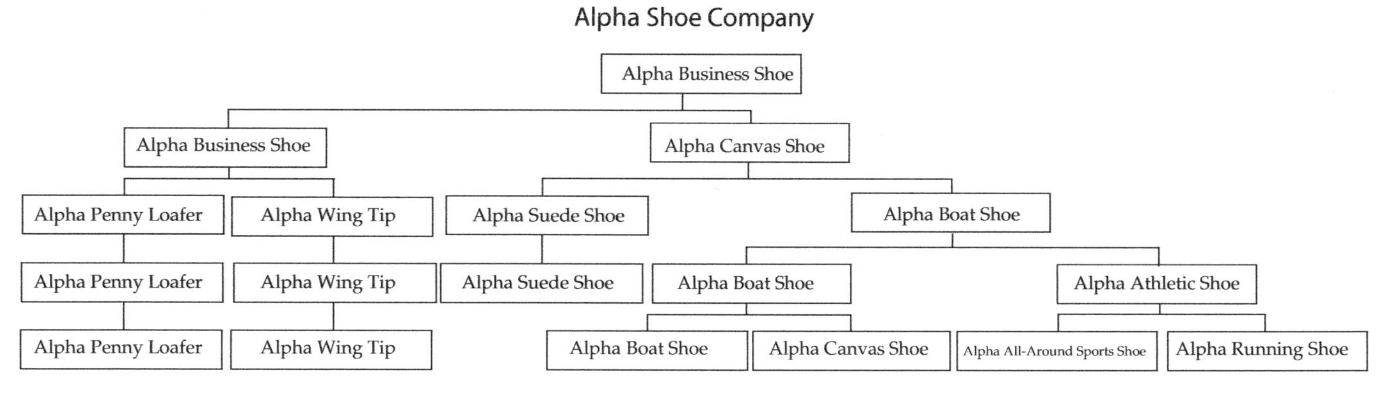

Exhibit 10.3. Sample Product Mix Map

As defined by David Aaker (1996), brand equity is "a set of assets and liabilities linked to a brand's name and symbols that adds to or subtracts from the value provided by a product or service to a firm and /or that firm's customers" (pp. 7-8). Such value translates to a bottom line (financial) impact. Indeed, the potential financial benefits of brand equity spurred the U.S. Internal Revenue Service in the early 1990s to consider the notion of taxing corporations on their brand equity as an intangible asset. However, the idea never materialized because of the complexity surrounding what brand equity is and how it could be measured.

A Brand Equity Framework

In his popular framework, Aaker (1996) says that brand equity is a function of five key components: brand loyalty, brand awareness, perceived quality, brand associations, and other proprietary brand assets (see Exhibit 10.4).

Brand loyalty is a measure of the customer's attachment to a brand (Aaker, 1996). Such attachment can be categorized into five distinct levels of loyalty. The lowest level of loyalty is no loyalty at all. These customers are indifferent about the brand and so responsive to price that they will often switch products based on price alone. The next level of loyalty comprises customers who have no reason to change because they are satisfied, habitual buyers. However, these customers will change if given a compelling reason to change. The third level of loyalty is satisfied buyers who will incur switching costs on switching products. These buyers will change if given a strong compelling reason, but because of the switching cost, they are less likely to do so. The fourth level of loyalty is customers who like the brand and consider it a "friend." At this point, customers are developing a personal relationship with the brand. The ultimate level of loyalty is committed buyers who buy the product despite any reason to change. Aaker recommends that to drive customers up to the higher levels of loyalty, companies must treat customers right, stay close to customers, measure and manage customer satisfaction, create switching costs, and provide extras to delight customers.

Brand awareness is the ability of potential buyers to recognize that a brand belongs to a certain product category (Aaker, 1996). Four distinct levels of awareness are given. The lowest level of awareness is no awareness at all. Basically, customers are unfamiliar with the brand. The next level of awareness is recognition of the brand. When

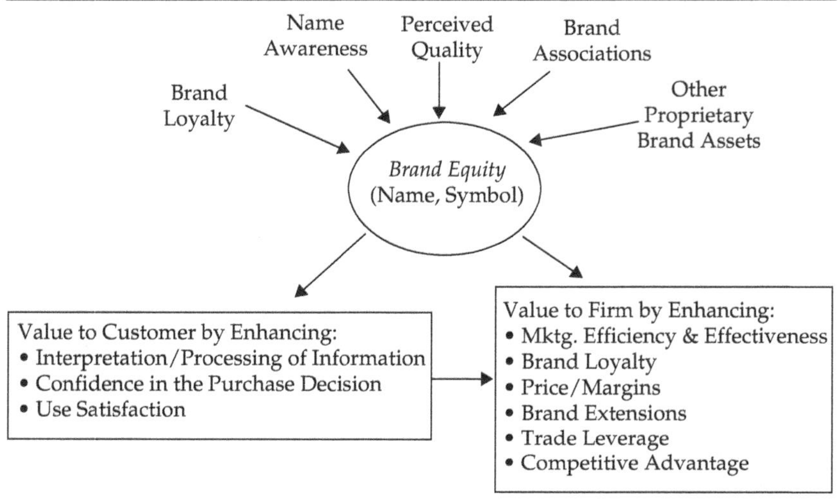

EXHIBIT 10.4. Aaker's Brand Equity Framework

SOURCE: Adapted with permission of The Free Press, a division of Simon & Schuster, Inc., from *Building Strong Brands,* by David A. Aaker. Copyright © 1996 by David A. Aaker.

prompted or cued, customers can remember what product category the product falls in after thinking about it The third level of awareness is brand recall. Customers can readily recall a product's category after just seeing the brand's name or symbol(s). The highest level of awareness is top of mind. When given a product category, customers will immediately recall the brand. For example, if asked to give a brand with the product category of cola soft drinks, a particular customer might immediately reply Coca-Cola. To create and maintain brand awareness, the brand should be different and memorable, associated with a slogan or jingle, connected to a symbol, regularly publicized, in full view at sponsored events, and used in conjunction with cues.

Perceived quality is the customer's perception that a product or service overall is excellent with respect to its intended purpose (Aaker, 1996). Perceived quality is portrayed as a continuum from low perceived quality to high perceived quality rather than as distinct categorized levels. The key influence driving perceived quality is product quality and service quality that meet customer expectations based on what the company says it is going to deliver. When expectations are not met, perceived quality will be judged as low; when met or exceeded, perceived quality will be judged as adequate or higher.

Brand associations are items in a customer's memory that are linked to the brand (Aaker, 1996). These associations would include personal experiences, promotion activities, and/or any other signal connecting to the brand. For example, a motorboat manufacturer conducted extensive market research to find underlying themes for why people buy boats. The company found that a segment of those interested in purchasing boats associated boats with the childhood experience of fishing with their fathers and grandfathers. This association was subsequently employed in advertising to elicit customers' favorable thoughts about how buying the company's motorboat would allow them to relive their youthful experience and share it with their family. In particular, advertising showed a young boy fishing with his grandfather on one of the company's new boats. To establish brand associations, Aaker (1996) recommends that the company must be consistent over time and consistent over elements of the marketing program.

The last component is other proprietary brand assets, for example, patents, trademarks, and channel relationships. Such assets tend to keep competitors from eroding the customer base (Aaker, 1996).

In the course of establishing and maintaining brand equity, efforts of measurement need to be undertaken. Aaker (1996) proposes eight variables that should be measured directly to track each of the components of brand equity, except other proprietary brand assets. Three additional market behavior measures are also recommended to provide a broader market view. These 11 measures and the corresponding brand equity component are as follows:

Brand loyalty:

1. Price premium: The amount customers will pay for the brand in comparison to competitor offerings
2. Customer satisfaction: Customers' happiness with the company's product and related services

Brand awareness:

3. Brand awareness: Salience of the brand in customers' minds

Perceived quality:

4. Perceived quality: Degree to which customers' expectations for performance and benefits are met

5. Leadership: Popularity of the brand based on such characteristics as top-selling brand in the category, customer acceptance, and/or recognition as technologically innovative

Brand associations:

6. Perceived value: The underlying reasons that customers view the brand as a good value for the money, given competitors' offerings and brands
7. Brand personality: Evoked images, elicited traits, and expressed interests that customers have with or connect to the brand
8. Organizational associations: Customers' opinions of the company and its bearing on the brand

Market behavior measures:

9. Market share: The branded product's performance relative to the performance of competitors' products
10. Market price: The market price of the branded product over time relative to competitors' products
11. Distribution coverage: Number of outlets providing customer access to the branded product

Obviously, multiple statistics and question items could be employed to measure each of the above variables. The key is to establish some level of tracking and regular reporting to uncover potential issues with the brand. Note that issues could be positive or negative in nature. Through a course of tracking and reporting, an improved understanding of a brand's equity is realized, and because of this understanding, better managerial decisions related to the branded product (branded product line) can be made.

■ A BRAND DECISION FRAMEWORK

Various decisions surround brand management. Exhibit 10.5 presents a framework that outlines these decisions, including the branding decision itself, brand sponsor decision, brand name decision, brand strategy decision, and brand repositioning decision.

The branding decision concerns whether to brand or not to brand a product/service. The purpose of giving a brand to a product is to give

Branding Decision	*Brand Sponsor Decision*	*Brand Name Decision*	*Brand Strategy Decision*	*Brand Repositioning Decision*
• Brand • No brand	• Manufacturer brand • Distributor brand • Licensed brand	• Individual names • Blanket family name • Separate family name • Company-individual name	• Line extensions • Brand extensions • Multibrands • New brands • Cobrands	• Reposition • No reposition

EXHIBIT **10.5.** Brand Decision Framework

it a distinguishable identity in the marketplace. However, a distinguishable identity is not necessary in certain cases such as generic and no-name products.

The brand sponsor decision concerns the channel level at which the brand will be given. A manufacturer brand is a brand that the manufacturer designates and that retains its brand characteristics (e.g., name, marks, trade characters, trade dress) throughout the channel. Examples of manufacturer brands include Oreo's (Nabisco), Tide (Procter & Gamble), and Colgate Toothpaste (Colgate-Palmolive). Manufacturer brands are sometimes referred to as national brands. A distributor brand also is possible, and these are sometimes referred to as private label brands. A distributor brand is a brand that a distributor designates and sells at its outlets. Examples of distributor brands include Arizona jeans (JC Penney), Craftsman tools (Sears), and Sam's Choice (Wal-Mart). Associations and professional groups are associated with licensed brands. In licensed brands, a group gives permission so that products can be sold with its name/brand on them. Merchandise sold with logos of the National Football League, National Basketball Association, and Major League Baseball are examples of licensed brands.

The brand name decision concerns the approach to choosing a brand name. Four possible approaches include individual names, blanket family name, separate family name, and company-individual name. An individual name gives the product its own identity, and thus, if the product fails, the company name and other company brands are not affected. The drawback is that additional resources are necessary to develop and proof a new brand name. General Mills uses this strategy with its offerings, that is, Betty Crocker, Bisquick, Gold Medal, Nature Valley. The blanket family name emphasizes a core name and connects this name with all new products. This name is typically the manufacturer's name. Heinz uses this brand name strategy, that is, Heinz ketchup, Heinz 57 sauce, Heinz mustard. The separate family name uses different names for different categories of products. Sears uses this strategy, as illustrated by the existence of Craftsman tools and Kenmore appliances. The company-individual name highlights both the company brand and the product brand. The intent of this strategy is to use the company brand name to accentuate the individual brand name. Kellogg's uses this approach with its products, that is, Kellogg's Rice Krispies, Kellogg's Corn Flakes, Kellogg's Raisin Bran.

The brand-strategy decision concerns the establishment of the brand in the marketplace. Five approaches are possible: line extensions, brand extensions, multibrands, new brands, and cobrands. In line extensions, the existing brand name is applied to a new size or flavor in an existing product category. For example, Kimberly-Clark's Kleenex line has comprised many line extensions, including Kleenex Facial Tissue, Kleenex Coldcare, Kleenex Expressions, and Kleenex Specialty Packs. In brand extensions, an existing brand name is applied to new product categories. Honda's use of its brand across various industries, such as automobiles, motorcycles, lawn mowers, marine engines, and snowmobiles, is characteristic of a brand extension strategy. Using the multibrand strategy, new brand names are introduced to the same product category currently served by the company. In this way, the company can serve multiple market segments. Procter & Gamble's Pamper and Luvs brands in the diaper market are indicative of a multibrand strategy. Marriott's use of multiple hotel brand names—Marriott Resorts, Courtyard by Marriott, Residence Inn, and Fairfield Inn—is a multibrand strategy as well. A new brand strategy is simply developing a new brand name for every new product category entered. The use of a new brand strategy would be predicated on the belief that the present brand would not provide a good association for the new category. The cobrand strategy represents a case in which a product bears two or more well-known brand names.Ingredient cobranding exists when the ingredients of a product include another product, for example, Betty Crocker Brownies with Hershey's Chocolate. Same-company cobranding exists when a company connects two or more of its brands into a new product, for example, when General Mills offers Trix-flavored Yoplait yogurt. Multiple-sponsor cobranding exists when brands of two or more companies are equally represented, as in the case of Dow Coming.

After a brand has been introduced into the marketplace, a brand repositioning decision may emerge. This decision concerns whether to change a brand or maintain the brand as is. Brands performing as expected would obviously remain unchanged, or they might be given more resources to strengthen their current image/identity. Brands performing below expectations could be repositioned to meet a different market or to better target the intended market. A brand continuing to perform below expectations would obviously be a candidate for harvesting.

■ THE BRAND SWITCHING MATRIX

An analytical method useful in brand management is the brand switching matrix. This matrix classifies purchase behavior so as to reflect certain characteristics about the marketplace and customers' brand loyalty.

The simplest way to construct a brand switching matrix is to survey customers about their previous brand purchases and current brand purchases. The data are percentages of customers buying each of the different brands in the survey. For example, it might be found that 33% of customers that bought Brand A in a previous purchase once again bought Brand A. This would suggest that Brand A's brand loyalty is about 33%. An effective way to organize the data collected is the matrix format shown in Exhibit 10.6.

Exhibit 10.6 specifically shows three different scenarios in a brand switching matrix format. As shown in the first grouping of Exhibit 10.6, 60% of customers who previously bought Brand A bought Brand A again; 35% of customers who previously bought Brand A bought Brand B; 2% of customers who previously bought Brand A bought Brand C; and 3% of customers who previously bought Brand A bought Brand D. This grouping illustrates a scenario in which two clear submarkets exist: It is apparent that Brand A's competition is primarily from brand B, and vice versa, whereas Brand C's competition is primarily from Brand D, and vice versa. The second group in Exhibit 10.6 illustrates a scenario where a dominant brand exists. The third group in Exhibit 10.6 illustrates a scenario in which all brands are relatively equivalent. The use of a brand switching matrix helps to illustrate these scenarios in a concise fashion.

Another way to read the data in the brand switching matrix is to consider the columns as the percentage of customers gained from a competitor and the rows as the percentage of customers lost to a competitor. For example, in Brand A's column of Exhibit 10.6, showing two clear submarkets, Brand A gains 60% of its own sales (keeps 60% of its sales) and gains 25% of sales from Brand B, 1% of sales from Brand C, and 3% of sales from Brand D. In Brand A's row of Exhibit 10.6, showing two clear submarkets, Brand A "loses" 60% of its sales to itself (keeps 60% of its sales) and loses 35% of sales to Brand B, 2% of sales to Brand C, and 3% of sales to Brand D. Note that each row adds up to 100%. Also note that the cell where Brand A gains from/loses to itself represents the amount of sales that Brand A keeps. This cell can be construed as representing, if not quantifying, brand loyalty, and thus, the diagonal of the matrix can be interpreted as brand loyalty. This suggests that brand loyalty for Brands A, B, C, and D is 60%, 70%, 65%, and 75%, respectively.

An additional use of the brand switching matrix is to estimate market share over time. To do this, the current market share of the differ-

Brand Bought in the Previous Period		*Brand Bought in the Current Period (t = 1)*			
		A	B	C	D
Two clear submarkets					
	A	.60	.35	.02	.03
	B	.25	.70	.03	.02
	C	.01	.04	.65	.30
	D	.03	.02	.20	.75
Dominant brand					
	A	.90	.03	.02	.05
	B	.40	.40	.10	.10
	C	.30	.05	.60	.05
	D	.40	.04	.06	.50
Equivalent brands					
	A	.40	.20	.18	.22
	B	.20	.35	.20	.25
	C	.27	.19	.30	.34
	D	.17	.18	.35	.30

SOURCE: Data from Lehmann and Winer (1997).

EXHIBIT **10.6.** Brand Switching Matrix

ent competitors must be given. The brand, switching matrix then serves to provide the probabilities of keeping or losing share over time. As shown in Exhibit 10.7, a brand switching matrix is constructed based on customers' purchase of the competing Brands X and Y. The current market share for Brands X and Y is 45% and 55%, respectively. After the next purchase, Brand X's market share is estimated to decrease to 43.5%, and Brand Y's market share is estimated to increase to 56.5%. These are calculated as follows: Brand X gains/keeps 60% of its share (.60 x .45) and gains 30% of Brand Y's share (.30 x .55), which summed equals 43.5%; Band Y gains 40% of Brand X's share (.40 x .45) and gains/keeps 70% of its share (.70 x .55), which summed equals 56.5%. Subsequent purchase iterations proceed in the same fashion using the newly calculated market share estimates.

Brand Bought in the Previous Period (t)	*Brand Bought in the Current Period (t + 1)*	
	X	Y
X	.60	.40
Y	.30	.70

Initial Market Share: Brand X = 45%, Brand Y = 55%

After the next purchase iteration (t + 1):
Brand X Market Share = (.60 × .45) + (.30 × .55) = .27 + .165 = .435 or 43.5%
Brand Y Market Share = (.40 × .45) + (.70 × .55) = .18 + .385 = .565 or 56.5%

After another purchase iteration (t + 2):
Brand X Market Share = (.60 × .435) + (.30 × .565) = .261 + .1695 = .4305 or 43.0%
Brand Y Market Share = (.40 × .435) + (.70 × .565) = .174 + .3955 = .5695 or 56.9%

Estimating long-run market share:
Brand X Market Share = (.60 × Brand X Market Share) + (.30 × Brand Y Market Share)
Brand Y Market Share = (.40 × Brand X Market Share) + (.70 × Brand Y Market Share)
Total Market = Brand X Market Share + Brand Y Market Share

or mathematically expressed as
$X = .6X + .3Y$
$Y = .4X + .7Y$
$1 = X + Y$

Solving for X,
$Y = 1 - X$
$X = .6X + .3(1-X)$ or $X = .3X + .3$ or $X = 3/7$ or $X = .429$
$Y = 1 - .429 = .571$

EXHIBIT **10.7.** Market Share Estimation Using the Brand Switching Matrix

The brand switching matrix also can be used to estimate long-run market share. Using the matrix of Exhibit 10.7, a set of simultaneous equations can be set up and then solved to estimate market share for Brands X and Y based on the given brand switching probabilities.

As shown, Brand X's market share is equal to 60% of its own share plus 30% of Brand Y's share. Brand Y's market share is equal to 40% of Brand X's share plus 70% of its own share. Given that Brand X's share plus Brand Y's share equals 100%, the long-run market share estimates (steady state market share estimates) are a 42.9% share for Brand X and a 57.1% share for Brand Y. (Refer to Exhibit 10.7.)

These estimates assume that the brand switching probabilities remain fairly constant. This assumption may or may not apply, depending on the marketing initiatives being employed by the competitors. However, the brand switching matrix can serve as a useful what-if analysis tool in determining if a marketing program designed to change brand switching behavior is cost-effective. For example, if we know that every 1% of market share represents $100,000 profit, is it worthwhile to implement a campaign to increase Brand X's loyalty by 5% at a cost of $250,000? As shown in Exhibit 10.8, a 5% increase in brand loyalty will increase Brand X's long-run market share by 3.3% (the new market share would be 46.2% versus the previous market share of 42.9%). The new campaign would conceivably generate $330,000 in profit (3.3 × $100,000) and thereby sufficiently cover the $250,000 budget. It, therefore, appears that the campaign is worthwhile to implement.

Current Brand Switching Behavior

Brand Bought in the Previous Period (t)	*Brand Bought in the Current Period (t + 1)*	
	X	Y
X	.60	.40
Y	.30	.70

Initial Market Share: Brand X = 45%, Brand Y = 55%

Estimated Long Run Market Share (Current Brand Switching Behavior): Brand X = 42.9%, Brand Y = 57.1%

Every 1% of Market Share = $100,000 Profit

(Continued)

EXHIBIT **10.8.** What-If Analysis Using the Brand Switching Matrix: An Example

Exhibit 10.8. Continued

Proposed Impact on Brand Switching Behavior After Implementing New Campaign

Brand Bought in the Previous Period (t)	*Brand Bought in the Current Period (t + 1)*	
	X	Y
X	.65	.40
Y	.30	.70

Brand X Market Share = (.65 × Brand X Market Share) + (.30 × Brand Y Market Share)
Brand Y Market Share = (.40 × Brand X Market Share) + (.70 × Brand Y Market Share)
Total Market = Brand X Market Share + Brand Y Market Share

or mathematically expressed as

$X = .65X + .3Y$
$Y = .4X + .7Y$
$1 = X + Y$

Solving for X,

$Y = 1 - X$
$X = .65X + .3(1 - X)$ or $X = .3X + .3$ or $X = 30/65$ or $X = .462$
$Y = 1 - .462 = .538$

Market Share Increase is 46.2% minus 42.9% or 3.3%. 3.3 × $100,000 = $330,000 Profit

Given that $330,000 sufficiently covers the $250,000 budget, implementation of the campaign would seem appropriate.

Key Concepts

- Product life cycle framework
- New-product strategy at maturity
- Product families and product platforms
- Product mix map
- Brand management

Chapter Questions

1. What are the four stages of the generic product life cycle framework?
2. What are the benefits and problems in employing the product life cycle framework for product planning?
3. What are some viable strategies to employ during the maturity stage?
4. What is the difference between a product family and product platform?
5. What is the purpose of a product mix map?
6. Why is brand management important?
7. What are the various drivers of brand equity?

Chapter Eleven

Special Topics in Product Planning: International Issues, Public Policy, and Intellectual Property

A variety of special topics are associated with product development and product management. Among these, three key topics are international issues, public policy, and intellectual property. The following discussion in no way represents an exhaustive discussion of each of the respective topics; it intends only to outline the underlying issues and product planning considerations.

■ INTERNATIONAL ISSUES

Two different sets of issues are emerging related to international product planning. The first concerns product design for international markets. The second set concerns management of global product development teams, that is, teams composed of members located in different places around the world.

Product Planning for International Markets

A useful framework for product planning considerations in international settings is given by Keegan (1995). This framework (shown in Exhibit 11.1) considers any necessary product changes and/or promotion changes to distinguish five strategies for introducing products to international markets. These five strategies include straight extension, communication adaptation, product adaptation, dual adaptation, and product invention.

Straight extension is simply the introduction of a product into a foreign market without any change to the product itself or the promotion campaign. As a result of the North American Free Trade Act (NAFTA), many U.S. grocery product firms are introducing their products into Canada and Mexico as straight extensions from the U.S. market. Product packages of these companies' products include both English and Spanish labels so there is literally no change to the product.

Communication adaptation is the introduction of the same product with changes to the product's promotion campaign. Four types of promotion changes are possible. The first is use of the same promotion message, varying only the language, colors, and name. However, this is not as simple as one would expect. As shown in Exhibit 11.2, in many cases, the product name or slogan in translation means something completely different than intended, often resulting in an embarrassing situation for the company. Colors, too, can have different meanings in different cultures, especially with regards to cultural taboos. For example, purple is associated with death in Burma and some Latin American cultures, white is a mourning color in India, and green is associated with disease in Malaysia (Kotler, 2000).

The second type of promotion change is to employ the same promotion theme but adapt the promotion copy to the local market. For example, Camay soap varied its commercial content across countries by showing a woman in U.S. commercials, a man in Venezuela, and a man's hands in Italy and France (Kotler, 2000).

The third type of promotion is the use of a global pool of promotions (e.g., advertisements) from which each local market chooses the most appropriate one. Also, allowing local market managers to design their promotions to meet country-specific needs within a given set of guidelines would be characteristic of this type of adaptation.

<table>
<tr><td colspan="2"></td><td colspan="3">Product</td></tr>
<tr><td colspan="2"></td><td>Do Not Change Product</td><td>Adapt Product</td><td>Develop New Product</td></tr>
<tr><td rowspan="2">Promotion</td><td>Do Not Change Promotion</td><td>Straight Extension</td><td>Product Adaptation</td><td rowspan="2">Product Invention</td></tr>
<tr><td>Adapt Promotion</td><td>Communication Adaptation</td><td>Dual Adaptation</td></tr>
</table>

EXHIBIT **11.1** Product Planning Strategies for International Settings

The fourth type of promotion is specifically designing a promotion campaign to target the local market. This essentially treats the foreign market as a separate target market in regard to the promotion strategy. A driver for using a distinct promotion campaign is the fact that different cultures respond differently to promotion media. For example, magazines play a major role in Italy but a minor role in Austria. Another driver for a distinct promotion campaign is country restrictions placed on promotion. For example, Greece prohibits coupons; France prohibits games of chance and limits premiums; Saudi Arabia discourages the use of women in advertising; and Norway prohibits cigarette and alcohol advertising.

Product adaptation is an altering of the product to meet local conditions or preferences, while the general promotion campaign remains basically the same. For example, cellular telephone manufacturers must alter their telephone technologies to meet the cellular system specifications in various global regions, for example, GSM in Europe; CDMA, TDMA, and PCS in the United States. This represents a regional product adaptation. Product adaptation can also be much more specific, depending on the situation. A country-specific product adaptation is Kraft blending different coffees for different European countries, because the British prefer to drink coffee with milk whereas the French prefer to drink coffee black (Kotler, 2000).

Dual adaptation is the altering of both the product and promotion campaign. In this way, the product and its associated promotion are tailored to meet the local conditions or preferences. As previously discussed, four types of promotion changes are possible. In the end, such promotion would likely promote the specific product features preferred by the local market.

Product invention is the development of a new product to meet local conditions or preferences. Two types of product invention are

• GM's Chevy Nova was marketed in Central and South America. "No *va*" in Spanish means"it doesn't go."
• The Dairy Association's huge success with the campaign "Got Milk?" prompted them to expand advertising to Mexico. It was soon brought to their attention that the Spanish translation read"Are you lactating?"
• Coors translated its slogan, "Turn it loose," into Spanish, where it was read as "Suffer from diarrhea."
• Scandinavian vacuum manufacturer Electrolux used the following slogan in an American campaign: "Nothing sucks like an Electrolux."
• Clairol introduced the "Mist Stick," a curling iron, into Germany only to find out that *mist* is slang for manure. Not too many people had use for the "Manure Stick."
• When Gerber started selling baby food in Africa, it used the same packaging as in the United States, with the smiling baby on the label. Later, they learned that in Africa, companies routinely put pictures on the labels of what's inside, because many people can't read.
• Colgate introduced a toothpaste in France called Cue, the name of a notorious porno magazine.
• An American T-shirt maker in Miami printed shirts for the Spanish market promoting the Pope's visit. Instead of "I saw the Pope"*(el Papa)*, the shirts read"I saw the potato" *(la papa)*.
• Pepsi's "Come alive with the Pepsi Generation" translated into "Pepsi brings your ancestors back from the grave" in Chinese.
• The Coca-Cola name in China was first read as *Kekoukela*, meaning "bite the wax tadpole" or "female horse stuffed with wax," depending on the dialect. Coke then researched 40,000 characters to find a phonetic equivalent *kokoukole*, translating into "happiness in the mouth."
• Frank Perdue's chicken slogan, "It takes a strong man to make a tender chicken," was translated into Spanish as "it takes an aroused man to make a chicken affectionate."
• When Parker Pen marketed a ball-point pen in Mexico, its ads were supposed to have read, "It won't leak in your pocket and embarrass you." The company thought that the word *embarazar* (to impregnate) meant to embarrass, so the ad read:"It won't leak in your pocket and make you pregnant!"
• When American Airlines wanted to advertise its new leather first-class seats in the Mexican market, it translated its "Fly In Leather" campaign literally, which meant "Fly Naked"*(vuela en cuero)* in Spanish.

EXHIBIT **11.2.** Slogans and Marketing Initiatives That Did Not Work in International Settings

pos-sible. Backward invention is the reintroduction of earlier product forms that are well adapted to a foreign country's needs. For example, National Cash Register reintroduced its crank-operated cash registers at half the price of modern cash registers and sold substantial numbers in technology-deficient areas of Latin America and Africa. Forward invention is the creation of a new product to meet a need in another country. For example, automakers develop vehicles to meet the local conditions of the marketplace. Vehicles designed for Europe and Asia are typically smaller than those designed for the United States. In certain cases, forward inventions developed by a U.S. company for a foreign market can be introduced to the U.S. market. Such is the case with Haagen-Dazs's *dulce de leche,* which was originally developed for Argentina. It was subsequently rolled out in the United States and Europe with much success.

International Considerations

If a decision is made to take a product to a foreign market, that market's culture and language need to be understood. Otherwise, a failure to understand the foreign market can be a frustrating experience as well as a major fiasco, as Exhibit 11.2 suggests.

Copeland and Griggs (1985) suggest an intriguing set of themes that companies should consider when trying to understand a foreign market. These themes—or "languages of the world" as Copeland and Griggs call them, provide a useful content on which to base a strategy for going into a foreign market with a product or service. These five languages concern time, space, things, friendships, and agreements.

The language of time recognizes that the perceptions of time differ across country cultures. People in the United States do not like to wait, whereas people in Latin America have a greater tolerance for longer wait times. Waiting also has different meanings for cultures. Consider the example of a U.S. businessman who was visiting an executive in a Brazilian company. After waiting a long time, the American businessman perceived that the Brazilian was uninterested in meeting him: In the United States, longer wait times are associated with stalling or trying to put people off. However, the Brazilian was trying to clear his agenda to avoid interruptions during the meeting, so from his point of view, the longer wait time meant that he greatly valued the U.S. businessman's visit.

The language of space recognizes that space has different meanings across country cultures. In the United States, personal space is valued, and thus, people's comfort zone when talking with each other is 1 to 2 feet of separation. In other countries, people stand closer to one another when they talk. Another facet of the language of space is being with other people. In the United States, individual success is valued, but in Sri Lanka, the individual is not as valued as the social collective.This hurt an American Express foray into Sri Lanka, which highlighted individual financial success and showed an advertisement of an individual on the beach. In Sri Lanka, the response to this advertisement was negative because the culture perceived the individual as a social outcast because he was alone on the beach.

The language of things highlights the different types of things that cultures value. Japan is a culture of minimalism. Because of this, Japanese homes typically do not have a lot of objects in them compared to the typical U.S. home. Another facet of things is gift giving. Japanese culture values gifts at the beginning of a business relationship, whereas U.S. firms do not exchange gifts until after a relationship has been established. Furthermore, how to present the gift and what gift to give are important. For example, in Japan, when presenting a gift, it is customary to allow time for the group to gather before making the presentation and to present the gift with both hands. Also, a group gift or a gift to each individual within the organization is preferred; it is considered extremely rude to present a gift to only one individual in a group. Appropriate and inappropriate types of gifts across countries include the following: Chinese colleagues prefer modest gifts such as coffee table books, ties, and pens but never clocks or anything made in Taiwan. Indian colleagues prefer sweets, nuts, fruit, elephant carvings, and candleholders but never leather objects and snake images. Japanese colleagues prefer items of Americana, scotch, brandy, or round fruits but never prefer gifts that come in sets of four or nine. Mexican colleagues prefer desk clocks, fine pens, and gold lighterbut not sterling silver items, logo gifts, or food baskets. Saudi Arabian colleagues prefer fine compasses and cashmere but never alcohol or pigskin products (Murphy, 1999).

The language of friendships indicates the differences across cultures with respect to personal relationships. For example, in nonmobile societies, individuals are less likely to want to expand their personal network. Mobile societies are more likely to welcome newcomers.

The language of agreements recognizes that the way people contract with one another differs across cultures. In the United States, agreements are often finalized through the use of lawyers. In Japan, people bow on an agreement. In Mediterranean cultures, a contract is not an end point, but rather, it shows that the parties are now serious about working with each other.

In addition to these expressed languages, there is a silent language involving signs, colors, and numbers. As previously mentioned, translation of product names and promotion copy and the colors used need to be carefully monitored to ensure that there is no misinterpretation and that local taboos are not being violated. Numbers can also have different meanings in different cultures. To reiterate, there is a need to truly understand the foreign market a company hopes to enter. Blindly entering a foreign market without careful study will undoubtedly result in problems.

Global Teams

The languages of the world also can be useful for managing another emerging international consideration, global product development teams. These teams are distinguished from other types of teams in that team members come from different countries around the world. Work by McDonough, Kahn, and Barczak (1998) found that global new-product team use is on the rise, and they speculate that by 2001, one in five new-product development teams will be global in nature. Factors driving this need are the global dispersion of company resources, expansion of corporate facilities around the world, and the difficulty and expense associated with relocating individuals to a central location.

Global teams have their challenges, however. In particular, they pose greater behavioral challenges than either co-located teams (all members are at the same physical location) or distributed teams (members are from different locations but within the same country). Global teams pose greater project management challenges than co-located teams. Behavioral challenges include generating trust among team members, achieving effective interpersonal relationships, and holding effective communication among team members. Project management challenges include identifying customer needs, ensuring that project goals remain stable, staying on budget, keeping on schedule, and having sufficient resources.

Research suggests that companies need to devote greater effort and time to meeting these challenges, providing more training to the managers of these teams, and putting into place organizational infrastructures to support these efforts. At present, global teams have been shown to perform less well than virtual or co-located teams, which is certainly not surprising given the greater project management and behavioral challenges they face. Limited company experience in managing global teams also may contribute to an inability to effectively manage these greater challenges and to improve their lower performance.

Communication appears to be one important factor for successful global product development teams. The work of McDonough, Kahn, and Griffin (1999) concludes that global teams have keen requirements for speed, volume, and richness of information. Regular use of the telephone among global team members appears to mitigate problems and achieve levels of communication that satisfy these three dimensions. More successful global teams also employ an affiliated set of communication mechanisms that include fax, teleconferencing, e-mail, and company databases. This affiliated set of communication mechanisms has complementary capabilities across the three communication dimensions, and firms that use these mechanisms appear to better meet global team needs. McDonough et al. (1998) also determined that a face-to-face meeting of the global project team at the beginning of the project is important to global team success. Such a meeting appears to provide a focus and direction for the global team. The recommendation is that team leaders and senior management allocate time and resources so that global team members can get together face to face in one location at the beginning of the project. In sum, global teams present unique challenges that product planners should be prepared to deal with, and global team communication is a must for addressing these challenges.

■ PUBLIC POLICY ISSUES

Five categories of public policy issues are product liability, environmental concerns, product/service performance, morality, and other public policy issues.

Product Liability

Product liability represents the vulnerability of a company to lawsuits because of inherent risks with the product, design defects within the product, manufacturing defects, failure to provide adequate instructions, or after-use dangers. Inherent risks generally cannot be avoided. However, efforts can and should be taken to minimize flagrant design defects, which present a dangerous condition to the user, overlook an essential safety device, and/or incorporate inadequate materials. Efforts also can be taken to minimize design defects through superior quality control procedures, as well as adequate instructions for use or warnings against harmful uses. With respect to warnings, these must be placed conspicuously on the product, communicating danger and instructing on how to avoid danger during and after use.

Should a lawsuit be filed against a company because of one of these issues or some other issue, four types of legal bases are possible. The first legal basis is negligence, which is defined as a personal wrong due to fault. The claim of negligence is that the product is defective by design and/or manufacture, and the company has failed to warn the public. Defenses to this claim are that the company was not negligent and that the product is not defective. If a company used substandard fasteners and, subsequently, the product broke apart, it might face a lawsuit based on negligence.

The second legal basis is warranty, which is the breaking of a promise or not fulfilling a promise. An implied warranty is based on the fitness of a product for a particular purpose, and an expressed warranty is a statement of fact made by the manufacturer (including any employee of the manufacturer). The defense to a claim of breaking the warranty would be that the supposed promise was .not implied by common usage of the product or that the supposed promise was not actually stated. A warranty case could surround promises by a salesperson about a product, when in fact, the product does not have features that satisfy those promises.

The third legal basis is strict liability or the responsibility of not putting defective products on the market. In a strict liability claim, negligence does not need to be shown, no direct sales need to occur, and no statement by the manufacturer will relieve the liability. Rather, strict liability centers around the issue of whether the company knew the product could cause harm in any way. The defense against strict liability is one of three possible responses: The customer assumed the risk on purchase, there was unforeseeable misuse, or the product is not defective. An interesting use of strict liability is found in a case involving McDonald's. A woman who spilled McDonald's coffee on her lap after purchasing it at a drive-through window and who was burned as a result sued McDonald's, basing her claim on strict liability. During the case, it was revealed that the McDonald's had determined that most of its coffee sales came via the drive-through, not from sales inside the restaurant. Because of this, McDonald's was shown to be using a poorer quality of coffee, which was brewed at scalding temperatures so that the usual drive-through patron could not drink the coffee right away. By the time the coffee was cool enough to drink, the patron was at a distance from the restaurant and not likely to return the coffee. (Research also indicated that patrons were likely to associate any unfavorable attributes of the coffee with its cooling down too much.) The court awarded the plaintiff in the case the exact sum of McDonald's profits from one day of coffee sales.

A fourth legal basis of lawsuits is misrepresentation of a product in the marketplace. That is, the company portrays the product as something that it is not, and based on this, the user gets injured. For example, in an advertisement, a helmet manufacturer showed an individual wearing one of its helmets while sitting on a motorcycle, even though the helmet was not a motorcycle helmet. A motorcyclist subsequently was injured while driving and wearing one of the company's helmets. He sued on the basis that he was misled to believe that the helmets were appropriate for motorcycle use. The plaintiff won the case and was awarded compensation. Possible defenses to the claim of misrepresentation can be that the way the company portrayed the product was truthful and/or that the buyer should have known better.

Environmental Concerns

Environmental concerns are a growing public policy issue for companies. Growing concern surrounds the raw materials going into products and the pollution caused by their manufacture, use, and disposal. Printed circuit board manufacturers have been criticized for the use of acid and chlorofluorocarbons (CFCs) in etching their boards; legislation has banned the use of CFCs, but the proper disposal of acid remains a controversial issue. Car manufacturers have historically been criticized for vehicle emissions, but a particular criticism has arisen concerning the re-emergence of large, gas-consuming sport utility vehicles. Computer manufacturers have been criticized for their lack of attention to disposal issues; many of the components in computers are inert materials and cannot be recycled. The computer industry has responded by engaging in efforts to recycle components. Overall, efforts toward making products more environmentally friendly are a timely consideration and may provide a competitive advantage.

Product Performance and Customer Service

Product performance concerns the assurance that a product or service will perform as specified. Extensive quality control and quality assurance programs must be implemented and monitored. Any quality problems must be documented and remedied, with documentation on how the remedy was enacted. This is particularly true for medical products companies, which must document all product manufacturing and testing procedures to satisfy Food and Drug Administration (FDA) requirements. Customer service and support is also a must. The company must be accessible to customers and willing to listen to them. Customer complaints need to be acted on, and customer questions must be answered to ensure proper use of the product. All and all, these initiatives help to achieve customer satisfaction, possibly leading to customer delight and, ultimately, leading to customer loyalty.

Morality

Morality deals with issues of whether it is justified to sell a given product. Controversial products include cigarettes, alcohol, and guns. Although individuals can decide whether or not to use these products, their sale and use has a broader impact on the general public.

Other Environmental Concerns

Like morality, politics, economic conditions, and media—among other things—can affect product offerings. A congressional or regulatory hearing on a pressing issue can persuade public opinion. Recent congressional hearings on health maintence organizations (HMOs) has influenced HMO business practices. The FDA's decision in 1969 to ban cyclamate, a synthetic sweetener, was a political one—although research suspected cyclamates to be carcinogenic, later investigation found the research to be suspect. Some European nations still allow cyclamates.

Economic conditions affect product planning. Recent economic crises in Asia have hurt overseas operations by major U.S. companies.

Media are an important influence on product planning initiatives, especially in the United States. Many new products succeed or fail because of favorable or unfavorable press. For example, recent coverage of the possible benefits of antioxidants, Vitamin E, and St. John's Wort has spurred a huge sales growth in the vitamin and herbal supplement market. In fact, such growth has attracted major pharmaceutical companies to the vitamin and herbal supplement market. Conversely, the negative press and word-of-mouth surrounding Olestra, Procter & Gamble's high-profile fat substitute, can be blamed for inhibited market growth and weak sales.

What To Do

Although environmental considerations should be addressed during the situation analysis, unforeseen circumstances may arise. To minimize such circumstances, upper management should be involved in product strategy and policy to ensure that the company image is not negatively affected by the product planning effort and that any potential shortcomings of the product offering are recognized before product launch. Concept, product, and market testing should be pursued to identify potential shortcomings, as well. Even though testing may slow down the product development process, in the long run, such testing may be well worth the effort.

In the event that an unforeseen situation arises, a crisis management program should be in place to address the situation. Upper management should be readily visible to ease customer fears and preserve the product/company image. In some companies, safety czars are used to plan the crisis management program and ensure product safety.

Ongoing education and public relations efforts by the company also help to assure customers and preserve the product/company image. Such education is most often directed out of an external affairs department.

■ INTELLECTUAL PROPERTY

The third special topic of intellectual property is especially critical in the course of new technology development. Protection of intellectual property is a must to ensure a competitive advantage. Such protection can come via a patent, a trademark, or a copyright.

Patent Protection

In issuing a patent, the government gives the inventor the right to exclude others from making, using, or selling the invention. The right-

extends for 17 years from the date of issue, after which the content of the patent becomes public property. A patent is the right to exclude others from making, using, or selling the invention—it is not the right to make, use, or sell the invention (a patent cannot conflict with state or federal laws prohibiting the making, using, or selling of such an invention). The patent right is usually considered a unique kind of personal property. It may be bought or sold, mortgaged, licensed, given, or willed to another nearly as easily as any other personal property.

To obtain the protection afforded by a patent, the inventor must make a full and complete disclosure of his invention. The invention or discovery must be not only new or previously unrecognized but also something extraordinary. An obvious or normally predictable result or something that an ordinary skilled person in the field could reasonably be expected to do cannot be patented. An idea cannot be patented. However, the machine, process, or thing into which the idea has been incorporated may be. There are seven categories of inventions or discoveries that may be patented:

1. An art or a process or method of doing something
2. A machine—an inanimate mechanism for transforming or applying energy
3. A manufactured product—anything made from raw material by hand, machine, and/or art
4. A composition of matter
5. A new and useful improvement of any of the above (original patents are often followed by numerous improvement patents)
6. A new variety of plant
7. A design—a particular pattern, form, or contour of a product may be patented. Design patents run for shorter periods of time than other patents. The prospective patentee may apply for a design patent to run 3.5, 7, or 14 years.

A patent application has three main components: (a) the petition, (b) the specification, and (c) the oath. The petition is addressed to the Commissioner of Patents and is essentially a request for a grant of letters patent to be issued to the applicant. The patent specification serves to clearly describe the invention, with drawings required in all cases to the point that they are meaningful. The oath is then taken by the applicant affirming that he or she is the originator of the thing for which the patent is being requested.

Trademark Protection

A trademark differs from other property in that part of its value is in its unique design. The intent of the trademark is to distinguish the goods of one manufacturer from similar goods of all other manufacturers.

Trademark registration continues for 20 years. If the trademark is still in use after the 20-year period, the company may renew it by filing an application to renew. Nonuse of a trademark for a 2-year period is prima facie evidence of abandonment of the trademark. A trademark also can be lost for a product name, if, after time, the product name becomes established as the descriptive term for products in the category. Such was the case for aspirin and cellophane.

Copyright Protection

The copyright is a form of legal protection for original works of authorship—literary, dramatic, musical, artistic—and for certain other intellectual endeavors. It gives the copyright holder exclusive right to copy, publicly perform, or display the work. A copyright protects the language used, but it does not preserve the ideas presented in the material. The life of a copyright is the creator's life plus 50 years beyond his or her death. Works for hire have a copyright duration of 75 years from publication or 100 years from creation, whichever is less.

KEY CONCEPTS

- Product planning for international markets
- Global teams
- Public policy issues: product liability, environmental concerns, product performance and customer service, morality, other concerns
- Intellectual property

Key Questions

1. What are the various approaches for entering international markets?
2. What are five important themes for approaching international markets?
3. What are some distinguishing characteristics of global teams versus other types of teams?
4. What are the legal bases underlying product liability cases?
5. Aside from product liability, what other public policy issues impinge on new product success?
6. How should one manage public policy issues related to product planning?
7. What are the purposes of a patent, trademark, and copyright?

Chapter Twelve

Product Development Best Practices

The previous 11 chapters provide an overview of the product planning process, product planning techniques, and inherent issues associated with and/or affecting product planning. In this last chapter, themes and evidence of product development best practices are given to guide product planning practice and bring about proper closure of this book.

A good starting point is *Business Week's* 1993 article entitled "Flops," which discussed product development failures and how to improve the chances of avoiding such failures. Six particular themes were listed to describe how a company can improve its success rate with new products (pp. 78-79):

1. *Ask your customers:* Don't develop a product just because the engineering department loves a new technology. Consult users and customers at every step from idea generation to commercialization.
2. *Set realistic goals:* A new product might be sure to produce $20 million in sales. So don't make it a loser by aiming for $40 million.

3. *Break down walls:* Passing a new product from one department to another risks potentially disastrous foul-ups. Instead, have research and development, marketing, and manufacturing work together from the start.
4. *Create gateways:* Don't let a product gather dangerous momentum. At each stage of a product's development, make sure it meets specific criteria of manufacturing viability, customer acceptance, sales support, and budget planning.
5. *Watch those tests:* A test market may succeed just because customers are sampling a new product out of curiosity. Don't get carried away by initial results. Test long enough to get a real sense of a product's potential.
6. *Do your postmortems:* Managers tend to run away from their flops. Don't. Formally review what went wrong and apply those lessons to the next launch. Reward managers who learn from their mistakes.

Business Week notes that failing to incorporate these themes can lead to various expensive mistakes. A sample of costly product development failures include:

Ford's Edsel = loss of $250 million
DuPont's Corfam = loss of $100 million
RCA's Videodisc = loss of $500 million
Time Inc.'s *TV Cable Week* = loss of $47 million
IBM's PCjr = marketing cost of $40 million

These illustrate the costs and amount of resources involved with the product planning endeavor, as well as the significant strategic role that product planning serves within corporations.

A similar set of best practice themes is provided by Urban and Hauser in their 1993 book entitled *Design and Marketing of New Products.* They prescribe the incorporation of these themes to ensure a greater likelihood of product development success. Note that these themes closely parallel the *Business Week* prescriptions:

- Listen to potential users early
- Evaluate opportunities
- Generate creative ideas
- Develop a core benefit proposition, for example, product innovation charter
- Integrate marketing, engineering, and production to deliver customer benefits (customer-oriented)

- Carefully design communication (collaboration versus communication)
- Forecast and evaluate profit potential before go/no go decisions
- Test the product and the marketing strategy
- Monitor customers and competition to assure continued improvement in the delivery of customer satisfaction/customer delight

Urban and Hauser (1993) also provide lists of reasons why products fail and succeed. Reviewing these lists, companies can be attuned to and identify potential pitfalls in the product planning process:

Reasons why products fail:

- The market was too small
- The product was a poor match for company
- The product was not new/not different from competitors' products
- The product offered no real benefit
- The product was poorly positioning versus competition
- There was inadequate support from the channel of distribution
- There was a high degree of forecasting error
- The product's launch was poorly timed
- There was a strong competitive response
- There were major shifts in the existing technology base
- There were changes in customers' tastes
- There were changes in environmental constraints
- There was poor repeat purchase or no diffusion of sales
- There was poor after-sales service
- The product provided an insufficient return on investment
- There was a lack of coordination between organizational functions
- There were organizational problems, including personality conflict within the company, and the organizational structure was not conducive to product development

Reasons why products succeed:

- The product matched customer needs
- The product offered high value to the customer
- The product was innovative
- The product was technically superior

- There was ample screening and analysis supported by an effective decision support system
- The competitive environment was favorable
- The product fit internal company strengths
- There was effective communication among company functions
- There was top management support
- There was an enthusiastic champion
- There was a new-product organization
- A new-product development (NPD) process provided structure, but there was some flexibility to adapt to unexpected difficulties
- The NPD effort avoided unnecessary risk
- The time from strategic commitment to launch was short
- There was a worldwide strategy surrounding the new product
- Quality was reflected throughout the product development process, and correspondingly, there was a commitment to customer satisfaction

Robert Cooper (1993) also provides a list of pitfalls that can contribute to new product failures and a mediocre new product program. These include

- A lack of market orientation, including inadequate market analysis, a failure to understand customer needs and wants, and insufficient attention to the market
- Poor quality of execution during the product development process
- Moving too quickly forcing the company to avoid doing or shortcutting certain key tasks
- Not enough homework on market and product definition
- A lack of product differentiation from competing products
- No focus, leading to a situation of too many projects, which forces a dispersion of limited resources, which, in turn, undersupports deserving projects

BENCHMARKING PRODUCT DEVELOPMENT PRACTICES

Every 5 years, the Product Development and Management Association (PDMA) conducts a benchmarking study on NPD practices to aid companies in assessing the sufficiency of their own company's product development process. Topics covered by the PDMA benchmarking study are varied, including process stages used, success statistics, techniques used, and issues. Below is a summary of key highlights from the 1997 PDMA *Drivers ofNPD Success* Report (Griffin et al., 1997):

NPD outcomes:

- NPD cycle time averages about 24 months for more innovative projects, down about 30% from 1990 data
- Companies typically start with seven ideas to generate one successful launch
- The success rate of new products that make it to the market has remained stable at 59%
- Sales of new products as a percentage of total sales is 32%

Processes:

- Nearly 60% of U.S. firms use a multifunctional stage-gate™ / phase review process
- About 39% of all firms do not use a formal product development process

Organizational management:

- Over 84% of the more innovative projects use multifunctional teams, whereas 40% to 50% of the less innovative projects use them
- Project completion dinners are the most frequently used team-based reward
- Project managers appointed by management are most likely to lead new product development projects

Tools:

- The focus of new market researchtools is obtaining better qualitative information, rather than quantitative information
- Market research techniques that respondents identified as important for new product development include voice of the customer studies, customer site visits, concept testing, and beta testing

- Engineering design tools that respondents identified as important for NPD include computer-aided-design (CAD), design for manufacturing (DFM) / design for assembly (DFA), concurrent engineering, rapid prototyping, computer-aided-engineering (CAE), value analysis, simulation, and failure mode and effects analysis (FMEA)

The study further distinguishes practices of better product development companies versus the rest-of-study sample. Better product development companies were defined as companies that are above the mean in relative success of their NPD programs, either the most successful or in the top third in their industry for NPD success and above the mean in financial success from new products. Overall, the study concludes that the most successful companies succeed not by using one NPD practice more extensively or better but by using a number of them together and more effectively. They do this by

- Measuring NPD performance and expecting more from the NPD effort. "Best" firms expect 45% of their sales to come from products commercialized in the previous 3 years
- Implementing a stage-gate™ / phase-review process and progressing to more advanced forms of an NPD process
- Starting NPD with a strategic planning activity
- Including more activities in their NPD processes
- Using multifunctional teams
- Driving product development efforts through specific new product strategies at both the program and project levels
- Quickly implementing new market research and engineering design tools

For more information about this study and/or PDMA, check out PDMA's Web site at www.pdma.org or call PDMA at 1-800-232-5241.

■ GOOD LUCK

It would be remiss to overlook the fact that luck plays a role in product planning success, too. However, simply relying on luck will not ensure continued product planning success. Rather, a greater propensity for sustained, long-term success is obtained through a systematic approach to product planning as prescribed in this book. Overall, it is hoped that this book has made such an impression on readers and that they will agree.

At this point, it is also hoped that readers appreciate the extensive breadth of topics and issues with which product planners contend, exemplifying the diversity of the product planning field. Just to remind readers of the extensive breadth of topics and issues in product planning, here are the topics that have been covered in the previous 11 chapters of this book, in sequence: Product Planning Basics, Strategic Planning, Opportunity Identification, New Product Organization, Concept Generation, Concept Evaluation, Technical Development, Market Planning, Launch, Life Cycle Management, and Public Policy and Legal Considerations.

In closing, I would like to offer my own version of a product postmortem. Specifically, I welcome readers' comments, experiences, and questions. Such feedback will help to build the knowledge base in this field called product planning and help to augment the book and its delivery so that it can best achieve its purpose of being an effective product planning primer. Feel free to contact me at the University of Tennessee, Department of Marketing, Logistics, and Transportation, 310 Stokely Management Center, Knoxville, Tennessee 37996-0530. Best wishes for successful product and service planning.

APPENDIX A

■ SITUATION ANALYSIS DATA SOURCES

The following is not an exhaustive list of data sources, but it does represent a good starting point for a situation analysis. Note that much of this list was compiled by Julie Wood, Information Consultant, Georgia Tech Library, Atlanta, Georgia, as a supplement for use in my product planning courses.

Sources for Identifying Standard Industrial Classification Codes and Industry Types

Standard Industrial Classification (SIC) Manual 1987. The Standard Industrial Classification (SIC) system classifies establishments by their primary type of activity. SIC codes are being replaced by the new *North American Industrial Classification System* (NAICS).

SIC Search Online (http://www.osha.gov/oshstats/sicser.html). This page from OSHA allows one to search SIC codes by keyword or to search for a code to retrieve a description of that code, or to view an outline of the SIC Code Manual.

North American Industrial Classification System 1997 and *NAICS Online* (http://www.census.gov/epcd/www/naics.html). This Web site contains correspondence tables: NAICS to SIC and SIC to NAICS.

Sources for General Industry Data and Industry Overviews

Standard & Poor's Industry Surveys. Features analysts' outlook, industry statistics, and comparative financial data for companies in key industries.

Encyclopedia of American Industries. Two volumes, one for manufacturing industries, the other for service and nonmanufacturing. Detailed industry breakdowns with history, overview, and recent developments sections.

Service Industries USA. Industry analyses, statistics, and leading organizations.

Manufacturing USA. Organized by SIC code, this source incorporates statistical tables from the Census of Manufactures and combines them with Ward's company information. Each industry analysis is enhanced with a state-level U.S. map showing industry concentration.

Forbes Annual Report on American Industry (http://www.forbes.com/forbes/SubSect/AnnualRe.htm). Provides comparative financial data on 1,280 companies in 20 industries.

Current Industrial Reports (http://www.census.gov/cir/www/index.html). U.S. Census Bureau data measuring industrial activity for selected products. Includes statistics on production, shipments, inventories, and so on.

Hoover's Industry Snapshots (http://hoovweb.hoovers.com/features/industry/industries.html). Surveys of nearly 40 industries. Historical information, current developments, financial data, and more.

Industry Web Sites (http://bd.dowjones.com/category.asp?CatID=6). Dow Jones Business Directory Guide to Business Web Sites.

Industry Link (http://www.industrylink.com/). Claims to be the premier directory of links to industry Web sites. Covers thousands of Web sites (resource and commercial), organized into 20 major industry categories.

Sources for Consumer Demographics and Behavior

Consumer surveys. Many magazines conduct surveys among their subscribers on every type of product or service that could be bought by consumers or, in the case of management publications, by business people or companies. Such studies provide information on such topics as brand preferences, buying influences, package size, and place of purchase. The following is a sample list of trade magazines that offer consumer survey information.

American Demographics Magazine (www.demographics.com). Four years' worth of articles are available via the Web site.

Drug & Cosmetic Industry. Magazine of manufacturing, formulation, research & development, packaging and marketing.

Food Technology. Food industry, trade, and research.

Beverage World
Carpet & Floorcoverings Review
Carpet&Rug Industry
Chain Store Age. Trade magazine for the retail market.
Chemical Times & Trends
Computerworld
Drug & Cosmetic Industry
Electronic Business
Food Technology.
Knitting International. This publication claims to be the "leading technical and management journal for hosiery, underwear, knitwear and knitted fabric manufacturers."
Lifestyle Market Analyst. Breaks down the U.S. population geographically and demographically. Includes extensive lifestyle information on popular interests, hobbies, and activities. Covers analysis of geographic markets, particular market segments, and consumer segment groups.
Pulp&Paper
Rubber World. Trade magazine for rubber and associated chemicals industry.
SocioAbs. Key source for research in workplace behavior and social trends.
Ward's Auto World. Trade magazine and annual report covering the auto industry.

Sources for Collecting Competitor Data

Rankings and Market Share: Print Resources

Market Share Reporter. Features published "top" lists and pie charts for a variety of market statistics related to industry. Accessed by company name, product name, or industry.

Dun's Business Rankings. About 8,000 public and private companies are ranked according to sales volume and number of employees. Companies are ranked within states and within 150 industry categories.

Ward's Business Directory of U.S. Private and Public Companies. Volume 5 of this directory ranks the profiled companies by SIC code category according to sales volume. Volume 8 ranks companies by NAICS codes. A total sales amount is given for each category, enabling an approximate market share calculation for each company.

The Forbes 500 Annual Directory. Lists and ranks the 500 largest publicly traded, U.S.-based companies, both industrial and service. The firms are ranked separately according to year-end sales, profits, assets, and market value.

Fortune magazine. Publishes a number of annual company rankings, including the Fortune 500 (published every April or May), the Global 500 (published in July), and the Service 500 (published in June).

Rankings and Market Share: Electronic and Internet Resources

Price's List of Lists (http://pop.circ.gwu.edu/~gprice/listof.htm). Compiled by Gary Price, Gelman Library, George Washington University, this site serves as a clearinghouse for internet-based lists of information, including rankings of different people, organizations, companies, and so on.

Fortune and Forbes Company Rankings within Industries. Provides rankings of top companies within particular industries (aerospace, beverages, hotels, insurance, metals, telecommunications, and many more). Brief profiles of the companies are included.

- Fortune 500 Industry List (http://www.pathfinder.com/fortune/ fortune 500/indlist.html)
- Fortune Global 500 Industry List (http://www.pathfinder.com/ fortune/global500/indlist.html)
- Forbes 500 Industry Listing (http://www.forbes.com/tool/ toolbox/ forbes500s/ asp/IndIndex.asp)

GaleNet (http://galenet.gale.com). Gale Business Resources Company and U.S. Industry Module features comprehensive information on 445,000 U.S. and international companies, thorough histories and chronologies of major companies, and in-depth coverage of major U.S. industries, including full-text essays, rankings, market shares, trade and professional associations, and statistical analyses.

Sources for Product-Related Data

Encyclopedia of Consumer Brands. This three-volume encyclopedia contains articles with bibliographies on about 600 popular U.S. brands. Examples of headings include brand origins, early marketing strategy, advertising, brand development, and competition.

F&S Index—United States. This index covers company, product, and industry information from financial publications, business-oriented newspapers, trade magazines, and special reports. The index also contains citations to articles on new products, technological innovation, and social and political factors affecting business.

Thomas Register Catalog File. Identifies which companies make what products. Includes a trademark index and some manufacturers' catalogs. Volumes 19 to 25 of the Thomas Register contain product catalogs of nearly 2,000 companies that are referenced in the Products & Services and Company Profiles sections of *The Thomas Register of American Manufacturers.* The Thomas Register Supplier Finder database is also available on the Web at http://www.thomasregister. com:8000/home.html.

Sources for Corporate Financial Data and Industry Statistics

Almanac of Business and Industrial Financial Ratios. Features Internal Revenue Service-based composite financial data covering about 4.3 million companies for 179 industries (arranged by SIC code). Tables feature 10-year trends in selected ratios and factors.

Predicasts Basebook. Gives charts of commercially published time-series data arranged by SIC, plus topics such as gross national product, population, and employment. Statistics include consumption, production, and wage rates.

Predicasts Forecasts. Gives forecast information on topics covered by Basebook.

Annual Report Gallery (www.reportgallery.com). This Web site lists annual reports that are available on the Internet and links to those reports.

1992 Census of Retail Trade. Lists retail industry statistics by geographic area, state, merchandise line, and subject heading.

U.S. Census of Manufactures (http://www.census.gov/econ/www/ manu-menu.html). Provides manufacturer statistics by industry type.

U.S. Census Statistical Briefs and Census Briefs. Lists industry-specific census briefs.

1993-1996 (http://www.census.gov/apsd/www/statbrief/)

1996-present (http://www.census.g0v/pr0d/www/titles.html# cenbrief)

Statistical Abstract of the United States (http://www.census.gov/ statab/www/). This source contains a collection of statistics on social and economic conditions in the United States. Selected international data are also included. The 1997 edition includes 97 new tables covering topics such as pet ownership and consumer finance.

Bureau of Labor Statistics (http://www.bls.gov/). The Bureau of Labor Statistics collects data and provides statistics and analysis on U.S. employment, unemployment, prices, living conditions, compensation, working conditions, productivity, international programs, and other topics.

County Business Patterns (http://www.census.gov/epcd/cbp/view/ cbpview.html). This is an annual series providing economic profiles of counties, states, and the United States. Data include employment, payroll, and number of establishments by industry.

State and Metropolitan Area Data Book (http://www.census.gov/statab/www/smadb.html). This is a collection of census statistical tables broken down by state and by metropolitan area.

Key Databases for Finding Articles and Information

ABI/Inform. Covers business and management topics including company histories, competitive intelligence, and product development. Topics include advertising, banking, broadcasting, computers, economics, foreign investment, health care, insurance, international trade, management, marketing, public administration, real estate, taxation, telecommunications, and transportation. The database contains citations and abstracts from over 1,400 U.S. and international journals and trade magazines.

Business & Industry. Contains important facts and key events dealing with public and private companies, industries, products, and markets for all manufacturing and service industries at an international level. Covers about 700 trade magazines, newsletters, and general business and international business dailies.

Business Dateline. Covers topics such as agriculture, company profiles, corporate strategies, executive profiles, financial services, high technology, manufacturing, marketing, regional business environments, retailing, and service industries. The database contains full-text articles from over 262 sources, including regional publications, press releases, and major newspapers.

EBSCO Business Search. Covers over 900 business-related publications, both scholarly and popular press.

Findex. Indexes research studies, surveys, and audits for all types of industries. The entries are divided into 12 broad categories: basic industries and related equipment; business and finance; construction, materials, and machinery; consumer durables; consumer nondurables; data processing systems and electronics; defense and security systems; energy, utilities, and related equipment; health care; media and publishing; retailing and consumer services; and transportation. The database also provides company profiles for 400 top corporations.

Lexis-Nexis. Contains over 5,300 publications. Many types of publications are included: newspapers (in English and many other languages), legal news, general interest magazines, medical journals, trade publications, company financial information, transcripts, wire service reports, government publications, law reviews, and reference works (such as the *Market Share Reporter,* the *Encyclopedia of Associations,* and *Ulrich's International Periodical Directory).*

NETFirst. Contains bibliographic citations (complete with summary descriptions and subject headings) describing Internet-accessible resources, including World Wide Web pages, interest groups, library catalogs, FTP sites, Internet services, Gopher servers, electronic journals, and newsletters. Records contain location information that can be used to connect users to resources of interest.

Trade Association Directories and a Sample of Useful Trade Association Web Sites

Associations Unlimited (http:/ /galenet.gale.com/). Part of theGaleNet resource.
Directory of Associations Online (http://www.asaenet.org/Gateway/OnlineAssocSlist. html). American Society of Association Executives.

The following is a sample list of trade association Web sites that track their respective industries and provide data and information either free or by fee. Many of these trade associations have their own market research staff.

American Automobile Manufacturers Association (http://www.aama.com/). Sales and market share data can be found at http:// www.aama.com/economic/amercar4.html; industry data can be found at http://www.aama.com/data/contents.html.
Cellular Telecommunications Industry Association (http://www.ctia.org).
Electronics Industries Alliance (http://www.eia.org).
Food Explorer (http://www.foodexplorer.com/). Provides information for food industry professionals.
Food Marketing Institute (http://www.fmi.org/food/). Food industry Web sites can be found at http://www.fmi.org/industry/resourcelist.html.
International Council of Shopping Centers (http://www.icsc.org/).
National Soft Drink Association (http://www.nsda.org).
Nation's Restaurant News (http://www.nrn.com). Links to industry Web sites can be found at http://www.nrn.com/links/ia.htm.
Toy Manufacturers of America (http://www.toy-tma.com/).

Appendix B

■ REFERENCE SOURCES FOR PRODUCT PLANNING

The following materials and reference sources are not an exhaustive list of product planning references, but they do represent a good starting point on which to base a product planning library and knowledge base.

Associations

American Marketing Association
311 South Wacker Drive, Suite 5800, Chicago, IL 60606
Phone: (800) AMA-1150 or (312) 542-9000
Fax: (312) 542-9001
www.ama.org

Commercial Development and Marketing Association
1850 M Street, NW, Suite 700, Washington, DC 20036
Phone: (202) 721-4110 Fax: (202) 296-8120
www.cdmaonline.org

Innovation Network
451 East 58th Avenue, No.4625, Box 468, Denver, CO 80216
Phone: (303) 308-1088
Fax: (303) 295-6108
www.thinksmart.com

Product Development and Management Association (PDMA)
236 Route 38 West, Suite 100, Moorestown, NJ 08057-3276
Phone: (800) 232-5241 or (856) 231-1578
Fax: (856) 231-4664
www.pdma.org

Project Management Institute (PMI)
Four Campus Boulevard, Newtown Square,
Pennsylvania 19073-3299
Phone: (610) 356-4600
Fax: (610) 356-4647
www.pmi.org

Technology Transfer Society (T2S)
2030 SW 34th Street, Box 160, Gainesville, FL 32608
Phone: (352) 955-0066
Fax: (352) 294-7802
www.t2s.org

Suggested Readings

Aaker, D. A. (1996). *Building strong brands.* New York: Free Press.

Altshuller, G. (1997). *40 Principles: TRIZ Keys to Technical Innovation.* Worcester, MA: Technical Innovation Center.

Bralla, J. G. (1996). *Design for excellence.* New York: McGraw-Hill.

Clark, K. B., & Fujimoto, T. (1991). *Product development performance: Strategy, organization, and management in the world auto industry.* Cambridge, MA: Harvard Business School.

Cooper, R. G. (1993). *Winning at new products: Accelerating the process from idea to launch* (2nd ed.). Reading, MA: Addison-Wesley.

Cooper, R. G. (1999). *Product leadership: Creating and launching superior new products.* New York: Perseus.

Cooper, R. G., Edgett, S. J., & Kleinschmidt, E. J. (1998). *Portfolio management for new products.* Reading, MA: Addison-Wesley.

Crawford, C. M., & DiBenedetto, A. (2000). *New products management* (6th ed.). Boston, MA: Irwin-McGraw-Hill.

Dolan, R. J. (1993). *Managing the new product development process: Cases and notes.* Reading, MA: Addison-Wesley.

Griffin, A., Belliveau, P., Markham, S., McDonough, E. F., Ill, Olson, D., &. Page, A. L. (1997, October). *Drivers of NPD success: The 1997 PDMA Report.* Chicago: Product Development and Management Association.

Kotler, P. (2000). *Marketing management: Analysis, planning, implementation, and control* (10th ed.). Upper Saddle Ridge, NJ: Prentice-Hall.

Kuzcmarski, T. D. (1996). *Innovation: Leadership strategies for the competitive edge.* Chicago: American Marketing Association.

Lehmann, D. R., & Winer, R. S. (1997). *Analysis for market planning* (4th ed.). Chicago: Irwin.

MacKenzie, G. (1996). *Orbiting the giant hairball: A corporate fool's guide to surviving with grace.* New York: Viking.

McQuarrie, E. F. (1993). *Customer visits: Tools to build market focus.* Newbury Park, CA: Sage.

McQuarrie, E. F. (1996). The market research toolbox: A concise guide for beginners. Thousand Oaks, CA: Sage.

Mentzer, J. T., & Bienstock, C. C. (1998). *Sales forecasting management.* Thousand Oaks, CA: Sage.

Moore, G. A. (1991). *Crossing the chasm: Marketing and selling technology products to mainstream customers.* New York: Harper Business.

Moore, G. A. (1995). *Inside the tornado.* New York: Harper Business.

Pinto, J. K. (Ed.). (1998). *Project management handbook.* Newtown Square, PA: Project Management Institute/Jossey-Bass.

Rogers, E. M. (1995). *Diffusion of innovations* (4th ed.). New York: Free Press.

Rosenau,M. D. Jr. (Ed.). (1996). *The PDMA handbook of new product development.* New York: John Wiley.

Ulrich, K. T., & Eppinger, S. D. (1995). *Product design and development.* New York: McGraw-Hill.

Urban, G. L., & Hauser, J. R. (1993). *Design and marketing of new products* (2nd ed.). Englewood Cliffs, NJ: Prentice Hall.

von Hippel, E. (1988). *The sources of innovation.* New York: Oxford University Press.

Wheelwright, S. C., & Clark, K. B. (1992). *Revolutionizing product development: Quantum leaps in speed, efficiency, and quality.* New York: Free Press.

Wheelwright, S. C., & Clark, K. B. (1995). *Leading product development: The senior manager's guide to creating and shaping the enterprise.* New York: Free Press.

Periodicals That Cover Product Planning Issues

Academy of Management Executive
Academy of Management Review
Brand Marketing
Business Horizon

Business Week
California Management Review
Fortune
Harvard Business Review
IEEE Transactions on Engineering Management
Inc.
Industrial Marketing Management
Interfaces
Journal of the Academy of Marketing Science
Journal of Business Research
Journal of Engineering and Technology Management
Journal of International Marketing and Marketing Research
Journal of Management
Journal of Marketing
Journal of Marketing Research
Journal of Product and Brand Management
Journal of Product Innovation Management
Machine Design
Marketing Management
Marketing News
Marketing Science
Nation's Business
R&D Management
Research and Technology Management
Research-Technology Management
Sloan Management Review
Strategic Management Journal

REFERENCES

Aaker, D. A. (1996). *Building strong brands.* New York: Free Press.

Altshuller, G. (1997). *40 principles: TRIZ keys to technical innovation.* Worcester, MA: Technical Innovation Center.

Association of National Advertisers. (1984). *Prescription for new product* success. New York: Association of National Advertisers.

Booz, Allen, & Hamilton. (1982). *New products management for the '80s.* Chicago: Author.

Bralla, J. G. (1996). *Design for excellence.* New York: McGraw-Hill.

Clark, K. B., & Fujimoto, T. (1991). *Product development performance: Strategy, organization, and management in the world auto industry.* Boston: Harvard Business School.

Cooper, R. G. (1982). New product success in industrial firms. *Industrial Marketing Management, 11*(3), 215–223.

Cooper, R. G. (1993). *Winning at new products: Accelerating the process from idea to launch* (2nd ed.). Reading, MA: Addison-Wesley.

Cooper, R. G., Edgett, S. J., & Kleinschmidt, E. J. (1998). *Portfolio management for new products.* Reading, MA: Addison-Wesley.

Copeland, L., & Griggs, L. (1985). *Going international: How to make friends and deal effectively in the global marketplace.* New York: Random House.

Crawford, C. M. (1987). *New products management* (2nd ed.). Homewood, IL: Irwin.

Crawford, C. M. (1997). *New products management* (5th ed.). Boston: Irwin.

Dhalla, N. K., & Yuspeh, S. (1976). Forget the product life-cycle concept. *Harvard Business Review, 54*(1), 102–112.

Dolan, R. J. (1993). *Managing the new product development process: Cases and notes.* Reading, MA: Addison-Wesley.

Fisher, R. J., Maltz, E., & Jaworski, B. J. (1997). Enhancing communication between marketing and engineering: The moderating role of relative functional identification. *Journal of Marketing*, 61 (July), 54–70.

Flops. (1993, August 16). *Business Week*, pp. 76–82.

Griffin, A., & Hauser, J. R. (1993). The voice of the customer. *Marketing Science*, *12*(1), 1–27.

Griffin, A., & Hauser, J. R. (1996). Integrating R&D and marketing: A review and analysis of the literature. *Journal of Product Innovation Management*, *13*(May), 191–215.

Griffin, A., & Page, A. L. (1996). PDMA success measurement project: Recommended measures for product development success and failure. *Journal of Product Innovation Management*, *13*(6), 478–496.

Griffin, A., Belliveau, P., Markham, S., McDonough, E. F., Ill, Olson, D., & Page, A. L. (1997, October). *Drivers of NPD success: The 1997 PDMA report.* Chicago: Product Development and Management Association.

Gupta, A. K., Raj, S. P., & Wilemon, D. (1986). A model for studying R&D-marketing interface in the product innovation process. *Journal of Marketing*, *50*(April), 7–17.

Hair, J. F., Jr., Anderson, R. E., Tatham, R. L., & Black, W. C. (1998). *Multivariate data analysis* (4th ed.). New York: Macmillan.

Hauser, J. R., &Clausing, D. (1988). The house of quality. *Harvard Business Review*, *66*(3), 63–73.

Holahan, P. J., & Markham, S. K. (1996). Factors affecting multifunctional team effectiveness. In M. D. Rosenau, Jr. (Ed.), *The PDMA handbook of new product development* (pp. 119–138). New York: John Wiley.

Kahn, K. B. (1996). Interdepartmental integration: A definition with implications for product development performance. *Journal of Product Innovation Management*, *13*(March), 137–151.

Kahn, K. B. (2000, January). *Benchmarking new product forecasting practices.* Flushing, NY: Institute of Business Forecasting.

Kahn, K. B., & Mentzer, J. T. (1998). Marketing's integration with other departments. *Journal of Business Research*, *42*(May), 53–62.

Keegan, W. J. (1995). *Multinational marketing management* (5th ed.). Upper Saddle Ridge, NJ: Prentice Hall.

Kotler, P. (1997). *Marketing management: Analysis, planning, implementation, and control* (9th ed.). Upper Saddle Ridge, NJ: Prentice Hall.

Kotler, P. (2000). *Marketing management: Analysis, planning, implementation, and control* (10th ed.). Upper Saddle Ridge, NJ: Prentice Hall.

Lawrence, P. R., & Lorsch, J. W. (1986). *Organization and environment: Managing differentiation and integration.* Boston: Harvard Business School Press.

Lehmann, D. R., & Winer, R. S. (1997). *Analysis for market planning* (4th ed.). Chicago: Irwin.

Lim, J. S., & Reid, D. A. (1992). Vital cross-functional linkages with marketing *Industrial Marketing Management*, *21*, 159–165.

Maltz, E., & Kohli, A. K. (1996). Market intelligence dissemination across functional boundaries. *Journal of Marketing Research*, *15*(February), 47–61.

Maslow, A. H. (with D. C. Stephens and G. Heil). (1998). *Maslow on management.* New York: John Wiley.

McDonough, E. F., Kahn, K. B., & Barczak, G. (1998, October 3–4). *Effectively managing global new product development teams.* Paper presented at the PDMA Research Conference Proceedings, Atlanta, GA.

McDonough, E. F., Kahn, K. B., & Griffin, A. (1999). Managing communication in global product development teams. *IEEE Transactions on Engineering Management, 46*(4), 375–386.

McQuarrie, E. F. (1993). *Customer visits: Tools to build market focus.* Newbury Park, CA: Sage.

Meyer, M. H., & Utterback, J. M. (1993). The product family and the dynamics of core capability. *Sloan Management Review, 34*(3), 29–47.

Moenaert, R. K., Souder, W. E., DeMeyer, A., & Deschoolmeester, D. (1994). R&D-marketing integration mechanisms, communication flows, and innovation success. *Journal of Product Innovation Management, 11* (January), 31–45.

Murphy, K. (1999, December 6). Gifts without gaffes for global clients. *Business Week,* p. 153.

Nussbaum, B., & Neff, R. (1991, April 29). High tech gone haywire. *Business Week,* pp. 58–66.

O'Connor, P. (1994). Implementing a stage-gate process: A multi-company perspective. *Journal of Product Innovation Management, 11*(3), 183–200.

Peter, J. P., & Donnelly, J. H., Jr. (1998). *Marketing management: Knowledge and skills.* Boston: Irwin-McGraw-Hill.

Pinto, J. K. (Ed.). (1998). *Project management handbook.* Newtown Square, PA: Project Management Institute/Jossey-Bass.

Porter, M. E. (1980). *Competitive strategy: Techniques for analyzing industries and competitors.* New York: Free Press.

Rogers, E. M. (1995). *Diffusion of innovations* (4th ed.). New York: Free Press.

Ruekert, R. W., & Walker, O. C., Jr. (1987). Marketing's interaction with other functional units: A conceptual framework and empirical evidence. *Journal of Marketing,* 51(January), 1–19.

Schrage, M. (1990). *Shared minds: The new technologies of collaboration.* New York: Random House.

Song, X. M., & Parry, M. E. (1993). R&D-marketing integration in Japanese high-technology firms: Hypotheses and empirical evidence. *Journal of the Academy of Marketing Science, 21* (Spring), 125–133.

Souder, W. E. (1987). *Managing new product innovations.* Lexington, MA: Lexington Books.

Ulrich, K. T., & Eppinger, S. D. (1995). *Product design and development.* New York: McGraw–Hill.

Urban, G. L., & Hauser, J. R. (1993). *Design and marketing of new products* (2nd ed.). Englewood Cliffs, NJ: Prentice Hall.

von Hippel, E. (1988). *The sources of innovation.* New York: Oxford University Press.

INDEX

About the Author

KENNETH B. KAHN (BIE, Georgia Institute of Technology; MSIE, Virginia Polytechnic Institute and State University; Ph.D. in Marketing, Virginia Polytechnic Institute and State University) is Assistant Professor in the Marketing, Logistics, and Transportation Department of the College of Business Administration at the University of Tennessee, Knoxville. His teaching and research interests concern product development, product management, sales forecasting, market analysis, and marketing strategy. He has published in a variety of journals, including the *Journal of Product Innovation Management, Journal of Business Research, Journal of Forecasting, Journal of Business Forecasting, IEEE Transactions on Engineering Management, Marketing Management,* and *R&D Management,* in addition to numerous conference presentations.

His industrial experience includes serving as an industrial engineer and project engineer for the Weyerhaeuser Company and a manufacturing engineer for Respironics, Inc. As a professor, he has worked with on product-planning related projects with a variety of companies, including 3M, Amgen, BellSouth, Borden, Cargill, Ciba Specialty Chemicals, Coca-Cola, Corning, Hanes/L'eggs, Hewlett-Packard, Kellogg, Mary Kay, Miller Brewing, Moen, Motorola, Nabisco, Schering-Plough, Symbol Technologies, and Xerox.

He is an active member of the Product Development and Management Association (PDMA) and is PDMA certified as a New Product

Development Professional (NPDP). A former PDMA board member, he is currently chairperson of the PDMA NPDP Certification Test Development committee. He is also active in the American Marketing Association, Academy of Marketing Science, and Institute of Business Forecasting.